T0154976

Humanity on a Tightrope

HUMANITY ON A TIGHTROPE

Thoughts on Empathy, Family, and Big Changes for a Viable Future

Paul R. Ehrlich and
Robert E. Ornstein

ROWMAN & LITTLEFIELD PUBLISHERS, INC.
Lanham • Boulder • New York • Toronto • Plymouth, UK

Published by Rowman & Littlefield Publishers, Inc.
A wholly owned subsidiary of The Rowman & Littlefield Publishing Group, Inc.
4501 Forbes Boulevard, Suite 200, Lanham, Maryland 20706
http://www.rowmanlittlefield.com

Estover Road, Plymouth PL6 7PY, United Kingdom

Distributed by National Book Network

British Library Cataloguing in Publication Information Available

Library of Congress Cataloging-in-Publication Data

The hardback edition of this book was previously cataloged by the Library of Congress as follows:

Ehrlich, Paul R.
    Humanity on a tightrope : thoughts on empathy, family, and big changes for a viable future / Paul R. Ehrlich and Robert E. Ornstein.
        p. cm.
    Includes bibliographical references and index.
        1. Social problems. 2. Social change. 3. Cultural relations. 4. Empathy.
    5. Globalization—Social aspects. I. Ornstein, Robert E. (Robert Evan), 1942–
    II. Title.
    HN18.3.E47 2010
    303.48'2—dc22   2010015306

ISBN: 978-1-4422-0648-9 (cloth : alk. paper)
ISBN: 978-1-4422-0649-6 (pbk. : alk. paper)
ISBN: 978-1-4422-0650-2 (electronic)

∞™ The paper used in this publication meets the minimum requirements of American National Standard for Information Sciences—Permanence of Paper for Printed Library Materials, ANSI/NISO Z39.48-1992.

Printed in the United States of America

PRE: For Ayelet Ruth and her generation
REO: For those who come next

Contents

PART I

CONNECTING WITH OTHERS
The Evolution of Humanity, Families, and Empathy

CHAPTER 1

On a Tightrope

HAVE you ever gone to the circus? Next time, watch closely the person on the tightrope trying to keep her balance. Notice what happens—you're grimacing, relieved, apprehensive, relieved again, hopeful, grimacing, and so on. Then look around; everybody else is tensing their muscles, moving left to balance while the tightrope walker tilts right, feeling apprehensive, then relaxed, tense again, sighing in relief when balance is regained. You are, automatically, feeling an intense connection and empathy with a stranger.

The need to expand our connections and cooperation with strangers is essential right now. All of us, citizens of every nation, are now in the same family, are now in the same boat, walking the same tightrope, like it or not. The worst problems of the human predicament are common to all of us, from climate disruption, loss of biodiversity, and poisoning of the environment to pandemics, gross economic inequities, and the threat of nuclear war. Our tightrope is a line from humanity's past to its future.

Like it or not, we're all now balancing on that same global tightrope—and that means we have to change our behavior.

We've got it in us to change. All human beings have a brain that evolved to give us an extraordinary ability to understand and to connect with others, but that primordial ability is much too limited for the complex world that we've created in the twenty-first century. Our global civilization is facing new and unprecedented challenges from many intractable problems. Daily we read about these dismal prospects, and it seems there's little we can do about them: climate disruption can cause increased starvation, and rising seas will generate crowds of refugees; there are new and scary pandemics, and toxic chemicals threaten health; there are large and small wars, discrimination, exploitation, gang rule, torture, economic inequality, and

3

on and on. But there is a lot that can and should be done regarding our predicament; it's time for big changes.

Of course, there's no simple, quick, and easy solution to make it safely to the end of the tightrope, to create a human society that is both sustainable and equitable, although many different solutions have been proposed. In the climate dilemma, these solutions range from simple things like lowering the planet's heat by painting roofs white in hot climates, to complicated and probably unworkable ones such as the formation of a world governing body that could control the energy economy of all nations. However, in spite of there being no easy answers, many more people could become aware of two closely related human characteristics—patterns of family affiliation and the capacity to empathize.* With this awareness, many people might be led to change their behavior, as well as that of the global community, so that environmental catastrophe might possibly be averted.

One of our society's major problems is that there is, as Barack Obama said in his Martin Luther King speech in 2008, an "empathy deficit." Most people don't relate to a broad enough part of humanity. We're often unable to "get into their shoes," to share their feelings, to understand their emotions. Empathy and sympathy are related but are not the same. Empathy is the ability to understand emotionally another's feelings and experience; we have empathy *with* someone. Sympathy means approving of another person's state or feeling the same; being in accord with them. We generally feel sympathy *for* someone. It is, however, difficult to feel sympathy for a person without some empathy. One can empathize with an individual reacting to, say, great provocation with an act of violence without being in accord with the action.

One hopeful sign for promoting change is the new understanding of how the human brain operates; we're not, as it turns out, just simple "economic men," cold-blooded rational decision makers. Out go the old models of connecting switchboards or computer-like structures. Instead the human brain/mind is highly influenced by the emotional tone of any situation, and emotions are essential to decision making. And it is the empathetic emotions that are falling short right now.[1]

And that empathy shortfall costs more than just a loss of emotional closeness. It affects how we see ourselves, our family members, and the "others" in our immediate life. It also affects how we see our nation, all the

---

Family is one of those words like *religion* that most people easily understand from context but have difficulty assigning a single definition. Here we use the term *family* to describe a wide range of affiliations that resemble in one way or other the relationships usually found among close relatives by birth or marriage.

people of the planet, and all of the planet's nonhuman inhabitants. Empathy's genesis traces in part to our long evolutionary history as a small-group animal—a uniquely intelligent creature that associated with a few dozen to a few hundred closely related creatures, all of whom lived in the same environment and had largely similar experiences and values. Empathy not only came naturally, it had natural limits—our distant ancestors in African forests and savannas did not ordinarily meet others with different worldviews. It wasn't until *Homo sapiens* left Africa and the species enormously increased its population, diversified culturally, and had contact with strangers that there was the possibility of an empathy shortfall. It is thus a relatively new development in response to our recent success as a species.

But now that the shortfall is here and well developed, eliminating it would be a first step, and to be sure, only a first step, to enable a new kind of world and aid a return to the family connectedness of our distant ancestors in Africa. This would be a human family reunion at a scale they could not have dreamed of.

We are not such a united family right now. Consider many people's inability to care for the condition of the poor today, to say nothing of feeling concern for how climate disruption will affect not just their own children or poor people on a distant part of the globe, but future generations of our species. That disruption could damage agriculture and fisheries so much that the more than one billion people hungry now could become three billion or more. It is unlikely that the descendants of our in-groups, of our own families, no matter where located, could avoid the fall from the tightrope—the mayhem and premature death that would result.

Why don't we register some of these possible civilization-ending threats? The costs of not acting now to lessen climate disruption could be extremely high, but we seem willing, even eager, to accept those costs rather than taking *relatively* inexpensive steps that would be beneficial even if the climate wasn't changing. Why don't we have more empathy for the people already hungry, and for the billions more who could well be hungry in a few decades?[2] Why don't more people realize that if we don't pay increasing attention to our most inclusive family, the human family, the denouement for all will likely be horrific?

We don't think it will be easy to get more people to emotionally join a global family. But we're writing this book because the first barrier to many if not most of the remedies for the human predicament is that we don't see the "other" people in this world as "us," part of the same people, in the same family, in the same . . . boat.

So, whether it will be easy or not, we think it essential to try. Making changes in how we view all our different families, how we all see and how we care for others, could be the beginnings of the move to a more unified, equitable, and secure world. And some of the latest research in fields like cognitive science, social neuroscience, and anthropology provide promising keys to our looked-for cultural evolution.

There are immediate behavioral solutions to problems such as inadequate health care, climate disruption, and the use of environmentally faulty energy technologies. All could be ameliorated by relatively small changes in human actions. For instance, there's much argument about health care in the United States these days, focused on financial issues such as the reimbursement schemes, insurance policies, and the need to give people without insurance access to care.

But just 10 percent of early deaths in the United States are the result of substandard medical care. About 20 percent are the result of social and physical environments, and 30 percent can be traced to genetic defects. *The biggest contributor to premature mortality, accounting for 40 percent of all unnecessarily early deaths, is unhealthful behavior.*[3] And our behavior is at the root of many other social problems: for example, automobile gasoline mileage will increase with tightening standards, perhaps overall by 15 percent by 2020, but changes in behavior, such as how we plan and execute our trips and attention to vehicle maintenance, could decrease fuel consumption by 30 percent tomorrow. The same, as we'll see, is true of energy use in buildings.

But even getting people to change their behavior connected to something as important to each of us as our health is extremely difficult—especially when sections of society are working hard to see that our diet gets worse. And getting Americans to be concerned about the health of those others, in particular the malnourished poor in our own nation or those hundreds of millions starving in distant lands, seems even more difficult—even though the more people who are malnourished, the greater the chances of epidemics that could affect *us*. The growing numbers of such people in close proximity to the animal reservoirs of disease are a prescription for novel and lethal diseases invading humanity.[4] The health of *them* influences *our* chances of reaching a ripe old age.

Americans don't seem to be bothered either that numerous other nations do a much better job of making all their citizens healthy. And many rich Americans don't seem to be concerned about the fate of the uninsured—after all, it's often said that if "those people" had worked diligently, they wouldn't be too poor to afford those shocking fees for their insurance and sky-high prices for often useless, harmful, or badly tested drugs. Helping them would cost too much.

Too expensive in the Rich Reactionary Dictionary means "might require raising our low marginal income tax rates." One bank executive said recently, about the prospect of receiving a smaller bonus and paying more taxes, "A lot of our folks have second and third homes and alimony payments and other obligations that require substantial current cash."[5] Taxes are seen in this lexicon as inherently evil, rather than a contribution that all of us need to make to run important parts of society. But taxes can be an expression of a society's empathy—its determination that all kids have a right to literacy and a healthy diet, even if their parents can't pay for it, and to freedom from abuse. Of course there are nonempathetic, economic reasons that can be given for using tax money on kids, but the record shows we can't achieve environmental protection, improve education, build roads, provide health care, and fund defense through market mechanisms. But, of course, taxes need to be well spent, and when they are, people should be made aware of it.

The Germans and Japanese use only a little more than half as much energy as do Americans and are just as affluent.* Raising the gas mileage American cars get might help a little, perhaps even in a decade. But immediate changes would result if Americans tomorrow started making fewer unnecessary trips by car, carpooling more, using public transportation, and walking and using bicycles for more trips. The energy dilemma would be helped by a general increase in empathy, so that even the rich would feel more for a poor family that had to give up a home than for a buddy who had to give up one of his executive jets.

And, in the long run, the biggest savings in energy use and the emissions of greenhouse gases (as well as the protection of human life-support systems) could come from redesigning both the United States and other nations around people rather than automobiles and by gradually reducing both the American and the global population. There can be no happy sustainable society if the population of the United States and the world keeps growing. But then, as the saying goes, what did posterity ever do for us? What business is it of ours to be concerned about the fate of future generations, especially when most economists tell us they'll be much richer than we are? Why should we have any empathy with them?

Is that attitude toward the future why the United States isn't moving in the direction of a sustainable society, adopting a humane population policy, and following Europe into a slow population decline? Is that why, at the Earth Summit in 1992, President George H. W. Bush declared forcefully, "The American way of life is not negotiable"? Why isn't it negotiable? It's

---

* It's a little more complicated because Northern Europeans, for example, live in more urbanized environments where energy use, as in transportation, is lessened. But the overall comparison still holds, because Americans use more energy in every category.

been in "negotiation"—in constant change—for the entire life of the republic. The "American way of life" altered enormously in America's first two hundred years, and the world has evolved dramatically since that "updated" way of life, of which the senior Bush spoke, was adopted in the middle of the twentieth century, right after the end of the Second World War. In addition, with all of the environmental problems facing society,[6] there is little reason to believe that future generations will be richer than ours. Indeed, as many now suspect, they are much more likely to be poorer. [7]

Indeed, why do policies that are self-defeating even for today's generations persist? Why is the United States so reluctant to aid the people of poor nations, often choosing instead to appropriate their resources? The government of the United States does relatively little, compared to other rich nations, to come to the aid of poor nations whose people are often living lives of misery and fails to lead by example in trying to solve the human predicament. Indeed, why isn't *any* nation taking adequate action to reduce threats like climate disruption, toxification of the entire planet, and the threats of pandemics and nuclear catastrophe?* What prevents people from making the behavioral changes that could lead to a sustainable global society?

A major reason is ignorance of all of our species' common fate and the shortfall of empathy: an emphasis on a very restricted concept of us and a relative lack of caring about them, with "them" including even our own as yet unborn descendants. Is it because those descendents—great-great-grandchildren and beyond—traditionally are not included in our extended family? Is that why we don't care about the long run?[8]

We need a change, an extension of our consciousness to be more inclusive of the rest of humanity. We need to identify with all other human beings and, to a much greater extent, relate to their needs, joys, and plights. With the conscious understanding that humanity is and must be one single family, people could begin to deal with many of our predicaments, avoid our big family being dysfunctional, and perhaps even extend our full empathy and membership in our family to future generations. To look at the question from another angle, why do we care so much more for "us" (as we'll see, *us* is defined in a complex and ever shifting way), and how can we change that? And it's worse than that. It's not just that we seem to lack empathy for others; our ignorance seems to make us lack empathy for ourselves! We fail to relate to the actual situation we're in—what shoes our own feet occupy—that to keep from plunging off the global tightrope requires us

---

* Some are trying mightily, such as Denmark and Norway, as are some cities in the United States, such as Portland, Oregon.

to cooperate with the others also trying to balance. And if changing behavior is difficult, changing consciousness may be even more so.

Our suggestions may often seem impractical. The changes we discuss will not always be pleasant or easy to achieve. We won't be describing a path to utopia; rather, we're trying to evaluate *what will be required* if we are going to change our behavior so that our global civilization can flourish rather than collapse.

But it's not all grim, really. If overconsuming societies could reshape their economies away from the produce-more, consume-more ethic, then work weeks could be shorter, vacation times longer, and learning opportunities more abundant; there would be more time available for adults to enjoy friends, to mix with their kids, and to stop and smell the flowers. That would be a form of "more for everyone" that could be sustainable and coexist with democracy. That many countries in Europe do so much better in this respect than the United States suggests that this is far from impossible.

In the United States the frantic pace of life often can block enjoying life. For instance, on a frigid morning in January, a sidewalk musician played the violin in a Washington, DC, metro station for about forty-five minutes. He started with Bach's Chaconne on a Stradivarius violin, and played five more classical pieces. Most of the some one thousand people who passed him paid no attention, a few slowed their pace, and after seven minutes, a woman threw a dollar in his hat without pausing. In the hour he collected $32.17 and no crowd.[9]

The musician was Joshua Bell, a world-famous violinist who ordinarily commands one hundred dollars or more a seat at concerts. The subway performance was part of a *Washington Post* experiment to see if people would recognize and appreciate fine classical music played by a street musician while they were on their way to work. It turned out that almost no one felt he or she had the time to stop and listen to some of the world's best music played by a brilliant musician on one of the finest violins ever made. A few empathized enough with the artist to pay a dollar for the performance. Small-group animals in swarms of strangers often fail to relate to them, as numerous stories of the New Yorkers' street behavior—such as simply walking around and ignoring someone who has collapsed on the sidewalk—attest.

One interpretation of the ignored musician was that appreciating beauty requires leisure and the proper setting. Of course, leisure seems a very rare commodity in our frantic society, where even young professional couples both feel obliged to work in order to accumulate the "necessary" items and live the "appropriate" lifestyle—placing ever more responsibility on paid caregivers to raise their children.

Indeed, since our hunter-gatherer ancestors worked much less than the average person today and rarely suffered the hunger that plagues some societies today, all people might reexamine the meaning of affluence and gradually decide that more relaxation and fewer possessions might prove a more desirable goal in life.[10] It's an issue of whether producing much compared to desires (the stone-age pattern) or producing little in relation to wants (today's pattern) is a better way to live—or whether something in between would be "best."

We might also think about the standards of affluence and social status that pertained in some chiefdoms. The best-known example is the Kwakiutl of the northwest coast of North America. In such societies it was *generosity*, not *accumulation*, that awarded status and leadership. Kwakiutl ceremonies, called potlatches, were exercises in seeing who could give away (or destroy) more goods and thus acquire more prestige. They demonstrated that patterns in today's United States are hardly hardwired into the human brain, although if you think about it, you can see signs of potlatch behavior in the conspicuous consumption in our own society (as in four-million-dollar weddings or taking a few dozen friends on an expensive cruise). What to do to reach a pleasant and enduring future, and when and how can we do it? Thinking about those things is what this book is all about.

CHAPTER 2

Empathy, and "Us" Family Members versus "Them"

Father Mother and Me
Sister and Auntie say
All good people agree
And all good people say
All nice people like Us, are We
And everyone else is They.
And They live over the sea
While We live over the way
But would You believe it?—They look upon We
As only a sort of They!

—RUDYARD KIPLING

WHEN we're born, we find ourselves in a family of one kind or another; around us we hear a language or two, observe a manner of housing and one or more patterns of work, a style of cooking and a regime of eating. And traces of that family and the world of our childhood persist through our life in all of us because of the way our brain develops. The brain gets organized in our earliest environment, it "picks up" the language(s) spoken around us, it absorbs one of various lifeways—farmers or nomads, Greeks or geeks—and it decides who is the safe "family" group, the "us."

While there are nuclear and extended families—and larger linkages such as bands, lineages, clans, tribes, chiefdoms, city-states, nations, and the like—we use "family" in this book in the broadest sense, since in ordinary speech it can range from single-parent plus child to "the family of

11

man." It also includes, metaphorically, the different language families, and families of people joined together in diverse groups of us as infantry squads, coworkers, professions, races, religions, cults, political parties, clubs, teams, fans, followers of a serial crime drama, criminal syndicates themselves, even friends on Second Life (the virtual world that now has millions of "occupants"), and on and on.

People get their basic us-others orientation early, but as they grow up in a modern society, their networks of affiliation expand and become much more complex. That expansion helps us to spread our empathetic feelings to more and more people as the population grows, but it does not solve the basic empathy dilemma, since networks also can be used to spread hatred. Feeling closer to some people, making them part of an "us," inevitably makes that new "us" feel more distant from all the rest, the "others," and makes us less empathetic (to say the least) with "them." With this old mind-set we see the prevalence of the "us" even in what we call ourselves: the names many tribal groups give themselves translate to "the people," as if they were the only real people in the world. This is the needed change point: our tribe, our family, our "us" needs now to become global and include all humanity because the behavior and impacts of humanity itself have changed so drastically in recent centuries.

The change is that human beings became, without any question, the dominant animals on the planet.[1] Once upon a time, the sum total of human beings consisted of a few hunter-gatherer groups that were, for the most part of their lives, separated from each other. These meager groups could clash or exchange members only on the rare occasions when they bumped into each other. They weren't saints; they had significant and very often destructive impacts on their environments and sometimes on other groups, but their ecological damage was only local or regional. Now ethnic or national groups live cheek by jowl with one another, and humanity's impacts are global and long lasting, and our species is endangering its own life-support systems and the infrastructure of the rest of the living world.[2] We need to change our ways.

To avert even more serious damage to the foundations of civilization, we have to change our minds about who is "us" now and act differently based on that new conscious mind-set. And we have to do it for all intents and purposes immediately—as crazy or impractical as that seems. That humanity, as a whole or a significant part, needs to evolve culturally and quickly has been widely recognized, but too many of the "solutions" to the dilemma of living in a world of seven billion people, coming from both the Right and Left, are often simply vague and hopeful wishes. Former Arkansas governor Mike Huckabee has said that the problems of law and order would diminish "if people behaved better." The Dalai Lama has said that we could solve many of the world's problems if people were more compassionate. All true, but these statements are too general. We need to start discussing *what* must be changed and *how* to do it. We're willing to go out on a limb to try to jump-start that discussion.

In our view, *what* we need to change first is the scope of our family feelings and our affiliations. They need to match the recent expansion in the scale and technological power of the human enterprise. *How* to deal with that expansion is the daunting question we'll tackle after examining the *what* more closely. And for this we need go into human evolutionary history for a bit. Stick with us.

Let's start at the most fundamental level, at the question of how early human beings, our ancestors, evolved such strong family feelings—the roots of us-them—to begin with. There have been many factors, not related to family structure, that researchers have suggested for the uniqueness and dominance of our kind, for humanity's successes in both increasing its numbers and transforming the planet. Bipedalism is one: human beings stand upright, and as a result have forelimbs that, relieved of the weight bearing of walking, can perform delicate movements. These forelimbs have become "hands." Our ancestors' meat-eating habit is thought important too, since meat's concentrated nutrition reduces the need for large stomachs and large jaws,* and the greater protein intake may well have allowed increased brain size, as did the invention of cooking, which made food more digestible and acquiring nutrients more efficient.[3]

But when all is said and done, the central factor in humanity's success is a *family arrangement that serves the needs of our big and complex brains.* Human beings have a long period of infancy compared with other mammals, including the primates, because our brains need to grow large. That need had to be filled outside of the womb, because large infant heads created anatomical difficulties for bipedal women delivering babies. That limitation on head size at birth causes modern human beings (and our more recent ancestors) to be born "premature," in the evolutionary sense, that is, long before we can care for ourselves.†

Indeed, biologist Sarah Blaffer Hrdy has recently reconsidered the very long period that the human brain requires to reach adult capabilities. It must absorb ways to function, to process stimuli, to control movements,

---

* Needed to chew all those tough veggies.
† The upright posture/narrowed pelvis necessitates birth early, and thus human beings are born with an immature brain that undergoes most of its growth and development in the external environment.

and to take in much basic cultural information. The extended stretch of an infant's helplessness normally requires care beyond what can be provided by a bonded couple alone.

In her recent book *Mothers and Others*, Hrdy argues convincingly that in the beginning, human beings were cooperative breeders. Unlike chimpanzees, our progenitors allowed—in fact, encouraged—other individuals, including adults of both sexes, to aid with child rearing. And that carries over now, in some cultures going to the point of permitting other females besides the mother to nurse the young. That level of cooperation was embodied in the wet-nursing practice from the 1600s to World War II. In Britain in the eighteenth century, a woman often could make more money wet-nursing than her husband could earn laboring.[4] With the introduction of breast milk substitutes, this practice has faded but far from disappeared in rich nations, but it remains common in less-developed countries. And, of course, employing "nannies" has remained common among the well-off.

Becoming a "cooperative breeder"—a species in which an extended family plays essential roles in rearing offspring and makes premature birth possible—was likely significant to our evolutionary success and remains key to our behavior today. Cooperative breeding leads to a long period of learning to interact with a variety of caregivers, and as a result, human beings are well prepared for a complex social life.

The human brain has a much more elaborate network of neurons (nerve cells) for facial recognition, for responding to others, and, recently discovered, for imitating others—for getting inside their heads—than has any other animal. We even have special face-recognition cells in our brains that respond to familiar people. As a result we can identify who is in our "tribe" to a greater extent than can our closest evolutionary neighbors, the chimps and the bonobos (sometimes called pygmy chimps). And the brain architecture is indeed special: recognition of faces isn't the same as recognizing other objects; brain damage can impair one and not the other. A head injury can leave you able to tell a cube from a ball, but not your brother from your sister—or vice versa.

The great benefits and difficulties of "family" orientation have their origin in this uniquely human manner of affiliation. The cooperation and empathy that it engages, is the basis of human success in dominating the planet. As Sarah Hrdy writes in *Mothers and Others*,

> Were it not for the peculiar combination of empathy and mind reading we would not have evolved to be humans at all. . . . Without the capacity to put ourselves cognitively and emotionally in someone else's shoes, to feel what they feel, to be interested in their fears and

motives, longings, griefs, vanities and other details of their existence, without this mixture of curiosity about and emotional identification with others, a combination that adds up to mutual understanding and sometimes even compassion, *Homo sapiens would never have evolved at all* [italics added].[5]

While no single factor was all important in developing our patterns of relationships, cooperative breeding is the most significant. For instance, we seem to be born with a capability for forging a close link to those we see, hear, and smell around us early on, the first family, no matter who they are. Babies spontaneously imitate their caregivers' expressions. Psychologist Andrew Meltzoff found that even a forty-four-minute-old infant could do it, about as young a research subject as is possible! The figure below shows a newborn baby (this one is a day old) imitating Meltzoff's expressions—a mirroring of others' behavior that is hardwired into the human brain.

Think what it means for a baby to be able to do this. The baby has never been able to see its *own* face—and therefore has no clue what it looks

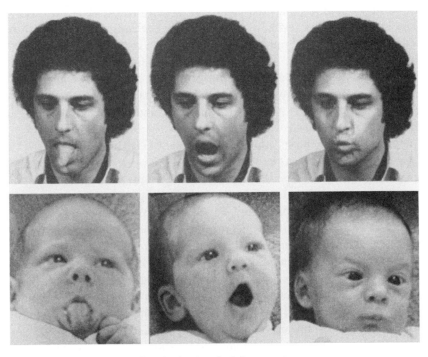

Infant imitating facial expressions
Courtesy of Andrew Meltzoff

like, how it moves—and yet the newborn can immediately link a visual image of a protruding pink triangle to an internal brain command to move the tongue, and can also make a connection between a white set of squarish dots inside of a dark pinkish, oval-shaped opening with his or her own brain's command to move the mouth. So we are certainly born with the ability to respond to and "know" at a most basic level what's going on inside others in our immediate surroundings.

And infants know when others are acting like them. In another of Meltzoff's studies, a fourteen-month-old infant sat across the table from two adults who were side by side. Two TV monitors were placed behind the infant, one displaying the infant who was at the table and the other showing a recording of another infant. One of the adults imitated everything the "live" infant did; the other imitated the actions of the infant on the recording. The infants at the table knew which adult was acting like them. They looked significantly longer and smiled more at the person who imitated them.[6]

There are newly discovered brain capacities that greatly expand our understanding of the human ability to understand, imitate, and empathize with others of our kind. It's that ability to be so aware of other individuals, know something about what is going on inside their minds, and empathize with them that enabled our species to become so cooperative. If you drop something near any two-year-old, she will stop and help you. Almost all children will do this without any prompting. But of course scientists need studies to confirm what we "know." Michael Tomasello of the Max Planck Institute in Germany has done the most thorough research on this with children of many cultures.[7]

The basics are these: Infants of fourteen to eighteen months meet a strange adult head-on. They see that the adult has a problem; it might be opening a cabinet door, picking up something dropped, cleaning up a spill. A typical result is that out of twenty-four youngsters, twenty-two help immediately without prompting.[8] This is apparently not a learned behavior, but as kids grow up, their tendency to help is either increased in scope or narrowed by being a member of a family group.[9]

As with any other capability, the human faculty for cooperation develops and expands as we grow. The good news is that this unique ability has allowed us to build cities where once there was only pristine land. The bad news is that we can build too many huge cities where once there was only pristine land. In doing so, we dislodge vital parts of our life-support systems. *The human capacity to conquer lands, plants and animals, and inanimate resources has now reached a point where a new scale of cooperation is needed to stay on the tightrope—if civilization is to thrive.*

The good news/bad news continues: the increased ability of human beings to cooperate enables a lawful state to exist for the benefit of its citizens, the creation of transportation networks to move people swiftly from place to place, and the use of science to design such networks—all to allow people to live almost anywhere on the land surface of the planet and to understand the world in general. That growing understanding has, among other things, resulted in increasing life expectancies for our species. But it has also enabled the very opposite of increasing life expectancies, mass murder, and it has complicated the role of empathy. Mass murder is an ancient human activity, seen in our lifetimes in Hitler's Europe, in Rwanda in east-central Africa, in the Congo, in Southeast Asia, and in the Balkans. The Nazis, as is well known, organized the coordination and cooperation of hundreds of thousands of people from many nations to aid in the killing of millions.

The recently discovered architect's plans for the Auschwitz gas chambers, in which more than a million people died, are just another indication of the careful and coordinated planning and organization people can use when dealing heartlessly with those "others."[10] The blueprints were among the original floor plans for Auschwitz-Birkenau (one of three Auschwitz camps), the extermination camp or *Vernichtungslager*, where at least 960,000 Jews, 75,000 Poles, and 19,000 Gypsies were murdered. Birkenau was the largest of all the Nazi extermination camps. The plans were initialed by the chief of the SS, Heinrich Himmler, and Rudolf Höss (who later commanded the camp) and date back to 1941.

Even in less-developed Rwanda, extensive cooperation was necessary to organize the 1994 mass murder. Hundreds of thousands of machetes had to be ordered, invoiced, paid for, and transported, in stealth, to scores of locations, and all this had to be arranged months in advance of their use. Excuses for their receipt had to be agreed upon: "There will be a large harvest this year." There had to be a working electricity network to run the radio stations, and speakers on those stations had to be coordinated and controlled to send out the prepared messages that would demonize the Tutsis.

Paul Rusesabagina, the manager of the Mille Collines Hotel in the Rwandan capitol of Kigali, whose defiance was portrayed in the film *Hotel Rwanda*, writes, "The message crept into our national consciousness very slowly. It did not happen all at once. We did not wake up one morning to hear it pouring out of the radio full strength. It started with a sneering comment, the casual use of the term 'cockroach,' the almost humorous suggestion that Tutsis should be airmailed back to Ethiopia. Stripping the humanity from an entire group takes time."[11] One tribe, the majority Hutus, were won over by a barrage of radio messages, rallies, and pseudo-history to the view that the Tutsi were an extreme "them" and were no longer classified as human.[12] Even though the Hutus had for decades lived among and even married Tutsi, they readily dehumanized the Tutsi into those "cockroaches." In his book, Rusesabagina says, "Priests help kill their congregations. In some cases, the congregations helped to kill their priests. Tutsi wives went to sleep next to their husbands and woke up to feel the blade of a machete sawing into their neck, and, above them the grimacing face of the man who had sworn to love them and cherish them for the rest of their life."[13]

Perhaps even more depressing is the complication that many of the Nazis who participated in the Holocaust are recorded as believing they were acting morally, indeed with empathy for their own family (they assumed they were like surgeons of the human body politic, cutting out the "cancerous" elements), and we suspect that the same is true of many Hutu killers. Rudolf Höss felt that the orders Heinrich Himmler gave out on behalf of Adolf Hitler were "sacred," and so he suppressed his natural empathy to serve what he believed was a higher moral cause. "I was not permitted to show the slightest compassion. . . . I had to carry on my task, to witness extermination and slaughter, to repress my feelings."[14] He expresses a recent extreme of the us-them morality that has plagued humanity for millennia. Höss's attitude supports the idea that ethics are culture and situation bound. And that means that one should follow the family's ethical standards regardless of the larger cultural or biophysical environment in which an extended family is embedded and despite any of the innate and natural empathy built into the structure of our nervous systems.

Höss's view brings us to one of our greatest challenges in trying to spread empathy—teaching people to empathize (not sympathize) with those whose behavior they find execrable. For many of us it is easy to empathize with a child or a parent who behaves in a way of which we deeply disapprove: "You were very wrong to do x, but you are my son, I can understand your action, and will still love and help you."

But empathy comes less easily to us, say, for Eric Harris and Dylan Klebold, who killed twelve students and one teacher and injured many others at Columbine High School in 1999. Nonetheless, it is important to understand their crimes. No one will excuse their behavior, but anyone who has been taunted, ostracized, and shamed in high school can empathize with the distress that led Harris and Klebold to their horrific acts. It is important to remember that empathy involves sharing another individual's feelings or emotions, and thus getting insight into the other's behavior. Those feelings and the behavior aren't always positive in themselves.

The idea that the features of a group's culture can only be judged from "within" that culture traces originally to the left-wing German Jewish anthropologist Franz Boas and his students. In the first half of the twentieth century, they developed what is known in anthropology as "cultural relativism." In its original form it was extremely empathetic towards non-Western cultures, holding that those cultures could only be judged in their own terms. Cultural relativism was developed as a counterpoint to the then prevailing ideas in anthropology that Western culture was the standard toward which all must strive—that there was an evolutionary sequence from primitive culture to barbarism to "civilization," usually the culture of a very white, upper-class Englishman. Or German. But as the Nazis took power in Germany, Boas retreated from his completely relativistic view. He could not justify Höss's behavior simply because Höss followed the ethics of the SS culture.* There has, of course, been a near-global repudiation of the SS culture from those who were and are now looking at it from the outside. But there has been a substantial effort to empathize with Germans of the post-Versailles era—to try to get inside their heads and to figure out what led many of them to give power to the Nazis or at least allow them to gain it, and then to ignore, support, or participate in genocidal projects.[15]

Anthropologists have, since World War II, considered it legitimate to make judgments of the effects of cultural elements on the survival of society or its treatment of its members or others.[16] But the question of who gets to make those judgments and the criteria by which they're made remains wide open.

This shift of attitude on cultural relativism is not helpful to the problem of spreading strong empathy and binding humanity into a single family; actions that elicit empathy can vary so greatly from culture to culture and depend very much on the cultural standards.[17] For example, empathy in most Westerners and many Muslims results in revulsion at the practice, originating in ancient Egypt and still common in parts of Africa and Asia, of female genital mutilation. But to many who practice it, it is not only ethical but essential.

The world is rife with such ethical problems rooted in our us-them small-group orientation. One of humanity's greatest challenges is to find ways to extend the family spirit globally, while finding ways to balance cultural diversity and relativism with a strengthening of empathy. It is a rather new challenge. As far as we can tell, a division of us from them among those scattered early hunter-gatherer bands was of little consequence, as there

---

* SS stands for *Schutzstaffel* (German for "protective echelon"), originally Hitler's personal guards. The SS was responsible for the majority of atrocities carried out by the Nazis. Note that our very use of the word *atrocities* shows our acceptance of the notion that outside judgments can be made of cultural norms.

were few "others" to meet in an empty world, and in many circumstances when groups were in proximity, their boundaries were rather fluid and an individual could transfer between groups with little difficulty.[18]

But divisions surely increased at the beginning of civilization. Some five millennia ago, as the people of the Indus valley moved south, they came into contact with Mesopotamians, whom they taught how to domesticate horses, make bronze, fashion weapons, and build and use war chariots.[19] This new technology and cultural lifeway completely disrupted the once peaceful and stable culture of the area, and the Mesopotamians, instead of raising sheep, took up stealing sheep and cattle from their neighbors.

In Mesopotamia the Indo-Aryans helped establish early cities and organized complex irrigation systems. They were pioneers in building a civilization and pioneers in what comes with it: demonizing ethnic, religious, or political "others" and fighting with them over access to resources. "Ethnic" itself, which is a Greek word for "a people," is in the New Testament used for those heathen "thems"—those not Christian, or Christianity's antecessor, the Jews, all the rest of . . . them.

No matter how bloody were the ancient battles—or the more recent Crusades, religious wars around the Reformation, Napoleanic wars, Little Big Horn, Isandlwana, Spion Kop, Balkan and world wars of the last century, or many "ethnic cleansings" (some still going on)—these conflicts have been geographically contained and their damage, though horrible, has been localized or regional. *But now we've entered a new, uncontained, and bloodless "battle" for creativity and compassion, where the very viability of global civilization is at stake.* And the battle isn't against an invasion of resource-hungry aliens from an extraterrestrial empire, which science fiction writers have often posited as a cause that would unite humanity. That's too bad, because human beings tend to stick together in the face of a common enemy, as New Yorkers did after September 11, Londoners did after July 7,* and citizens of Mumbai did after November 26–29.† Rather, the "common foe" is the actions of that weirdly cooperatively breeding small-group animal that has gained dominance over everything but its own behavior. The situation is summed up in a famous phrase from the noted intellectual Pogo on a 1970 Earth Day poster: "We have met the enemy and he is us."[20]

However, there *has* been substantial movement for that battle against humanity's own dark side: Over the past few millennia the human race has

---

* The 2005 bombings by English Muslims that killed some fifty-six people and injured about seven hundred.
† The 2008 terrorist attack by a Pakistani terrorist group in which almost two hundred died and many more were wounded.

progressed, ever so slowly and unevenly, toward becoming a united family that might meet the threat. Gradually the small families of our primate ancestors (who we'll meet in chapter 3) fused into larger units. Some five thousand years ago, Menes (or Narmer) was the king who, at least in myth, united Upper and Lower Egypt. Then "Egyptians" became an "imagined community"[21]—the first very large-scale family.

The ancient Greeks saw the Trojan War, which they claimed happened almost two millennia after Menes' reign in Egypt, as the first moment in history when they came together as one people with a common purpose.* This unification, whether it was mythical or not, became part of the ancient Greek heritage and was solidified by the staging of the first Olympic games in 776 BCE. This common heritage, along with their cuisine, and their common lifeways at one fell swoop gave the later Greeks a strong sense of both national and cultural identity.

The Greek identity was defined simply: if you spoke Greek and had the same values as other Greeks, you were one with all the other Greek-speaking peoples. More than 2,500 years ago, 150 city-states in ancient Greece became united under the Delian League. This formed the basis of one eventual country, even though various league members were classified enough as "them" to be battled in brutal conflicts, including the Peloponnesian War that saw the league break up.†

Associated with, or a product of, a widening of family, national and political unification has been accelerating since the Industrial Revolution. Three centuries ago, almost two hundred communities occupied and divided up what is now one country, France. One hundred and fifty years ago there were some seventy "Germanies"—duchies, fiefdoms, feudal tracts—then there was one, then two, and now there is again one. Italy, after Garibaldi, followed suit, and deliberately tried to solidify its national pride in World War I when it battled a mélange of ethnic families called

---

* Historians still question whether this war really happened, and if it did, whether it could really have gone on for ten years and whether it contained the episode of the soldier-filled hollow Trojan horse. However, Troy itself has been unearthed.

† Of course, subsequent Greeks, who some two hundred or so years later were the heirs to the lands Alexander conquered, were more fluid in their family organization. The Ptolemys, who took over Egypt, which was then an isolated land, acted like pharaohs inside Egypt and repaired to Alexandria on the sea and lived there as Greeks. The Seleucids, whose dynasty reached from what is now Syria to Asia Minor, lived as adaptive monarchs, country to country, and blended in with the social structure of each. See Stanley Bury, Arthur Cook, Frank Ezra Adcock, Martin Percival Charlesworth, Iorwerth Eiddon Stephen Edwards, John Boardman, and Frank William Walbank, *The Cambridge Ancient History*, vol. 2 (Cambridge: Cambridge University Press, 1966).

the Austro-Hungarian Empire. Now France, Germany, Italy, Austria, and Hungary all are part of the European Union, and all but Hungary have the same currency, the euro (Hungary plans to adopt it as soon as it can meet the financial criteria).

Of course, as a counter example, the unification of the colonies into the United States was likely more a case of a shared hatred to British rule than spreading empathy. Lack of that internal empathy was vividly illustrated by the Civil War. Interestingly, after that war there was a subtle psychological shift in how the family of the United States was viewed. Before the war one would say, "The United States *have* good relations with other countries"; after the war, "The United States *has* good relations with other countries."

But while most politicians (and likely political scientists, economists, and pundits) think the world is better off with large national units, as we'll discuss, Earth's political landscape is riven with breakaway groups wishing to belong to smaller rather than larger national families.

There's another sign, in addition to the fusion of polities, that the peoples of the world are gradually moving toward one family: where once there was a tower of Babel throughout the world, a world in which there are more than eight hundred languages spoken in New Guinea alone, now one needs to know only Chinese, Spanish, English, Arabic, and Hindu to have a conversation understood by more than half of humanity.

While once the world's people spoke some 7,500 languages, that number will likely be halved by 2100. Even though language losses may be due to less-than-progressive factors such as imperialism, it nonetheless is easier for most to be empathetic with those who speak the same language. On the other hand, the cost of this increasing linguistic unity and possible spread of empathy, is that losses of languages take with them a valuable part of humanity's cultural heritage.

So extended families have been growing, and over the long haul, empathy has spread, largely for the better but sometimes for worse. One surprising indication of the spread of empathy is that the relative number of the deaths in wars and conquests has been declining throughout history. Almost as many people were slaughtered during the Mongol capture of Eurasia some eight hundred years ago—when the human population was about one-sixteenth today's size—as died in World War II. Indeed, warfare (as opposed to other forms of violence) seems to have evolved with agriculture, and estimates indicate that bloodletting among early farmers could have been even worse than that perpetrated by the Mongols.[22] The notoriously belligerent Yanamamo lost more than a third of their males in warfare, and casualties in the frequent wars among early inhabitants of Mesopotamia were reported to be heavy. By contrast, in the American Civil

War, the bloodiest conflict in U.S. history, only about one in forty adult males (fifteen to sixty years old) were killed in battle.

Perhaps more telling, there's no record of the "others" feeling sorry for the tens or scores of thousands beheaded or blinded when city-states were conquered by the Assyrians, or for the hundreds of thousands who died gruesomely, often impaled on stakes, when Shaka built the Zulu nation. But many in other countries were empathetic with what happened to Jews, Cambodians, Southern Sudanese, and Tutsis in their more recent holocausts, and many today are empathetic with the situation of the residents of the Gaza strip and with the lives of women under Taliban rule. So while *us* in opposition to *them* is more than alive and well, a global *us* is spreading, but its increase has been too gradual and haphazard. Almost everyone is to some degree empathetic with other people, but the strength and reach of that empathy needs rapid reinforcement. We all need to be able to put ourselves more readily in the shoes of others, even others we now view as "them."

We, the authors, have seen in our lives some signs of the ongoing change, of the spread of empathy and the broadening of family-like groups. When a student in 1964, REO went to a farewell party for a friend who was going to Mississippi to help register "Negro" voters.* They then went out for a drink, and both wondered before saying goodbye what he would find there. Farewell it turned out to be, for REO's friend, Andy Goodman, found death a few weeks later, along with two other civil rights workers.

A decade before that, PRE and a colleague, the late Ralph Barr, organized white and black students into groups to sit in restaurants that refused service to Negroes during lunch time. The groups would not be served, but the restaurants wouldn't make any money either, and after many threats of violence (but none carried out), the restaurants of Lawrence, Kansas, were desegregated.

It was the first time any one of us in Kansas had been involved in a group activity where the members had several different skin colors. A few years ago, at a retirement party for another friend, who was chancellor of a college, there was another new experience. There were scores of people present: heads of fire departments, state senators, mayors, CEOs, entrepreneurs, museum directors. The striking thing: all of them were African American. It was almost impossible to believe there was a time, in recent memory, when very few African Americans could vote freely, let alone become president.

The racial mix is growing and spreading, in part because of increasing communication and familiarity with exotic cultures and mores, fostered by

---

* REO, here and in subsequent uses, indicates a personal example from author Robert Ornstein; PRE indicates a personal example from author Paul Ehrlich.

increased media attention, global travel, and even food, and in part because of a growing global labor market leading to increasing migration (and, sadly, sometimes to more, not less, us versus the others). At a recent get-together at a favorite café in Paris, REO found that the staff was very different from the French he expected: a Polish barista, a Greek server, a baker from the banlieues, whose family is originally from francophone Senegal. All now have a common currency; all keep in touch with families via the Internet, and all use fast trains and very cheap flights to visit their family homes. Years ago scores of different currencies were used in Europe, and no one would think of going to Brussels for lunch.

Work too is different now. In doing a new website, REO received photos from a collaborator on the East Coast, sent them to another in Mexico to check, and sent them to a third in god-knows-where for captions; when the photo stage was done, the website went off to Australia for writing. The website will be available to children in Kenya or New Guinea who might share a cheap laptop.

In addition, PRE coedited a text on how to conserve biodiversity, a text whose chapters were written by people scattered all over the world and that will be made available globally, without charge, on the Web.[23] And he now has regular meetings with colleagues around the world in the computer-simulated virtual world of Second Life.

We've all seen dramatic examples of the spread of empathy in difficult circumstances. Innumerable people have been displaced by war and killings, but the events show both aspects of empathy—that of others who are willing to accept strangers into their cultural family and that of those transplanted who are willing to "read" the recipient culture and fit into the new family.

A nine-year-old boy grows up in the tight-knit society of Southern Sudan, knowing everyone he sees, including all his aunts, uncles, and cousins. He plays one day in the bush and hears screams that soldiers are killing his family and burning his village. He runs with others, far, far away—first to Uganda, then to Kenya, becoming one of the "Lost Boys" of the Southern Sudan. Then, after many trials, he is airlifted by aid agencies to Boston, a place where he sees more people on the "T"—the underground transit system—in a morning ride than he knew in his village so long ago. He's made the transition from a small agricultural community in which he was familiar with everybody to the modern world, completing a transformation that has taken the West two millennia.

At first, without the basics of family and extended family, Mangok Bol was "lost" once more. But he got accustomed to seeing thousands of strangers daily, learned English, and finally became a graduate student at Brandeis.

He keeps in touch with his wife, another "lost" person from the Sudan, via instant messages. She is living, however, in Australia. He sent us this story via e-mail. Modern transport and communications can make family relationships more "extended" than one could imagine before World War II. And the ability of human beings to adapt rapidly to entirely new family systems is attested by stories like Mangok's (his full account is appended in the notes):[24]

My first surprise landing at JFK International Airport was the large numbers of people present at the airport at that time, a crowd of the kind that I have never seen before. What puzzled me about this crowd was that each individual in the crowd seems to pay no attention to others passing by them. After carefully looking at the airport crowd and how fast they were walking, I was totally convinced that life in America was going to be a strange one. I told myself that these American were not welcoming and appreciative of other people coming to their country. My reaction to American life was a frustration from somebody from a place where you almost know everybody to a place where you almost don't know anybody, even those who live in the same building with you. Massachusetts was my final destination, joining my distant cousins who came ahead of me.

My first day in Boston, Massachusetts, was amazing except that I was overwhelmed by the cars on the street in downtown Boston and the number of people wandering around in downtown. I remember asking my caseworker at some point whether something important was going on in the city but he laughed and said, all these people you are seeing here are just walking around or doing some shopping. The caseworker explanation did not make any sense to me whatsoever. What surprises me the most was that nobody seems to care about the presence of another person walking next to them? I thought that everybody knew each other but I was wrong and I would learn this later as time went by.

The urge for small-group/family membership remains strong in the electronic age via new media that promote social networking. Sites such as Facebook and Second Life are splendid tools to keep in touch and to communicate what one thinks about—almost anything from favorite recipes to political ideas—but they also can magnify differences and conflicts and increase the dissention and discord between groups. As with much of modern communications, these extended ways of association amplify any tendency, be it socially useful or dangerous to others.

The expansion of communications—from writing, printing, and telegraphy to radio, cinema, TV, the World Wide Web—has increased awareness of the values and needs of the cultures of "them." It has led to a multiplication of international institutions and treaties, a boom in international travel and migration, and, as we pointed out previously, a decline in the diversity of languages.[25] The television and other media coverage of the horrors faced by U.S. troops and the fate of enemy civilians was a factor in loss of support for the Vietnam War among Americans. Now communication is at a dramatic high point: the globalization of information, especially visual, has made people aware of the culture—the nongenetic information possessed corporately by their extended family—of the "others," to the degree we both once hoped would help bind humanity more into a single family. Technological advances have made social networking possible at a scale never seen before.

But the expansion of media channels, including millions of blogs, has an unhappy downside of encouraging polarization. Any individual—right wing, left wing, pro-choice, pro-life, racist, antiracist, religious, atheistic—can find a media outlet that will represent his or her prejudices almost exactly. Hate the idea of a charismatic Democratic president? Watch Fox News. Believe all the problems of the world trace to economic and power inequities? Read the *Nation* or the *New York Review of Books*. Believe invading Iraq and Afghanistan was to spread democracy? Watch Wolf Blitzer on CNN. Want snappy right-wing slogans? Tune in the *Rush Limbaugh Show*. Think the End Times are upon us? Go to the Rapture Ready website. One effect this wide array of media orientations clearly has is *reducing* empathy for other groups. This may be partly responsible for the growing political polarization in the United States, indicated by the December 2009 first-time passage of a major social bill (health care) in the U.S. Senate on a straight party-line vote.

But, as we have also indicated, polarization is not the only reason all is not sweetness and light on the "spreading empathy" front. Unhappily, the old saw "familiarity breeds contempt" often appears to be more to the point in today's world. Or, to put it another way, the old liberal-education idea that knowledge leads automatically to tolerance doesn't appear to be correct—at least on the time scale within which action is required.

Persians spend a lot of time demonizing Israelis, who in turn demonize the Israeli Arabs, the other Arab societies, and the Palestinians; while within Arab society, Sunni Muslims attack the Shia, Shia attack Sunnis, and the Sunnis of Sudan attack the Christian Central African blacks living in the south. Catholics and Protestants have clashed for centuries in Ireland; Crips hate Bloods, mestizos, and blue-eyed blancos in different gangs; fans of one soccer team attack fans of the opponent, causing international incidents; and in the

Balkans, there are so many imagined family groups that can be persuaded to kill one another that even specialists in geopolitics can lose track.

In addition, the digital technologies that have so aided globalization—especially cell phones and the Internet—have empowered groups such as Basque separatists and Islamic fundamentalists to disrupt the human family in ways impossible to imagine a half century ago. And cell phones have a new use: they are great for triggering roadside bombs.

Such disruption of empathy happens almost every day with Internet rumors and accusations about celebrities' sex lives and politicians' creeds. For instance, a *Washington Post*/NBC News poll of May 7, 2010, found that more than 14 percent of Americans (called "birthers") claim that Obama was not born in the United States and thus he is not eligible to be president.[26] Not one of "us" then.

In part, the issue is the biologically trivial but socially powerful one of skin pigmentation. Outright lies about Obama's appointees clog the blogosphere, with the obvious goal of having his presidency fail. The bloggers and their representatives in Congress show no empathetic consideration for the potential millions or billions of victims of such failure. One can say the same thing for the long and successful efforts of corporate interests to conceal the seriousness of climate disruption, in the same way they did for decades with regard to the dangers of smoking cigarettes.[27]

Why does the job of empathy disrupters seem so easy? Part of the answer is our small-group history, which makes a man like Barack Obama seem to be so "other" to many Americans.* But when we say we're a small-group animal, what exactly do we mean? The anthropologist Robin Dunbar and his colleagues, in an innovative series of studies over the years, have offered a new and startling perspective on how human beings became so successful. It builds on the thesis that Hrdy presents, although the Dunbar group's work is separate and focused not on the number of caregivers but on the size of the immediate family group itself. Human beings, you

---

* It was true of African Americans as well. The former mayor of San Francisco, Willie Brown, an African American himself, wrote in the *San Francisco Chronicle* on October 18, 2009, of his initial reactions to working with a politician with a "them" name. "The president's visit was a far cry from his first fundraiser here in 2004. He was just a state senator from Illinois running for the U. S. Senate, and I took on the job of filling the Waterfront Restaurant at $250 a head. Being from the age when Cassius Clay became Muhammad Ali and lots of other blacks took on Muslim or Africanized names, my first question when he called to ask for my help was, 'What's your real name?' 'It IS my real name,' he replied. 'Nobody named Barack Obama is going to get elected to anything,' I said. Fast forward to November '08. The telephone rings day after the election and I hear this voice: 'Hello, Willie Brown. This is President-elect Barack Obama.'"

may have noticed, along with other primates are very social animals. Our lives revolve, as said, around other people, what they're thinking of us, what we're thinking of them, and in less industrialized cultures how we can either cooperate with them or fight them to get resources (come to think of it, it's not so different in our lives).

This intense social life is connected to our unusually large brains with a large percentage devoted to the cerebral cortex (the outer layer of tissue on the brain, center of cognitive abilities). And Dunbar shows that the size of species' living groups is related to brain size, specifically neocortical volume, in non-human and human primates.[28] The neocortex, with something like one hundred million meters of neural wiring, is the center of human "higher" mental functions such as speech, problem solving, and imagination.* That volume is related to the number of relationships that we can keep track of. Dunbar also found that social grooming in primates maintains groups, and the amount of time devoted to social grooming correlates well with group size.

Given the large human cortex, Dunbar's number (now a classic in the field) is that about 150 individuals is the size of most human groups where people relate often enough to have strong bonds based on direct personal knowledge.[29] And it seems to have been the case throughout our history. Neolithic villages in Mesopotamia are of about the same size. Twenty to twenty-five dwellings seems to be the typical size of a number of village sites dated to around 6500–5500 BCE, and anthropologist John Oates estimates village population sizes of 150–200.[30]

And Dunbar's 150 occurs frequently in contemporary human society. The Hutterites (a fundamentalist group that lives and farms communally in South Dakota and Manitoba) average about that number of individuals in a group, and they regard 150 individuals as the limiting size for their farming communities: once a community reaches this size, steps are taken to split it into two daughter communities.[31] Academic research groups in the sciences usually consist of up to two hundred individuals, but rarely more. Most armies have a basic unit of about 150 men. This was as true of the Roman army as of modern armies since the sixteenth century.[32] The size of a company in the U.S. Army in World War II was 100–250 men, with companies in combat infantry units surprisingly close to 150 soldiers.

And in everyday life, the number is pretty much the same. Dunbar found that the average number of recipients of Christmas cards in his survey was 153.[33] Dunbar has documented this rough number in scores of other situations, from singing groups to an exhaustive study of the number of people one

---

* The neocortex is most recently evolved thin outer layer of the hemispheres of the brain, which is characteristic of and limited to mammals.

could ask to find a person in another country. In one study he asked people to see which person they knew who could help to send a message to, for instance (our examples), a goat herder in Greece, a Filipino boatman, and the like. In each case the person would try to think of someone, like Aunt Mary who went to Greece last year or the waiter at the local South Asian restaurant. The questioning went on (it was exhausting as well as exhaustive) until the unfortunate subjects in the study could think of no additional new friends. And the number of people one might use to search the world? It was close to 150.

With much speeded transport, cinema, radio, TV, and the Web, we're more united globally than even our Victorian ancestors, but our brains' limitations retard the spreading of empathy because of the limited number of people we can keep in our organic Facebook. But that communication network can speed the spread of disinformation and hate as fast as information that will spread empathy, while threats to our global civilization are arriving much faster than the human family is unifying and cooperating in keeping our common balance on the tightrope of civilization. Those threats require that we somehow speed up the realization that all humanity is a single family, with all of us having similar genetic endowments, needs, goals, and vulnerabilities, as well as connected fates. We're not Pollyannaish that creating a global family can be done, but it is the one thing that's *required* if humanity is to create a sustainable society.

The story of how cultural evolution got around that Dunbar number is straightforward. The human population has grown from a few million individual beings scattered throughout the globe ten thousand years ago to almost seven billion today. That's roughly a thousand people now for every one person then. During that period people found advantages in organizing themselves into many different kinds of groups and in learning to associate themselves with larger and larger family-style units—most with population sizes far beyond the Dunbar number. Indeed, a few people now even feel some allegiance to everyone—to that entire human family. Dramatic changes in group allegiance have even gone on during our own lifetimes, while humanity's population size has roughly tripled. But those expanding allegiances tended to spread empathy beyond the built-in capacity of our brains to form strong face-to-face relationships. Cultural evolution produced advantages to being empathetic with complete strangers, and that's the trend we must accelerate.

Even with that spread of empathy, the us-versus-others scenario is now a key barrier to creating the new level of cooperation needed, both within and between countries, to solve the human predicament. *Our* families, however extended they become, still make us wary of people of other families. That arrangement, which was once likely beneficial in small, isolated communities, now blocks us from dealing with many of the common problems that face humanity (for instance, climate disruption or the threat of pandemics), even when many are aware of the need for cooperative solutions. So is the end of the story an inevitable catastrophe? Not necessarily. Lowering that barrier, a descendent of the Dunbar speed bump, could allow the citizens of a globalized world to find their way to a more secure and sustainable future. But speed is of the essence—we are degrading our life-support systems much more rapidly than we are spreading our horizons of concern.

We hope that humankind can overcome its family history and surmount the global challenges it faces; after all, as we said, it's come a long way toward that already. It's time for a big change, analogous to "growing up." And the analogy isn't so far-fetched. If we, as human beings, would step back and look at ourselves, we'd glimpse a more radical viewpoint: we'd realize that our species, *Homo sapiens*, is in its "adolescence."* Early on, our species comprised a few scattered family bands in Africa, groups that were often isolated from one another. Eventually *Homo sapiens* spread around the world. Humanity has had its amazing growth spurt since the Industrial Revolution, increasing some sixfold in size.

Now we need to act in a way appropriate to our mature size and new power, as a clumsy teenager has to put aside childish things to act like an adult. Just as an adolescent has not fully developed the frontal lobes of its brain that supply social skill and restraint, our global society has not yet fully developed the institutions that would supply the same skill and restraint on an Earth-wide scale.

But it's possible; people have changed behavior in such fundamental areas as the number of children per family considered desirable, the propriety of slave holding, kindness to animals, voting, race relations, gay rights, and even smoking (one of humanity's most addictive habits). The changes took place when the need was identified and accepted by many. And when it comes to empathy, as we'll see, we now know that what may turn out to be the basic mechanisms, "mirror neurons" that respond to the actions of others, are built into our brains.

Today we citizens need to decide where and how to make similar big changes that would help the formation of a genuine global family as an additional "place" to which to pledge allegiance. That aim is recognized as important by many: the new president of the United States said in his inaugural address, "We cannot help but believe that the old hatreds shall someday pass; that the lines of tribe shall soon dissolve."

---

* Human beings have been in existence for something like a fifth of the average life span of a mammalian species, and a fifth of a human life span is roughly the end of adolescence.

CHAPTER 3

The Seeds of Family Values and How They Sprouted

BEING born into a small-family group consisting of close relatives was the experience of our ancestors for millions of years. And traces of our early ancestors' families persist to this day in all of us. Our relationships with our parents and kids, how many children we ourselves choose to have, our employer, the football team we root for, our religion, our political party, our nation, and our favorite soap opera are all partly determined by the values that evolved in those ancient families. These values trace back to the very beginnings of humanity, and made it possible for us to become Earth's dominant animal. And these values are partially responsible for the paradox of dominance—the paradox of why so brilliant a family organism behaves in ways so stupid that it may have planted the seeds of its own destruction.

To get closer to those roots, to fully understand family and empathy, we need to begin nearer to the beginning of our evolutionary history and our biology. And we should start with the marvelous brains without which there would be no articulated family values. Human beings evolved big brains under several evolutionary pressures. Big brains allow their owners to deal successfully with an array of options, to adapt to environmental variability.

A bear is a classic omnivore—an eater of both plant and animal foods—and bears have big brains. If a bear eating berries spots a fawn hiding in the grass, it can switch its diet instantly. If the berries run out, the bear can go down to the river and try its luck fishing, and we've all seen the YouTube videos of bears finding the plentiful garbage cans in our national parks and even figuring out how to get into a parked car with cookies (and hopefully not the kids) inside.

In contrast, caterpillars are classic herbivores, and most are restricted in their diets to the leaves of one plant or to a closely related set of plants. A small-brained caterpillar can't make choices; if the plant that provides its food dries up suddenly and the caterpillar can't find another of the same kind, it simply dies. The big dinosaurs, both herbivores and carnivores, had proportionately small brains and couldn't do anything about the climate change following an extraterrestrial body's collision with Earth some sixty-five million years ago. They couldn't adapt to the freezing cold that ensued, and their only "choice" was to go extinct.[1] Only the little birds survived to represent the dinosaurs today. But the bear must pay a penalty for its adaptability; it must supply its proportionately larger brain with a greater percentage of the energy it takes in than the caterpillar or dinosaur must deliver to their relatively tiny control centers.

One thing that a big brain allows is a sense of self. We human beings have a sense of self; however, that "sense" is not limited to human beings—other primates seem to "know themselves," at least to a limited extent. In its simplest form, a sense of self is seen in great apes such as chimpanzees and even in monkeys. When a dab of paint is placed on a chimp's face and the chimp is given a mirror, the chimp touches and examines the unusual spot.[2] This is often thought to indicate that they have at least an elementary sense of self.*

Other experiments suggest that chimps and at least some other great apes have that sense well developed. This is a sense completely missing from some other social beings, such as leaf-cutter or Argentine ants, whose "groups" may contain tens of millions or even tens of trillions of individuals, with (presumably) no theories about what's going on in the minds of their fellow in-group ants;[3] there is just a set of genetically programmed responses to chemical and tactile clues.

Human beings have far larger brains and need to make much more complex environmental choices than do dinosaurs, bears, or even chimps. The evolution of big brains in human beings was in part a response to the growing ability of a highly social primate to perceive, imagine, and project the thoughts of others of their group and to see themselves as individuals, separate from those others. Our ancestors had developed that sense of what others are thinking, feeling, and intending, something we, today, employ constantly.

Those ancestors had a sense of self and realized that other beings had not only their own senses of self but also intentions that might differ from their own. It's a realization that human children start to acquire, according to some researchers, as early as twelve months. At age two or two and a

---

* Of course, it might only indicate that the animals have a good idea of what a mirror is, but the general point is probably true.

half, children begin to realize that other people can actually have a different idea of what's going on than they do. This is a mental development that is beyond that of adults from other species, with the possible exception of chimps and other great apes.

The classic studies involve an experimenter, children, and candy. The experimenter shows a child some candy in a pink box while this child is sitting next to another child or, for the convenience of the study, a doll. The other child (or doll) is asked to leave the room, and the candy is moved from the pink box to a blue box. Before the other child (or the doll) returns, the child who remained is asked, "Where will he look for the candy?" Young children say, "The blue box," because that is where the candy actually is. Older ones say, "The pink box," because they know the other child has a different understanding, even if incorrect. This sense of what others think is called, in unfortunate jargon, "a theory of mind," and it speaks to a knowledge of self and a knowledge of different selves or different minds of others.[4]

Before one can identify with a family, whether nuclear, extended, or extremely extended, it is necessary to identify oneself as distinct from others. A sense of self and a "theory of mind" are both fundamental to a sense of belonging to a human family. In early families, there was an important third prerequisite—an ability to recognize kin. This is widespread among animals. In higher primates it may be based on familiarity—the ability to recognize faces or odors. In chimpanzee troops and hunter-gatherer groups, the cohorts of individuals were most often closely related to one another. Indeed, one can imagine that even in groups that exchanged individuals for reproductive purposes, most of the sexual exchange occurred between neighboring bands with a high degree of genetic affinity.

In addition, even chimpanzees have an uncanny ability to recognize visually who is related to whom. In the lab they can match up father-son pairs on the basis of photographs alone. Face recognition, either of compatriots or leaders, remains a major feature of family-based organization in human societies today. In early human settlements, the entire group presumably was an extended family, as in the Southern Sudan today. It would typically consist of close genetically related individuals who recognized each other by sight and, perhaps, their body odor as well. So, there are limits to the number of other people with whom each of us can relate—Dunbar's number, again, around 150 in most cases.*

How did families evolve, and are there universal or near-universal principles upon which they are organized? How did us versus them get going

---

* Before, of course, the Internet, Facebook, MySpace, Twitter, Second Life, and god-knows-what else.

in our hairy and unwashed precursors a long, long time ago—despite (or because of) the evolution of empathy?

Great ape mothers—female chimpanzees, bonobos, gorillas, and orangutans—all cling jealously to and keep very close contact with their offspring. They nurse and protect them and do not allow other individuals to gain access to them. And the offspring cling tenaciously to their mothers. Those ape kids do not grow up with a family; they grow up primarily, and early on almost exclusively, with mom alone. Human family preferences are different from those of the other ape species, and these differences trace to our brains.

Remember, it's not that human babies who are born at seven or eight months are the only "preemies"; *all* of our kids are born, in the evolutionary sense, prematurely. Human beings are premature in that there is a long period of juvenile helplessness as the brain grows and matures. Compare how quickly our pets develop; six weeks after birth, a kitten can survive on its own, and a horse can walk and follow its mother almost immediately upon being born.

Enormous brain growth and development is required for an individual human being to learn to live in his or her locale and social milieu. Human babies must even learn to see—infants can't see as do adults. Their lengthy helplessness requires a great amount of attention from their primary caregivers, who are almost always their mothers. Mothers' caring duties limit their other activities. Human beings produce the slowest maturing and most "costly" primate babies to raise, but moms cannot and do not perform this difficult and complex job all by themselves.

Given this period of helplessness and vulnerability, and the great amount of effort required for rearing and educating the young, you'd think that the population problem would be too few of us surviving, right? Strangely enough, human beings reproduce faster than their closest primate relatives.[5] Sarah Hrdy emphasizes that some of the most important aspects of adult human psychology trace to our evolutionary divergence from the other great apes in family arrangements, as human ancestors increasingly became cooperative breeders. As she says, "No other social creature is capable of feeling quite so 'lonely' even when surrounded by familiar conspecifics."[6]

So there has been a very long history of *Homo sapiens*' social interactions focusing on a "family" of a few adults, their offspring, and an assortment of helpers. Those arrangements, which permitted relatively high reproductive rates compared to other great apes, got our basic units as human beings started on the road to becoming the dominant animal on the planet.

Evolutionary biologists initially spent a lot of effort trying to show how a bonded pair of human parents developed, since they erroneously believed that this was the early human condition. That idea is virtually dead, but it contributed to the common notion that the ideal human family resembles that of seven-year-old Theodore ("the Beaver") Cleaver of the 1950s situation comedy *Leave It to Beaver*. It is, like many other myths, understandable—and comforting. The very wholesome parents, June and Ward Cleaver, and their very wholesome twelve-year-old son, Wally, struggle to keep the rambunctious Beaver in line in their very wholesome suburban home, in their very wholesome suburban community.

The Cleaver-style family remains a representation of the natural state of humanity as imagined, by and large, by the American advocates of "Christian family values," a safe life in a world unsullied by the complexity of social arrangements. It is the world that lives on in the imagination of conservative politicians, the American Family Association, and the American Society for the Defense of Tradition, Family, and Property. The second of these two organizations has given us the following definition:[7] "By family we mean that institution based on monogamous and indissoluble marriage. The family is the basic cell of the social body and in entire accordance with the natural order of things. In it, one finds the stability of society and an ideal climate for the formation of children. Moreover, the family was elevated yet higher by Our Lord Jesus Christ who instituted the sacrament of Matrimony."*

In the real world, this definition applies to one form, and even today not the most common form, of what is often called a "nuclear family." The reality is summarized by social scientist Judith Bruce: "The idea that the family is a stable and cohesive unit in which father serves as economic provider and mother serves as emotional caregiver is a myth. The reality is that trends like unwed motherhood, rising divorce rates, smaller households and the feminization of poverty are not unique to America, but are occurring worldwide."[8]

Above all, it is important to recognize that the family that is "in decline" in the minds of many politicians is an idealized family version that dates

---

* "Of all the seven sacraments, Matrimony is the most widely challenged in the Catholic Church. It has also been the main cause of disunity in Christianity"; from the Real Presence Association, a Catholic faith–based website, quoting John A. Hardon www .therealpresence.org/archives/Marriage.htm (accessed May 12, 2010). From the same author we have this statement: "At the heart of Protestantism is the denial that Christ instituted the Sacrament of Matrimony. Moreover, no Protestant denomination in the world believes that marriage cannot be dissolved with a right to 'remarry,' not once, but as often as a nominally married husband and wife want to." John A. Hardon, "Matrimony: The Sacrament of Fidelity and Procreation," Our Catholic Faith, www .ourcatholicfaith.org/articles/Matrimony%20-%20The%20Sacrament%20of%20 Fidelity%20and%20Procreation.html (accessed May 12, 2010).

back only several decades or so, and in the United States "not a lot further than the 1950s." As Sarah Hrdy says, "Even though there was only a blip in time when a single-wage earner could reliably and predictably support an average family, this myth of the nuclear family, with a nurturing mother at home and a providing father at work, became an American ideal."[9]

In short, *there is no reason to believe that the stable, small-nuclear-family values have ever been a dominant feature of families in a real society.*[10] Until recently, most societies were structured into extended families, characteristic of agricultural societies. Such families featured males often controlling several females in polygynous relationships,* early marriage age with matings determined by parents, couples starting out living in the parents' home, complicated economic exchanges accompanying marriages and extending to rather distant relatives, and an absence of today's notion of romantic love but the presence of a high fertility rate.[11] Without a doubt, the idea of romantic love as expressed by the troubadours of the High Middle Ages was of courtly love, and *not* of one that existed between husband and wife.

Then, as societies industrialized, there arose individualistic marriages centered on post-teenage couples in romantic love. Eventually, these pairs set up a residence separate from the parents immediately after marriage, and had much more distant interactions with siblings, cousins, and other kin. But mom and pop and the kids—nuclear families like the Cleavers, based on the love of husband and wife and with dad earning and mom tending hearth and offspring—live on as the prototypical family situation in the popular imagination of the West. The family definition is often expanded to include various relatives living in the same household (grandma helping with the kids) or elsewhere (Uncle Leo in Miami), or all people identified as kin—the invite list of genetically related people for the family reunion plus those associated with them by marriage.

The great variation that occurs among human societies even today makes "family" in the narrowest sense difficult to define beyond stating that almost all comprise bonded, sexually or genetically related individuals, who cooperate more with each other in their productive and reproductive lives than they do with most other individuals.

For most of human history, however, the key to family "success" has not depended upon whether the female attracts a male to help raise her young, but instead upon how many individuals beyond the father (sometimes technically called "alloparents") were available and willing to help with the offspring.

---

* Technically, *polygyny* is one male bonded to more than one female; *polyandry* is one female bonded to more than one male; and *polygamy* is either.

That "dad, mom, and 2.4 kids" ideal model doubtless traces in part to the recently reduced child mortality rate in the West, where public health interventions like immunizations, clean water and sanitary waste disposal, health inspections of food supply, and social programs have reduced the deaths from having inadequate child care. In the past families had to have more caregivers if the children were to survive—including more children to serve later as alloparents.

The model family doesn't mesh with the family structure of our distant hominin ancestors.* It doesn't even mesh with Judeo-Christian biblical "family values," which, after all, valued polygyny—the amazing King Solomon supposedly had seven hundred wives and three hundred concubines.[12] Those "biblical values" included the notion that brides who were not virgins, or women who had been raped, should be stoned to death, as should a woman and man who have an adulterous sexual encounter.[13] The empathy deficit was gigantic in biblical times when people followed brutal and sadistic gods, and it still is in cultures that allow men to abuse women within and outside of their families.

People can form intimate family associations that diverge dramatically from what born-again Christians visualize. The best-studied exception to the rule is kinship and social structure in the Na (pronounced "Nay"), a minority people of southern China.[14] The Na culture has neither husbands nor fathers—the males involved in sexual reproduction are not involved in the family groups. The majority of families in Na society occur as matrilines (groups based on common descent traced through females). The matrilines are the family units of production. Reproduction, however, is mostly accomplished by a system of promiscuous covert "visiting" by men who do not otherwise participate in any family activities.

The overt goal of male-female relations among the Na is sexual pleasure, but males are also viewed as giving gifts to the matrilines by allowing women to get pregnant. The necessity for intercourse to produce children is recognized, but a genetic contribution from the male is not. The sperm is seen as a contribution that allows development to start, as exemplified in the Na sayings on the topic: "If the rain does not fall from the sky, the grass will not grow from the ground" and "Having a good time [making love] is a charity to the woman's household." The Na expand on this: "In mating, the aim of the woman is to have children, and the aim of the man is to have a good time and to do an act of charity."[15] The Na see vows of male-female fidelity as shameful, as it involves a negotiation or exchange that is

---

*Hominins are all forms of human beings after our line diverged from that of the chimpanzees.

counter to their customs.[16] Children are not associated with their fathers, and in many cases are unaware of their identities (not surprisingly since women frequently have dozens of lovers). Girls are associated with their mothers, boys with their maternal uncles, who serve the same sorts of roles that fathers do in other societies.

There is a powerful anti-incest taboo within each matriline, with sanctions that include death. Siblings live and eat together all their lives, and raise the kids produced cooperatively. A Na man told an anthropologist that children are closest to their mothers, maternal uncles, and brothers and sisters, and that it would be shameful to leave mom and sis to get married. Thus among the Na, the fathers clearly do not bring home the bacon, and generally the children are well taken care of by their alloparents. If there is a crisis leading to a shortage of either males or females, the Na's complex adoption procedures can be used to remedy the situation.

What *might* mesh with the concerns of those focused on the illusory "standard" nuclear family is that in humanity's early family patterns, the *nurturing traditions were automatically carried forward because they were required for survival*. Now that link has been largely broken by modern medicine and social programs, and the result, according to some psychologists, is a decline in the emotional well-being in increasing numbers of children who survive despite the absence of the close care from numerous alloparents. Sarah Hrdy considers family values today and asks, "Are we losing the art of nurture?"[17] In some parts of society that may be the case. In any case, young human beings are clearly best off surrounded by caregivers, but in some segments of modern societies that is less and less likely—with consequences that can only be guessed.

How families arose among our distant ancestors will doubtless remain a topic of controversy and contentious research.[18] There may be no single story about the origins of the family, beyond the point that cooperative breeding played an early and key role. At the time of the early hunter-gatherer bands, there probably was little distinction between the band and the family. Everyone was related to everyone else, social structures were egalitarian, children were routinely raised cooperatively,[19] and emotional closeness was supplied to children as often by other group members as by parents, other group members who were normally fairly close relatives.

Equally important, the group was coherent enough for everyone to recognize and know everyone else—and even when families migrated from one group to another, the groups were small enough so that the facial recognition mechanism in each individual's brain was likely to store all group members.*

---

* As in the Southern Sudan today described by Mangok Bol.

Since the majority of people encountered day in and day out were kin, it may well be that the face-recognition module in the brain was also part of a kin-recognition module. Many young children seem to think they know everyone—all grey-beards are "grandpa." Originally, that was probably the case, with recognition extended if a new individual joined the group. But much more social learning is required today.

However early human families evolved in the beginning, it seems clear that they are the rock upon which the us-them distinction was built. Our first experiences don't determine our character completely and irreversibly, as Sigmund Freud thought, but they do influence strongly how the connections inside the human brain get wired up.

Think of the modern diversity of human cultures, languages, and lifeways and the various adaptations to the world's environments that show a flexibility far beyond that of our distant ancestors. Human brains are wired by early experience so that their possessors can speak one of several thousand languages and can live in the heights of the Andes or below sea level, in the desert near Khartoum or in the near-sea-level swampland of Bangladesh or even in a Manhattan high-rise. Our species can do so because of our "prematurity"; as a result of human babies' early birth, the human brain comes into the world with many uncommitted and even unborn brain cells.

The human brain's development, more than any other, takes place after birth in the external environment. The sounds of the language one hears, even in the womb through the abdominal wall; the living and shelter patterns; the family relationships; the eating and food-gathering patterns; and the other prominent features of the environment are picked up by the developing brain. There are critical periods in that brain's development. For those exposed to many languages, the one heard and spoken most during the first six or so years becomes the dominant language.

This brain customization happens through a process that the biologist Gerald Edelman has well named "neural Darwinism."[20] During the development of an animal (including us), enormous surpluses of neurons are produced, and groups of those brain cells that get stimulated repeatedly (as in those that recognize certain speech sounds or those that receive a specific kind of visual stimulation) win the competition and get wired up in a network of connections, while the other associations just fade away.

If even a short period of stimulation from the outside world is lacking, there may be a permanent deficit. For example, REO got hit above the eye in a baseball game when he was five, and to protect the possibly injured right eye, his doctor put a patch over it. That right eye is permanently less sensitive in the dark than is his left eye, a deficit due to just a week of wearing an eye patch at the "right," or, really, wrong, time in his brain's development.

All human lives first begin with one family structure, one set of physical structures surrounding us, one language structure, the structure and style of means and lifeways—such as what we eat, when we eat, and even in what order different dishes are consumed. We establish our view of the world based strongly on this early experience—and those early onset worldviews require much effort to modify.

That is clearest in learning a language: think how difficult it is for an adult English speaker to become fluent in Japanese (and vice versa) and how easy it is for all Japanese kids to learn Japanese. While all human beings are greatly shaped by the experiences of the first few years, in our first family, the crunch is that now humanity is faced with the monumental task of dealing with those seven billion other people, all of whom have had different early life experiences.

The Evolution of "Them"

FROM their earliest days, our forbears organized themselves into small groups and, over the past sixty millennia as they scattered out from their African homeland to occupy an "empty" world, they needed to stick together. There was an important consequence for our evolution; for many, many thousands of years, most of our ancestors saw almost no "outsiders" on a daily basis and had no allegiance except to those who lived in close proximity—their "troop," their own kind, their family in one sense or another.

These latter people, recall, were almost all genetic relatives, even ones who had transferred from nearby groups. This was the first extended family, and it was as natural a unit for *Homo sapiens* as is the pack for wolves. But the ability to recognize some people as close kin means that we classify others as not being kin.

There is a lot of evidence that kin versus non-kin distinctions are programmed into our brains by our genes and early experiences. For example, our inherited tendency seems to be to consider as kin anyone we see day in and day out when we are young. Thus in Israel, where there are strong incest taboos, unrelated children raised together in kibbutzim from an early age rarely marry. The rules against copulation with kin "misfire" and keep unrelated people from mating.

Brother-sister marriages were encouraged in some situations, such as those that were necessary to preserve wealth and status in royal lineages in ancient Egypt, in the Inca kingdom, and in Hawaii; "us" was about as closely controlled as it could possibly be. And it's not so uncommon to have close relations with close relations: parent-offspring incest is found in many cultures and was likely common in Western society, especially in Victorian times.[1] But whether incest regulation was a feature of our ancestral hunter-gatherer bands is difficult to assess, especially since taking spouses from outside the band doubtless was common as a way of making alliances with other groups.

Incest avoidance, by diverse arrangements in different bands, could well have been one of the ways of determining who associates with whom in hunter-gatherer societies. But on one basis or another, early groups certainly built their own distinctive cultures—their own "our" culture, passed on from generation to generation and different from the strange rules and habits of other groups, "their" cultures. This worked well as long as Earth was sparsely populated; as a result, the difference between us and them may have been more often than not a source of wonder and interest as "our" groups met "others" to exchange information, goods, foods, and even women.

Then as human populations increased and began to settle down and practice agriculture, and as accumulated property could be passed on to future generations, an enormous variety of family structures developed. Along with that development came codes and rituals, seen in the first records of the Mesopotamian civilizations. The law code of Hammurabi, who ruled Babylon from 1792 to 1750 BCE, contained complex rules (to be enforced, of course, by the appointed bureaucrats) about family issues that ranged from regulations about inheritance, divorce, and adoption, to the property rights of women. And way back then, the Assyrians were already trying to conquer other groups to spread their "us," their religion.

Diverse family structures were natural responses to the tasks that families had to accomplish—as in the relaxation of incest taboos with the purpose of preserving family power. In any case, far from having a standard "nuclear family" for humanity, the variety of family arrangements, of who are us and who are them, and whose gods and customs are "right," became stunning.[2]

Trying to figure out the environmental correlates of family arrangements is a cottage industry in anthropology. It's sometimes literally the case: why, in some societies, does a wife move into her new husband's home, and in others the husband moves into the wife's home?[3] Why do some families trace descent through the male line and others through the female? Why was polygyny (one man married to more than one woman) frequent in some societies? Polygyny was common among biblical patriarchs and is nowadays allowed in Muslim countries under Sharia law, with men having up to four wives. Why does Tibet have polyandry (one woman married to several men) as a traditional marriage form? What explains the Na? In each system, the "us and them" varies.

In Islamic countries, additional women sexually bonded to a man in a polygynous marriage can be "us"; in Christian countries, they most definitely are "them"!

Anthropologists trace the evolution of a variety of family patterns to changing conditions. For example, descent traced through females probably developed with the shift from hunting and gathering to agriculture. Women, who in bands primarily foraged, became attached to the land as they took over care of crops and domestic animals. Women got to know land and crops, and the less they moved around, the more they produced for the family. Thus "matrilocality"—the woman staying in her birthplace at marriage, with males moving to them—became advantageous.

In some societies, men are permitted to "lend" their wives to other men—sometimes relatives, sometimes not. In the United States today, one common marital pattern is serial polygyny or serial polyandry—a man or a woman who marries, divorces, and remarries one or more times. This can lead to an astounding diversity of family relationships, of who's us and who's them. One couple we know calls their three kids his, hers, and ours.

The rules about sexual activities outside of the family also vary widely and are often ignored today in the United States, dramatically by holier-than-thou politicians. The most religious states[4] have the most births out of wedlock.[5] On the other hand, concubinage (the taking of a second, more-or-less-permanent but lower-status, socially acceptable wife-like partner) or the taking of mistresses (secret or socially approved) have been traditional relationship patterns in many societies, as in France today.[6]

The bottom line is that beyond the hunter-gatherer band, human societies organize into subgroups for production and reproduction based on genetic (brother-sister), marital (husband-wife, partner-partner), sexual (husband-concubine), and power relationships (paterfamilia-slave). The forms of organization have differed in detail from group to group and from environment to environment, and so has how empathy is expressed. Compare the "normal" reaction of a Western brother if his sister is raped with the reaction of a brother in some Islamic societies, where it is considered "normal" to stone the raped sister to death. Such variability is a consequence of a species that has evolved as a cooperative breeder, has moved into diverse environments, and then has begun to construct its own ecological niches and cultural adaptations on an unprecedented scale.

As the human population increased and as the groups became larger, their organization naturally became more complex—as needs arose to manage large farms and irrigation projects, to build roads, and for military defense (or adventurism). This opened the door to splitting society into the organizers and the organized, officers and enlisted men, the rulers and the ruled. In addition to kinship by genetics and marriage, the other kin-like relationships would become a way of organizing societies. Now our society needs to go further beyond the nuclear family, beyond the organizers and the organized into superior associations.[7]

Since sight is our primary sense, it is not surprising that when extending their families, people usually include others who seem visually similar. The most prominent aspect of human appearance is skin color; it's often the first thing we see of someone approaching from afar, even before we can tell male or female.

The skin color of human beings is variable in nature, and it has been changing as people migrate around the planet. The direction of natural selection for skin color depends primarily on how much of the sun's rays individuals are exposed to (those rays have complex beneficial and detrimental effects). Our ancestors' original dark skins became lighter after they left the blazing sun in Africa some sixty thousand years ago and moved through diverse environments over the entire planet.

The palest racist in 1960s Alabama was a light-skinned descendant of black Africans. The African American in Cambridge, Massachusetts, using cream to lighten her skin is anticipating a likely evolutionary trend if her descendents remain in such a dreary, overcast climate. Of course, the sociocultural aspects of "race" have interacted with natural selection to produce today's complex patterns. The selection gradients that produced the original geographic differentiation have been largely overwhelmed by rapid migration and interbreeding and what is known technically as *positive assortative mating* (people's tendency to mate with others of similar skin hues or other characteristics).

As complex as is the geographic distribution of skin color, it is not matched by variation in hair structure, height, or head shape. This is why the races that early scientists and most laypeople today imagine to be biological units simply don't exist. Yes, human beings vary greatly geographically in superficial characteristics; no, those differences don't divide them biologically into races.

Race is real in society; it is created culturally as a family extension and is the source of pervasive discrimination, the extreme of us and them. It's a weak point in the human tendency to show at least some empathy to other human beings. We suspect that racism is an ingredient of a small-group animal's attempts to retain family-like small groups to belong to—and that involves defining many other people, especially ones different from those closest to us in childhood, as being out of the group. While skin color is a handy tool for creating that separation and remains a powerful factor,[8] religion (and gender) also comes into play, as do imagined differences in descent or class membership. The results—from slavery and the subjugation of women to the Holocaust, the extermination of the *kulaks* in the

Soviet Union, and the genocide in Rwanda—are an all too familiar part of human behavior.

Genocides and political mass murders are recurrent phenomena—since World War II, nearly fifty such massacres have happened, killing between twelve million and twenty-two million civilians, more than all victims of internal and international wars since 1945—but these events rarely induce responses by policy makers.[9] A key to promoting genocide is defining people as an out-group and, usually, creating stories that exaggerate greatly any innate differences to justify exclusion from humanity. Making up these kinds of stories and their resultants have been demonstrated many times in schoolrooms.

The "hero of the month" in Jane Elliott's fourth-grade Iowa class in the spring of 1968 was Dr. Martin Luther King Jr. When King was shot later that spring, the students wanted to know why their hero had been killed. It was then that the teacher decided to teach her students from this all-white community about racism.

On the day after Martin Luther King Jr. was assassinated, Elliot, in a now famous study, demonstrated how quickly prejudice, both positive and negative, could develop. She separated the class into two groups by one physical characteristic—those who had blue eyes and those with brown. Elliot told the class that blue-eyed people were stupid and lazy and were not to be trusted. To identify them quickly, Elliott handed out strips of cloth that fastened at the neck as collars. The brown-eyed children happily put the shackles on their blue-eyed counterparts.

Next, Elliott withdrew her blue-eyed students' basic classroom rights, such as drinking directly from the water fountain or taking a second helping at lunch. Brown-eyed kids received preferential treatment, were allowed to boss around the blues, and were given extended recess.

Elliott recalls, "It was just horrifying how quickly they became what I told them they were." Within thirty minutes, a blue-eyed girl named Carol had regressed from a "brilliant, self-confident, carefree, excited little girl to a frightened, timid, uncertain little almost-person."[10]

Prejudice works both ways: the brown-eyed children excelled under their newfound superiority. Elliott had seven students with dyslexia in her class that year, and four of them had brown eyes. On the day that the browns were "on top," those four brown-eyed boys with dyslexia read words that Elliott "knew they couldn't read" and spelled words that she "knew they couldn't spell." Prior to the study the students had no opinions, of course, about each other based on eye color. Elliott taught them that it was all right to judge one another based on eye color, but she did not teach them how to oppress. "They already knew how to be racist because every one of them knew without my telling them how to treat those who were on the bottom," says Elliott.

And on other days, Elliott told the students she had made a mistake and the blues were "on top," and the same bigotry resulted. So the children saw and experienced firsthand what prejudice was like; in this the experiment was a success. Elliott also observed that on days when students were part of the inferior group, they showed lower test scores, less enthusiasm, and more hostility toward activities in the classroom.*

There is a tendency to extend the family beyond the sexually bonded, and there are some patterns that seem to transcend species borders. When human and chimpanzee societies resort to violence, "bands of brothers" are often formed. Chimp intergroup violence is carried out by the strongest individuals—primarily by groups of young males. In addition, those males are ones that are closely bonded (and often closely related). In human beings the patterns are similar. In Sparta, homosexual relationships among younger and older warriors created pseudokin bonding valuable in combat.†

Even in modern warfare, those in combat fight by and large not for principles but for their family—the comrades with whom they have bonded, their band of brothers. In the Second World War, one major element in the impressive success of the badly outnumbered *Wehrmacht* was the German army's policy relating to replacements. When an American GI was killed or wounded, a new infantryman was drawn at random from a replacement depot (a "repple depple" in the army slang). Military historian Stephen Ambrose wrote, "Most of the replacements got to the most dangerous place in the world—unknown, unknowing, scared, bewildered."[11] Many of the replacements were killed or wounded within a few days of joining units at the front, before they could bond into the family of their squad or platoon.

In contrast, Germany's *Wehrmacht* carefully kept men from the same towns together in infantry units, and replaced casualties with soldiers from home as well. The German command appreciated the value of family

---

* This has since been repeated with dramatic results elsewhere, with both children and adults. There are, of course, some major ethical questions raised by the original experiment— particularly the concept of "informed consent." For fourteen out of the next sixteen years that Elliott taught in Riceville, she conducted the exercise. In the white enclave of Riceville, fighting racism was not looked upon by most as an honorable duty. As a result of Elliot's work, kids beat up her own children. Her parents' business lost customers. Elliott and her family received regular death threats. And each fall, parents called Elliott's principal and said something like, "I don't want my kid in that nigger-lover's classroom!"

† Pseudokin are what we call people or groups with relationships to others that resemble, in certain respects, those of true kin.

bonding among men in combat (*Kameradschaft*).[12] It tried to keep the boys actually doing the fighting in units of pseudokin reminiscent of those that fought in the only documented "war" among chimpanzees. Raiding squads of male Kasakela chimps, one of two groups studied by Jane Goodall at Gombe Stream on Lake Tanganyika, wiped out the community of the Kahama chimps to their south in a series of deadly forays.[13]

When human populations grew to the point where kinship couldn't hold things together, the problem of control became more severe and threatening. For instance, the small Polynesia islands of Tikopia and Mangaia had quite different cultural trajectories. Both faced severe resource constraints imposed by the small size of their islands. The Mangaian society destroyed most of its resource base and degenerated into warfare and cannibalism. The Tikopians, in contrast, instituted population control, sometimes by quite brutal methods such as encouraging young men to take suicidal canoe voyages. They converted their island into an orchard and achieved sustainability—a population size that could be supported by local resources generation after generation. Why the difference? Archaeologist Patrick Kirch speculated that it was the relative size of the islands. Tikopia is tiny, 1.8 square miles—PRE walked over a mountainous quarter of it in a few hours. Everyone had to know everyone else. Mangaia is larger enough (20 square miles) for groups of kin to occupy a valley of "us" distinct from the next valley of "them."

Problems of control were not all that emerged as human populations grew and agricultural societies developed. In hunter-gatherer groups, just about all members possessed the same culture. The exceptions were few—perhaps a hunter with a favorite productive spot for placing rabbit snares, a group of women who knew the medicinal properties of a certain plant, a canoe builder who had a special way of lashing on an outrigger support, a shaman whose mentor had taught him a secret incantation.

When early human beings were a small-group animal actually *living* in small groups, there was little need for a complex institutional organization. Food choices were limited and things that were poisonous were well known—restrictions based on direct experience were passed on directly. People ate the food the foragers brought in. There was no need for a Food and Drug Administration or inspectors who tried to make sure that restaurants were sanitary or even a Nuclear Regulatory Commission.

A war leader took the young bucks off for a ritual battle against the neighbor group—there was no draft board, no army versus navy or infantry versus cavalry, no Texas super contractor like KBR* lobbying for contracts

---

* Formerly Kellogg Brown & Root.

to rebuild the group's village, no Blackwater* to hire to kill "them." No court system was needed to decide who sinned or was sinned against; public dispute settling involved all those with a stake in the matter, or the execution of an agreed-upon malefactor took care of the problem. Inequities within the group were relatively minor—meat, the most critical and desirable resource, was likely rather evenly shared. In hunter-gatherer groups, the opportunities for accumulating wealth were limited by the problems of spoiling (meat) and carrying valued objects as the group roamed.

It wasn't until after the agricultural revolution some ten thousand years (just some five hundred generations) ago that a sedentary lifeway provided the basis for the wealth-based social structure similar to that of today. As farming became more efficient, it eventually made it possible for one family to produce more food than it needed, in turn freeing others to take up other specialized occupations as blacksmiths, priests, soldiers, bureaucrats, and so on. In addition, being sedentary made it possible not only to accumulate goods but also to pass them on to the next generation.

That shift resulted in a growing *culture gap*, as specialization increased and people were trained into separate and distinct occupations. No longer did any individual know the majority of the nongenetic information possessed in the aggregate by their extended family. This knowledge was, rather, concentrated increasingly in the hands of an assortment of groups of pseudokin—priests of a certain god, decorative artists, pyramid engineers, specialists in siege warfare, and so on. In the past few centuries that gap between people and between peoples has widened at lightning speed, and it has resulted in the failure of individuals living in industrial societies to be familiar with even one thousandth of a percent of their society's culture. Think of the gap as one between what society as a whole knows—all knowledge stored in brains, libraries, computers, photos, films, structures, and so on—and what the average person knows.

Today a European, Japanese, or American, even one with experience in many work areas, cannot possibly store more than a miniscule part of the group's culture. Here's a personal example: given the correct pile of parts, neither of us would know how to assemble a computer, let alone describe the processes by which the parts were manufactured, the provenance of the materials they embodied, or the methods by which those materials had been gathered and processed. And we've both used computers daily for four decades.

That specialized knowledge is now the reserve of one or more groups of pseudokin, the guild or profession, with extended family ties to one another. The members of the extended families would, in the computer case, include

---

* Now Xe.

(but not be limited to) computer scientists and engineers. Such pseudokin often have strong associations with each other and often try to strictly limit their family size (think American Medical Association or taxi cab drivers). Other examples of the culture gap abound. Most city dwellers have no idea of soil preparation or planting schedules essential to farming. A computer scientist at Stanford was said to have thought that milk was manufactured. A professor of English once wondered aloud to us as to how "they" put the egg albumen and yolk "into those neat little shells."

Culture gap examples draw laughs from files sent around on the Internet and from clips of Jay Leno's famous "Jaywalk," where Leno asks questions to random people on the street. For example, the question "What is the highest court in the land?" gets blank stares even when "Diana Ross" is given as a hint; "What is meant by a jury of your peers?" draws the comment "Aren't they those things that stick out from the beach into the ocean?" and "Where is Afghanistan?" is answered with "next to Arkansas." In another example of culture gap, former president Ronald Reagan said after a trip to South America, "Well, I learned a lot. . . . I went down to [Latin America] to find out from them and [learn] their views. You'd be surprised. They're all individual countries." Maybe he was joking.

Something as directly important to individuals as the legal system is barely comprehended by most. Nonetheless, society can continue well enough with attorneys having near exclusive knowledge of jurisprudence and with surgeons alone knowing how to remove a tumor (although most individuals would benefit enormously from some knowledge of the law and medicine). But society seems unlikely to survive when most voters remain ignorant of such topics as how the climate works, the relationship between biodiversity and ecosystem services, the key points of the second law of thermodynamics, the roots of racism, and so on. The culture gap about how the world works results in an industrial society becoming maladapted to the biophysical realities of Earth.[14]

Disparities of wealth and power developed naturally as the culture gap widened. Ruling families emerged, as the need developed to coordinate and control ever larger groups of people. Methods of control and construction were known primarily to the ruling class; for most laborers, the culture gap was already a factor. Wealth, then as today, meant access to information, and access to information produced wealth.

Egyptian dynasties were a classic example, where power was usually held by closely related individuals and religious ideas (and a need to employ farm labor outside of the growing season determined by Nile flooding) led to efforts such as pyramid building. Religion played a controlling role in most societies long after the pharaohs disappeared from the scene. That kings and their families exercised the power of a god ("divine right") and were the embodiment of the state is typified in the saying usually attributed to Louis XIV of France: "L'État c'est moi" (I am the state). In the twenty-first century, one American president claimed he was helped in ruling by talking to a supreme being (we think the advice he got was clearly lousy, or perhaps his hearing needed a checkup).

As societies became more complex, another family-related phenomenon appeared—formal institutions. Their origins may be traced to what economists today call social capital. We are all familiar with capital, the money we have, and with built capital—everything from homes and machinery to cars and toys, from which we enjoy a steady stream of real or psychic income. We pay careful attention to measuring and depreciating that capital. Another form of capital that societies account for carefully is human capital, the education and skill attainments of the labor force.

And biologists and economists are recognizing *natural capital*, the resources of the biosphere—minerals, fresh water, organisms that are components of ecosystems, and the like—that support our civilization.[15] Some of the services of natural capital include ameliorating the climate, keeping the atmosphere breathable, pollinating crops and protecting them from pests, providing flows of vital fresh water, preventing floods, and supplying wild foods from land and sea.

Social capital is more subtle, but it is nonetheless real. At its simplest, it might be seen as the division of labor and mutual support that makes a family a more effective unit than the sum of its individual members. Dad might be a great hunter, but without mom to gather a steady stream of tubers and watch the kids, or without the kids to trek to the streamside and return with water and firewood, the family would be a much less efficient producing and reproducing machine. The family with social capital and institutionalized arrangements is much more efficient. PRE's father worked nearly full time earning a living, while his better-educated but less-employable mother focused her attention on the rearing and educating of the children.

You might ask, isn't the family enough? Why do we need formal institutions at all? Human brains evolved not only to plot, plan, and maneuver our own lives but also to adjust our behavior to those other plotting, planning, and maneuvering individuals with whom we can empathize or who are our deadly enemies and whose minds we try to read. Our empathetic abilities doubtless evolved in part to deal with the complexities of social and particularly sexual relationships. And it's important to note that the complexity of the information early people needed to understand about other individuals must have set rather strict limits on group size—even modern brains can't deal with understanding thousands of close associates, let alone billions. That's where institutions come in.

Formal institutions add to social capital by organizing social contacts. They are a version of the family writ large. They are hierarchical, usually with the analogs of dad, mom, kids of various ages, and grandpa (president, chief deputy, various levels of bureaucrats, retired chairman of the board), and often a loyal group of people who presently or previously had contact with the institution and value it. Roman Catholicism, New York University, the United States Marines, the Sierra Club, and al Qaeda are all examples of formal institutions.

Successful institutions are essential to achieving a sustainable global human family, institutions especially designed to spread empathy and regulate treatment of the global environment. Developing such institutions is a daunting prospect for a generation surrounded by obvious institutional failure, from the frequent inability of the United Nations to suppress conflict and the ability of climate "deniers" to slow progress in trying to reduce the threat of climate disruption, or the U.S. government's failure to stem the activities of Wall Street risk takers, and the persistent empathy deficit that blocks solving the problems of poor peoples and nations.

Many people, following economist Milton Friedman and the Chicago School, believe that capitalism, as little restrained by government as possible and with little empathy with "losers," is the ideal state of the economic system. This economic position is epitomized by the views of Alan Greenspan, the former head of the Federal Reserve. Greenspan is an adherent of the radical Ayn Rand philosophy, which emphasizes "ethical egoism," the dominance of individual rights (including property rights), and laissez-faire capitalism, enforced by a very limited government. Rand was adamantly opposed to any idea of altruism—her empathy shortfall was legendary. Greenspan's influential view finally met its end after the financial crisis of 2008–2009. In the crisis, untrammeled risk-taking by bankers almost brought down the world economy. Such a disaster wasn't supposed to happen.

> "I made a mistake in presuming that the self-interests of organizations, specifically banks and others, were such as that they were best capable of protecting their own shareholders and their equity in the firms," Greenspan said at a House hearing last October under questioning from Rep. Henry Waxman (D-Calif.).
>
> "In other words," said Waxman, moving in for the kill, "you found that your view of the world, your ideology, was not right, it was not working."
>
> "Absolutely, precisely," said Greenspan. "You know, that's precisely the reason I was shocked, because I have been going for 40 years or more with very considerable evidence that it was working exceptionally well."[16]

The solutions of how best to organize complex society vary with the definition of "best." That is especially the case if one wants to make that society a global, imagined family with lots of empathy throughout. Some people and groups try to preserve a presumed natural family-type structure, with a dictatorial "father"; others want to imitate a family with lots of teenagers rebelling and wishing to share power. Imposition of Chicago School laissez-faire policies in Chile led to impoverishment, torture, and death for many people, but greatly enriched a few.[17] In few places has the persistence of a giant empathy deficit, of a lack of caring for "them," been more obvious.

Now nearly seven billion people live in a global economy in which many countries are classified as "developing," but aren't going to be developing at all if the development goal is to have a per capita consumption at something like current U.S.-Europe-Japan level. If we believe that every member of the human family should have access to clean water, nutritious food, adequate clothing and shelter, education, a livelihood, and leisure time, today's situation is a major institutional failure of attempts to organize a global effort to help.

Even if one doesn't accept that position, the failure to provide those things to billions of people is very dangerous. That's because gross inequality breeds terrorism, providing the often-educated terrorists with a made-to-order excuse for carrying out murderous attacks: that the very rich do relatively little to help the very poor and in various ways appropriate the resources of the poor. Furthermore, the impoverished increasingly will have access to weapons of mass destruction; and they already are in the North Korean arsenal.

The superrich may not end up with their heads on pikes, but even now diseases that incubate in the less well-off threaten everyone. A sensible society would design, maintain, and modify institutions that would increase empathy and guard everyone against such threats. We should have the ability to do so, and do so quite rapidly despite the extreme complexity of the problems, if history is any guide.*

After all, our species has already shown great imagination in creating institutions and structures for allegiance, for defining in-groups and,

---

* Of course, we're not so naïve as to think that the problems of the lack of development can be solved by good feeling and empathy alone. Some of the problems are discussed in Paul Collier, *The Bottom Billion: Why the Poorest Countries Are Failing and What Can Be Done about It* (Oxford: Oxford University Press, 2007), and others very well in Tania M. Li, *The Will to Improve* (Durham, NC: Duke University Press, 2007). Understanding what needs to be done is certainly a start.

by exclusion, various degrees of "them." For instance, communal ties in medieval England were supplied by the extended institutional family of the church, and belief in purgatory was an important device for building local communities. The "bede roll," which was a list of the dead who had prayed with the community, was a device for tying people to their ancestors, and reading the role helped to create a sense of a shared past, as well as a sense of a possible future family community in heaven. This made those in other villages "them" at one level, but the "big them" of non-Christians were different at another level. As in most monotheistic sects, nonbelievers, heretics, infidels, and the like, as history has abundantly shown, are the "big them," often targeted for conversion or killing.

One common allegiance-spreading device in increasingly huge populations is to extend the family to close friends who are distinguished by courtesy kin titles of "uncle" and "aunt." Many less personal groupings are also built on the cultural foundations of what originally were based on genetic and marital kinship. Most of these *ultra extended families* use kin family terminology liberally, and automatically create a "them" in the process.

Shakespeare wrote of men joined in a military venture as a band of brothers, and male organizations very often call themselves brotherhoods or fraternities. These range from a wide variety of unions (Brotherhood of Teamsters, of Electrical Workers, etc.) and veterans groups (TLC Brotherhood of Southeast Asia veterans*), to prison gangs (Aryan Brotherhood) and activist religious organizations (Muslim Brotherhood, dedicated to nonviolent creation of a global, just Islamic empire, but also inspiration for Osama bin Laden and others dedicated to violence). From the Freemasons to football teams, brotherhoods are everywhere, as are "old boy" networks.

Many organizations of women are called sisterhoods, and members refer to each others as sisters. These include feminist organizations (Global Sisterhood Network), organizations to promote certain groups (Black Women in Sisterhood for Action), transsexual support groups (The Sisterhood), and Christian religious groups (Evangelical Sisterhood of Mary). In Jewish religious congregations there is usually an organization made up of females without genetic connection called the sisterhood, which even in orthodox groups may be involved in fund-raising despite the generally inferior position to which women are consigned in those congregations. Members of sororities, curiously enough, consider themselves sisters. Priests are often called "father" in the Catholic Church, and they are only rarely biological fathers. The pope heads the family as the Holy Father; heads of convents are "mothers," symbolically, if not often in actuality.

---

* TLC = Thailand-Laos-Cambodia.

Other organizations are simply referred to or considered as families. Some of these families hardly have the feel-good family values. The Gambino crime family is a good example. Its origins trace to 1931, in a war between two earlier criminal gangs, led by Guiseppe "Joe the Boss" Masseria and Sicilian newcomer Salvatore Maranzano. The war was ended by the assassination of Masseria. It was all arranged by Masseria's underling, Charles "Lucky" Luciano. Luciano invited his chief to lunch, stuffed him full of veal, linguini, red wine, and, courtesy of four accomplices (while Luciano went to the bathroom), bullets.

Luciano was in collusion with the Jewish thugs Bugsy Siegel (one of Masseria's murderers) and Meyer Lansky, who were central to a multiethnic crime family that became known as Murder Incorporated.[18] "Lucky" quickly arranged the murder of Maranzano. That left a final old-timer to run the family, Vincent Mangano. Another of the Masseria firing squad, Murder Incorporated's vicious Alberto Anastasia, killed his way to the top of the Mangano family, finally finishing off first Philip Mangano, Vincent's brother, and then Vincent himself. Anastasia, in turn, was involved in many killings until one of his underlings, the cunning Carlo Gambino, had him shot to death in a barber chair, took over, and gave his name to the famous Gambino crime family. Patricide was a common feature of crime family structure, a truly destructive form of pseudokinship.

This wasn't exactly the mom, pop, and 2.4 children–style of ideal family values, but members of these Mafia crime families lived by certain institutional codes of behavior and levels of "themness." Anastasia was killed because he had had a witness against bank robber Willie Sutton killed. That act violated gang family values since killing "civilians" was forbidden— because it threatened the safety of the family! The code of *omertà* (silence) bound all family members—no one could "rat out" other members. The Mafia's origins were in the hills of Sicily over a thousand years ago, and the association strove to become a family based on their common Sicilian background. The behavior of the original Mafia family gradually deteriorated in the United States, but even as a collection of thugs it retained some of its family origins. For example, Luciano was assaulted and almost killed in 1929, but refused to rat out his family-member attackers.

Japanese corporate culture considers the firm a family—although the protective family aspects are fading as affluence recedes. University communities—faculty, staff, students, graduates—sometimes refer to themselves as family members: the Stanford family, the Harvard family, and so on. After September 11, Stanford Faculty Senate chair John Rickford began the first senate meeting of the new academic year with a moment of silence in memory of members of the "extended Stanford family" who perished during the attacks. Informal groups of friends are probably the most common collections of pseudokin, and the most common in-groups that differentiate between "us" and "them."

Recently a colleague referred to a very diverse group of ecologists and economists who had become friends over the years working together at meetings on the Swedish island of Askö as the Askö family.[19] It was appropriate, from PRE's viewpoint, because he had formed close ties of friendship with many of the participants, taken vacations with them, enjoyed spas with them, corresponded frequently, and looked forward to the workshops as a virtual family reunion—and PRE's feelings were clearly shared.

The nation is the largest family, an "imagined community" of pseudokin in which people relate to others they have never met, whose names they don't even know, but who they assume also relate to them. Nations are united by language, culture, and, especially, history (real or imagined), and they are family-like in the sense that people often feel related to dead kin they have never met ("founding fathers," "those who here gave their lives that that nation might live"), or to future descendents as yet unborn ("Will future generations of Americans salute us?"[20]). Think of the moments of silence, when pictures of service members killed in Iraq or Afghanistan are shown, that now often follow news programs on public television.

Nations have often shown extreme extensions of family concepts. Germans marched into the Soviet Union in 1941 for the fatherland; Russians gave their lives in defense of the motherland. "Uncle" Joe Stalin led the latter; "Uncle Sam" sent huge amounts of military supplies to aid him and them.

In many nation-states, the state and the nation are not the same. Think of the state of Great Britain and the nations of Scotland, Ireland, and Wales; the state of Russia with nations such as Chechnya; the state of Iraq with the Sunni, Shia, and Kurds; and so on. So nation-states have their own laws and foreign policies that may not be popular with all the nations they represent.

Inside nations, constant pressure is often placed on those who deviate from some cultural norm; over the centuries the dominant Han culture of China has attempted to alter the system of a "them," the Na, but with minimal results. In 1956 the communist government made a major attempt to institute monogamous marriage as the standard. This "communist morality" was based on a pseudo-evolutionary religious theory of marriage patterns in which the Han system (male-female monogamy) is seen as the highest stage. It's a view reminiscent of those of many Western religions, and in the United States is a stimulus to the persecution of Mormon polygyny. Indeed, the certitude of the Chinese communist cadres dealing with misguided "others" is very much like the certitude of religious fundamentalist "families" in the United States determined to deny marriage to monogamous gay couples.

There is substantial cultural "stickiness" in trying to spread empathy internationally. France and Germany do not become friends overnight. (After World War I, French prime minister Georges Clemenceau was rumored to have commented on the possibility that the Rhineland would become a separate state, "I like Germanies so much, I wish there were three of them.") The human many-small-groups approach to the world with its built-in sense of group differences tends to make us persist in having an in-the-family versus outsider viewpoint. But our small-group attitudes are maladaptive when humanity has developed technologies that make it possible for one overextended family to wipe out another and even threaten the existence of human civilization.

Today, erroneous ideas regarding the origins, nature, and, especially, the immutability of different sets of family values (ours, right; theirs, wrong) is once more helping to lead humanity to tragedy. Since we can't transform into solitary animals, building a sustainable world had better involve reaching some agreement to disagree on many family values. The agreement would be within some generally accepted limits (e.g., ethical systems should minimize oppression of members of our families [us], or members of them—systems that, for instance, from our viewpoint, should not allow unequal treatment of women[21]). The stick-to-small-groups momentum is great, but once recognized, the incentives to change, to assure the very survival of our precious families, are enormously greater.

To recap, antiquated ideas of family values divide the world into sets of us and them, divisions that are reflected in politics, in education, in unnecessary conflicts inside countries and between nations, and in the way we deal with the environmental crisis.

Islamic extremists kill hundreds of people in Mumbai and try to encourage a civilization-wrecking nuclear war because "they" are trying to foist their Western family values on "us"—in that case, us being fundamentalist Islamists. Hundreds of thousands have now died in Darfur, and three million died in Pol Pot's Cambodia, in part because people in the West don't often come to the aid of those who don't look like family. Many of the American soldiers in the Vietnam War found that killing the North Vietnamese and Viet Cong was easier to take when the foreigners were considered "gooks."*

---

* Communist insurgents in South Vietnam, who called themselves the National Front for the Liberation of South Vietnam.

It's not always thus; in Haiti after the great 2010 earthquake, it looked like the United States was helping, although at one point Haitians died because the U.S. military stopped airlifting desperate cases to Florida hospitals* in a dispute over who would pay for their treatment.[22]

The astounding tragedy that took place in Rwanda in 1994—in which approximately 850,000 people were killed, most hacked to death with machetes, one by one, in about two months—illustrates how easily a new family structure can be imposed. But the creation of a "them" goes on in a less bloody way today. Unfortunately, the media in the modern world are more oriented to "truthiness," as Stephen Colbert has put it, than truth itself. A good example is the swift-boat campaign during the U.S. presidential election of 2004 that cast doubt on whether Senator John Kerry had earned his medals and had told the truth. Was Kerry a patriotic, loyal, American "us," or a member of the unpatriotic "them" who had criticized our national family at a time of war? As in Rwanda, the anti-Kerry campaign was organized to begin slowly and to have the effect build up over time.

A group calling itself the Swift Boat Veterans for Truth first set up a website that was very critical of Kerry's war activities and made several specific accusations against him. These "Swifties" made an anti-Kerry television ad, and promoted the anti-Kerry statements of several veterans who also had served on swift-boat crews in Vietnam. It seemed ludicrous, since Kerry was given a Bronze Star for bravery, while his opponents, George Bush and Richard Cheney, both, through their own convoluted efforts, had dodged combat.

The Kerry campaign dismissed the accusations of the Swifties, saying they were a politically motivated group financed by people close to George Bush and conducting an election-year smear campaign. And challenging a documented war hero seemed preposterous. But the smears were repeated so often that it became believed, not by all, but by enough people in a close election to help George Bush. And at the start of the campaign the group had little money, but they used the power of us versus them successfully. They used the fragmentation of the media to their advantage, finding small segments and websites who were violently opposed to Kerry, feeding them information, and after building up these numbers, went after larger fish, in this case Fox News. From there it spread.[23]

Similarly, as we noted earlier, coordinated campaigns of deliberate lies have been launched on the Internet by the right wing, attacking Barack Obama and some of his key advisors as a group of "them"—communists, czars, socialists, abortionists, eugenicists, and so on, some of it based on Obama being a "them" on the basis of skin color. The campaign to make

---

* That might well have been an ordinary screwup, though.

Obama a "them" has increased Obama's difficulty in taking leadership toward humanity dealing with the global environment crisis as a single family.

We must note, however, that whereas much of the present divisiveness that wracks the U.S. government and its failure to deal adequately with a whole array of crucial empathy- and environment-related issues, a fair ration of blame can be assigned to the Left, which often has been unhelpful or worse. Some conservative positions on issues ranging from immigration reform to limits on government are at least worthy of a thorough hearing. After all, the two presidents whose administrations did the most for conservation were both Republicans—Teddy Roosevelt and Richard Nixon. And sometimes continuing to do something proven to work may be better than innovation (as the Cabrini-Green example we discuss later illustrates). Where is Edmund Burke when we really need him?*

Bad behavior causes us continuous problems, sure. But you must remember that unlike all the other social mammals that exist or have existed on the planet—wolves, lions, marmosets, chimps, australopithecines, and so on—only humans have occupied the entire globe and now organize their social relationships in groups of billions. Remember, we're an adolescent species in the midst of an unprecedented social experiment of crisscrossing family values.

There are a lot of big changes needed as we start to grow up.

---

* The brilliant Irish-Anglo statesman (1729–1797) who was the father of modern conservatism.

PART II

CHANGING OUR MIND AND CHANGING THE WORLD WE MADE

CHAPTER 5

The Neuropsychology of "Us"
The More Alike We Are,
the More We Like

I'm a woman, so I like Hillary. I'm black; I like Obama. But I'm also
grumpy, so I like John McCain.
—POLITICAL CONSULTANT DANNA BRAZILE,
discussing the U.S. presidential election in early 2008[1]

THE history of humanity is one of a growing complexity of our affiliations—from the original bonding among members of early hunter-
gatherer groups and family rule (pharaohs to Habsburgs) to larger, more
amorphous groups (courtesy aunts, Uncle Sam, fraternities, sisterhoods,
soap opera actors, movie stars, novel characters). And we have been truly
ingenious in finding ways to separate "us" from "them." Just remember this:

> Gilead then cut Ephraim off from the fords of the Jordan, and when-
> ever Ephraimite fugitives said, "Let me cross," the men of Gilead would
> ask, "Are you an Ephraimite?" If he said, "No," they then said, "Very well,
> say Shibboleth." If anyone said, "Sibboleth," because he could not pro-
> nounce it, then they would seize him and kill him by the fords of the
> Jordan. Forty-two thousand Ephraimites fell on this occasion. (Judg.
> 12:5–6, NJB)

There are other ways than the accents used by the men of Gilead that
we now use to maintain what is "us," our family allegiances, at any moment:
body scarification, emblems, tattoos, style and color of clothes, flags, chants,

secret handshakes, passwords, rituals, restricted meetings, and the like. Our identity is multiple and those ones that cross families and groups often produce contradictory values. Symbols help to keep us in line. Symbols are, however, like clothing and color, often just superficial: Suzanne Vega, a contemporary song writer says, "Songs brand us a part of a tribe. We can pick and choose what tribe we belong to. Goth, emo, hippie, punk, folk, alternative, for example."[2]

Our symbols of us, like the accents of Ephraimites, can still put our lives at risk, as when a New Yorker magazine writer describes a man killed because he wore red—the wrong color to wear in a favela. Red and black are all right, the writer was told, because they were the symbol of a football team, but red alone was the symbol of another gang.[3] Similarly, in Los Angeles in 2008, a young boy was gunned down on a corner that was part of a gang's territory. The explanation: "Anybody who wears blue and green out there knows he's in the wrong place." The boy didn't know, as he was just visiting his cousins and went out for a stroll in the neighborhood.

Our multiple identities shift constantly, and we don't usually notice the shift. And our empathy shifts with it. Our immediate surroundings change our minds more than we think because the mind is set up for the short-term. If we are surrounded by people with similar dress, with signs or banners, our thinking shifts and we often tend to take more extreme positions.

Have you ever wondered why so many religions and other pseudokin associations (even the Yakuza, the Japanese gangsters) wash before meeting? It's because just washing hands allows people to feel that they "wash away" their sins, and lessens their regret about unethical behavior.[4] Cleanliness in one sphere primes it in another. It strengthens the "us" in us, and the positions we hold against the "others."

This is why people in political rallies demonize the opposition "others" without a second (or, really, first) thought, why people in mobs sometimes commit excessive acts that they would never perform if by themselves or in a small group. Think of how the word *dirty*, specific in its literal sense, moves in our lexicon to cover other dealings: a dirty politician, a dirty trick, a dirty movie. We have to be more aware of these unnoticed ways we "change our mind." This tendency of the mind can be turned to good use.

Such mind changing happens through what's called "priming." Whatever is in our consciousness at any moment brings up a host of associated thoughts and ideas. In the standard experiment used to demonstrate this priming, people look at words displayed, very briefly, on a screen, and the time to recognize them is recorded. It's found that we're likely to recognize the word *pear* more quickly just after seeing *apple* than after seeing the word *bulb*.[5]

Priming of the mind has profound effects on judgment, mental stability, and our view of others. In one study some people entering a shopping center found a ten dollar bill placed there by psychologist Alice Isen.[6] They were followed and were given a survey covering a series of topics. Compared with those who didn't find the money, their refrigerators were rated more reliable, their prospects for world peace were higher, and their future seemed brighter! A good ten dollar investment! No wonder there are now so many free samples in the supermarkets.

Personal "reality" changes drastically when confronted with new information. When we see an image of conflict or strife (for example, a British subject seeing results of an Irish Republican Army attack in England), a host of negative feelings is stimulated and an us-versus-them attitude increases. What happens in the larger society primes changes, although sometimes these changes are surprising. After the July 7, 2005, bombing attacks in London, one might have expected that depressing event to make people more depressed. But the suicide rate dropped![7] Indeed, the saturation bombing of German civilians by the Royal Air Force in World War II did not have the expected discouraging effects on German morale.[8]

Nowadays websites and media reinforce group feelings. The large minority of people in the United States who are Christian fundamentalists are inundated by reiteration of certain interpretations of the biblical book of Revelation. Such inundation changes how they see the world. Here is a verbatim quote from a typical End Times website:

> It is increasingly obvious that the time of our Lord's coming is drawing near. Prophecy is being fulfilled daily, and at a faster pace than ever before. Whether you believe in a pre-tribulation rapture, or believe Christians will be witness to the full tribulation, wrath, and final judgments, matters not. The beginning of birth pains and the signs of the times should have the same effect on all of us. It should motivate us to save as many souls as we can in the time that we have left. The Great Commission tells us to be disciples to all nations, bringing the message of salvation through Christ to all people. If the Church is raptured before the tribulation, it is important that we leave behind an explanation for the trials and judgments those left behind will face. How else will they recognize the deception of the anti-Christ and seek instead the truth of the Bible?[9]

Such reminders do change behavior. A colleague who teaches religious studies in the South has to advise his students routinely that they really should study for finals, because it is unlikely that the End of Days will happen before the End of Term. And it isn't an easy sell, either! Maybe in 2012 it *will* all end.

In the past few years, there's been a revolution in the understanding of how human beings communicate and empathize with others. The most striking and the most important discovery is that the brain has a network of neurons that responds to the actions of others. This provides a possible neural basis for empathy. The research began in the mid 1990s, but REO first heard about it at a conference on brain and consciousness in 1998 in Tucson, Arizona, and didn't believe it at first.[10]

Vittorio Gallese, who traveled to the conference to present his work, is a brain researcher in an important neuropsychological laboratory in Italy. At the meeting, Gallese told REO that his lab had found cells in the premotor areas of the brain that react to the actions of others, a phenomenon many scientists did not believe could exist (and, to be honest, there is still some controversy today).* This reaction was discovered due to a set of coincidences after lunch one day. In the early 1990s, at the University of Parma, the head of the lab, Giacomo Rizzolatti, was working on a long-term project to record electrical activity from neurons in the premotor cortex of macaque monkeys. The premotor cortex is involved in the planning and initiation of movements. Thus, different cells in this area are usually activated when an animal makes a movement, such as grasping or arm moving. To find out which cells are active, in these studies sensitive microelectrodes are inserted deep in the brain and the activity of the cells is monitored. In a typical recording, and after a lot of searching in the brain, when the monkey grasps an object, one can record specific premotor neurons as they fire in action.

What followed lunch that day was an unexpected discovery. The story goes this way: the lab workers didn't shut off the recording devices after the morning session, so the devices were still on when the workers returned from lunch. One of Rizzolatti's graduate students had an ice cream cone for dessert, which he ate in full view of the wired-up monkey. To his surprise, the electrodes suddenly began to signal a spike in cellular activity in the premotor cortex, even though the monkey was motionless.†

Some neurons fired when the monkey made certain movements—like bringing a piece of food to its mouth—and, surprising to all those in the lab, they also fired when the monkey simply watched someone make similar movements. When the monkey watched someone perform an action,

---

* This first study was done with the lab animals already being analyzed, macaque monkeys, but confirmatory findings have been done in human beings.
† There is question as to whether this account is exactly true or a "laboratory legend," but the basis, that the "mirroring" neurons were discovered by accident in this lab are true.

its brain seemed to simulate the action. These are the renowned "mirror neurons," as Rizzolatti later dubbed them, that we mentioned earlier. They are part of the brain system that is responsible for our ability to understand the actions of others. While some claims for these neurons are overstated and there is the mistaken counterclaim that only monkeys have been found with them, it's important to realize that such groups of neurons have been discovered in human brains via MRI studies.[11]

Mirror neurons in the appropriate motor cortex fire when we see another person picking up a package, as if we're internally rehearsing the action, a kind of consistent internal imitation. This continuous process of putting ourselves in another's place presumably forms the basis for our innate empathy and our ability to understand via this inner rehearsal what is going on in other people's heads. This ability of ours is stronger than that in any other species and, as Andrew Meltzoff's experiments with young babies showed, seems to be with us from birth! And it is this tendency that we, the authors, hope will be strengthened to allow our kind to make the adaptations necessary right now.

The us-them distinctions have proven beneficial in some circumstances—as when groups build on solidarity to solve common problems, for example, black pride, feminism, union movements, company solidarity. These promoters of solidarity have often led to an eventual reduction of us-them. We would like to see the us-them divisions that lead to a collective assault on our life-support systems (e.g., we won't limit greenhouse gas emissions because they won't) replaced by solidarity building in the global human family that would preserve those vital systems. One possibility would be to employ the Internet, which has helped people with less-unifying agendas to move awareness of their cause to new heights. Although the "swift-boating" results were not exactly to our liking, similar techniques might be used for promoting a greater understanding of our common family.

If through the techniques employed by the Swift Boat Veterans for Truth, people can so easily believe in transparent falsehoods, they clearly can be influenced to act in aid of their own survival and that of their children and their civilization. They can be made to believe that the common enemy in Pogo's immortal words *is* us (more specifically, our behavior) and that we must cooperate and unite to defeat the old behavior patterns. The Internet ad campaign methods that can be used to convince people of the need to change are well known to marketing professionals and ideologically oriented think tanks. There has, however, been a natural reluctance on the part of environmental and social scientists to adopt the same techniques that are now used to peddle soft drinks and SUVs, to spread lies about health care and climate disruption, and to ruin the reputation of politicians trying to do the right thing.

Modern cognitive neuroscience yields fresh insights on our allegiance-divided selves and on how conflicting ideas and ideals are handled by the brain. It also can provide an opportunity to develop more flexibility of responses and empathy in a way more suited to the complexities of the modern world. As we have noted, through information campaigns, appropriate framing, and priming, individuals and societies have "changed their minds" about many important and deeply held attitudes and behaviors.

Now those changes must be expanded to include behaviors even stickier than smoking and family size: caring for the needs and wants of all of today's people and those of future generations. We need a new grouping of people concerned with the fate of everyone. This grouping does not need to replace our manifold families but adds a critical family on top of all the others. And we can get clues from current family structures of how we might build that family; societies whose individuals and family-type groupings are treated more equally thrive in comparison to less-equitable societies.[12]

One way to progress toward a more *sustainable* global society is to work for a more *equitable* global society. An obvious approach to this goal is to emphasize, through education and communications systems, that everyone is better off in the absence of gross economic divides, racism, sexism, and religious prejudice. Equally obvious, striving to reduce overconsumption is also key. Awakening has already come to some; successful individuals now often use their resources to improve the condition of all humanity.

There are several good recent models of such philanthropy in action: Bill Gates and Warren Buffett are each contributing more than thirty billion dollars to the Gates Foundation with its focus on health and education. George Soros recently announced he would devote one billion dollars to research in clean energy technology and one hundred million dollars into helping policy makers get good advice on environmental issues. One of PRE's friends has invested much of his fortune and his life into making Stanford a great university while also supporting other useful enterprises.

Another promising, but small, development is that a group of rich Germans late in 2009 launched a petition that called for their government to make wealthy people pay higher taxes. These rich Germans feel that members of their group have more money than they need, and that the extra revenue from putting some of those funds into taxes could well support economic and social programs that would aid Germany's economic recovery. "The path out of the [economic] crisis must be paved with massive investment in ecology, education and social justice," they say in the petition. Those who have "made a fortune through inheritance, hard work, hard-working, successful entrepreneurship, or investment" should be paying more to alleviate the crisis.[13]

We could all build on such attitudes, to see others as being like ourselves and as having a common fate. It should be easy—after all, all human beings are closely related genetically! But it takes special effort, special knowledge, and perhaps special people like those Germans.

There are neurobiological barriers to the recognition of deep sameness, barriers that overemphasize the small differences in our daily life. Many people, especially outsiders, would think that there is little difference perceptible between an Irish Catholic and an Irish Protestant; indeed, the psychiatrist Willard Gaylin has written that they couldn't be differentiated "in physical appearance, speech patterns, Irish traits, Celtic humor or even cultural values."[14] But psychologists in Northern Ireland have shown that *any child can tell them apart.* They know what to look for.

The human penchant to create distinctions was at the root of the division in Rwanda into Hutu and Tutsi, as the actual origin of differences, if any, is unclear. In his 1863 *Journal of the Discovery of the Source of the Nile*, British explorer John Hanning Speke indicates that he was fascinated by a group of leaders in what is now Rwanda, a group who drank milk and ate mostly meat, were a bit taller and lived a bit like the Masai. He contrasts this group with the shorter villagers who he claimed were obviously destined to be low-level workers, a pretty crazy idea. But Speke's conclusion that there were distinct "races" present came to fruition many years later when there were nearly a million deaths in the Rwandan genocide.[15]

There are basic human predispositions; our brain evolved to make it easier for us to like those who are related to us genetically, as judged by familiarity, more than nonrelatives. Cultural inertia in ways we limit the range of our empathy seems explicable when the tendency to prefer those who look like us is built into the human central nervous system. What's going on in our brains when we encounter people of different degrees of relatedness? David Brooks, a political commentator for the *New York Times*, wrote about how we judged the candidates in the 2008 and earlier elections:

> [Voters are] not sure that candidate—John Kerry, Michael Dukakis, Al Gore—is like them, shares their values, shares their basic life experience. The question is still asked of Barack Obama, "Is he like us?" And whether you like it or not, the way people measure such questions is through the use of symbols, whether it was Michael Dukakis sitting there in the tank, or John Kerry wind-surfing, or John Edwards's $400 haircut, people care about the symbols when they're saying, "Is that guy like us?"[16]

Some innovative work allows us to visualize how artificially adding a bit of one's genetic similarity to a person makes us like them better.

Consider the Clintons for this illustrative example. Imagine you are one of the people in the left column of the figure below. In the middle are photos of Hill and Bill. Those on the right look like the Clintons, but there is a subtle difference: about a third of the image, not enough for the viewer to really notice, is contributed (via digital manipulation—morphing—by two Stanford researchers) from the faces on the left.

When asked to pick which Clinton image they preferred, the people on the left chose the one with a part of them morphed into it, although they were unaware of its composition. This is an important finding, for it shows that we like familiar people even more when they are, undetectably, made to look more similar to us.[17] This is a simulacrum of what goes on in daily life as we sort out the people in our world. Perhaps, since early human groups were inbred, that convergence in appearance between oneself and others who surrounded us early makes us feel more comfortable—that we are with our family. Thus is the appeal of those who are more similar to us. We use

Faces on the far right include 35 percent of faces on the left
Courtesy of the Virtual Human Interaction Lab, Stanford University

this example because it is purely visual and easy to understand, unlike a similarity by affiliation or interest. And our empathy for those who look like us (such as genetic relatives) is at its extreme when we've been filmed for a performance of some kind and watch the film. When we make a mistake, we find it especially agonizing to see; our empathy with ourselves is strong indeed—and hardly unexpected since for essentially all of our evolutionary history the possibility of watching ourselves perform did not exist, so our neural mechanisms haven't developed the ability to distinguish us from those that simply look like us.

In the contemporary world our lives, as we have indicated, expand outside the initial family unit (whatever its size) and we form many different levels of affiliation—to friends, schoolmates, workmates, teammates, mates of all kinds, even characters in movies, soap operas, and novels. And it is cheering to realize, from the viewpoint of solidifying a global human family, that physical similarity is easily overridden by familiarity that can breed affiliation and empathy—even with imaginary individuals. Think of how we identify often with the characters in movies or TV shows, and we are sad when the season ends or the fictional characters suffer or die—especially characters in a series you have been watching for years.

All this emotional connection, even when you know the characters do not exist. People, real or fictional, who we see a lot trigger the same mechanisms that make us consider those we saw much of in early childhood as kin. REO finds that every June and for several months afterward he suffers from an as yet non-*DSM-IV* disorder called NBA withdrawal;* PRE was so dedicated to players on the Brooklyn Dodgers from 1940 to 1955 that he had to go "cold turkey" to cure his addiction after the Boys of Summer finally won a World Series in 1955.

Modern people have access to new methods of affiliation never before seen in the two hundred thousand years of our species' existence. Groups on small cruise ships or otherwise traveling together develop family-like characteristics in a matter of a week or so. We like objects or even people that we see over and over more than the unfamiliar, and we even see them as more similar to ourselves![18] Familiarity can also breed content.[19]

Some six million people were involved directly in Princess Diana's funeral, lining the route of the funeral procession. They were people who considered her a family member because of continual viewing of her in the media. Six million is roughly the number of people who existed on the

---

* *Diagnostic and Statistical Manual of Mental Disorders* is an "official" compendium of mental diseases produced by the American Psychiatric Association. Its last revision was the fourth (IV) in 1994 and 2000.

planet when agriculture was invented, and who were divided into many tens of thousands of bands. Late night TV show hosts and others with much media exposure get streams of letters, starting with a familiar salutation ("Dear Jay") and written as if to sibling or spouse.

PRE has found himself feeling affiliated to people he has met only as avatars (cartoon substitutes for the real people who operate through them) in a discussion group on Second Life. It seems especially easy on Second Life since you can't be put off by a person's appearance or dress—although weird avatars (which one can create to represent one's true self) can be off-putting to some. The factor governing this strange affinity is how alike we perceive people: if they are similar to us on one dimension (say, sense of humor or position on a controversial topic) we can consider them "us"; if not, they're "them."

This was captured in a CNN interview in 2002 between Paul Begala, a Clinton White House associate, and J. C. Watts, then a congressman. Begala began, "Let me say, I'm a liberal. You're a conservative. That's not our biggest difference. I'm white, you're black, and that's not our biggest difference. I'm a Texas Longhorn [this is a football team; Begala's not, actually, a beef cow] and you're an Oklahoma Sooner and—"

"That's our biggest difference," Watts said.

"That's the biggest," agreed Begala.[20]

They found their *alike spot*. It's a basic part of us, to seek the "alike." How does it begin? Children effortlessly learn new behaviors from watching others. Parents provide their young with an apprenticeship in how to act as a "like" member of their culture long before verbal instruction begins. We find our "alike spot" by imitation. Andrew Meltzoff, who did the ground-breaking study of the ability of a forty-four-minute-old child to imitate, says, "Infant imitation is connected with the perception of others as 'like me' and understanding others' minds. . . . Others who act 'like me' have internal states 'like me,' achieve a goal and concomitant facial expression and effortful bodily acts."[21]

In the populous and complex modern life, we're torn between our different identities and inundated by "contact overload"; we can be at the same time female, middle class, black, foodie, Buddhist, rock music devotee, Oprah fanatic, Raiders fan, Ford buyer, Democrat, and much more. We're pulled one way and another, and without being noticed, by the influences of the moment. And these identity issues are not trivial: they have very large effects on how the world works.

Many Americans view Israelis as "us," and pour billions of dollars into Israel, while paying less attention to the fate of the devastated Palestinian others. Muslim countries view the Palestinians as "us," and threaten to wipe out the Israeli others and their supporters. And all human families are held hostage to the possible results. Similarly, we pay too little attention to the fact that Sunni and Shia Muslims each consider themselves families—so that in foreign policy we see Iraq as a monolithic country and pay too little attention to the complex allegiances that make many Iraqi Shia more pseudokin to many Iranians than they are to Iraqi Kurds or Sunnis.*

Our shifts between different identities is most often unnoticed by us, but it can have dramatic positive or negative effects, since we all belong to different groups at the same time. Some of the most compelling recent evidence for the importance of perceived family-type resemblances concerns what occurs when people are made acutely conscious of their membership in one or another of the different family groups in which they are members.

When different family "identities" are brought to the fore, behaviors change drastically. Amazingly, an individual's performance on intellectual and athletic tasks is shaped by their awareness of the current stereotypes about one of the groups to which she or he belongs.[22] There were important studies done at Harvard University in 1999 by Margaret Shih and her coinvestigators of this phenomenon.[23]

The participants in this research were a group of Asian women who were made aware that this was either a research project about women (who are stereotypically worse at math than are men) or that it was on the subject of being Asian (and they are stereotypically better at math than members of other ethnic groups). The results show that Asian women do *worse* when taking intelligence tests when they think it is a test of their gender, and they do *better* when they think it is a test of the supposed Asian superiority over whites. How they do depends upon whether their allegiance to women or to their Asian background is at the top of their consciousness when the test is administered.

This finding, which is named "stereotype threat" by the originator of this line of research, Claude Steele, has been expanded to explain the common finding of many African Americans' lowered performance on standard testing. The impressive body of work Steele and associates have built up demonstrates that performance deficits are widespread for individuals who are aware that the family group they are identifying with at the moment is considered inferior.

Steele and Joshua Aronson and colleagues first studied high-achieving African American students at Stanford who took the verbal GRE (Graduate

---

* Like many other ex-empire countries, Iraq was just drawn up on a map by the British without consideration for divisions among peoples within the country, joining in the old saying, two oilfields and three tribes.

Record Examinations). They were divided into groups and each group was given a different understanding. One group was told that the test was measuring individual intelligence. The other group was told that it was just a formality and not a test of ability at all. So what happened? The stereotype of different racial ability that was activated by the instructions had their effect: the African American students did much worse when they were told that the test was a measure of intelligence than if they were told it was just a formality. Steele and colleagues write, "In situations where the stereotype is applicable, one is at risk of confirming it as a self-characterization, both to one's self and to others who know the stereotype."[24] So stereotypes about your different family memberships can affect your behavior, depending on which allegiance is foremost in your mind.

The same thing happens to many different groups of people: the elderly do worse on memory tests if someone refers to the idea that aging can reduce cognitive ability. Other studies reveal similar effects: women do better on spatial tests if reminded that they attend a college whose students perform well on such tasks; male golfers putt more accurately if exposed to a stereotype that members of their sex are better at putting than those of the opposite sex. Jeffrey Stone, of the University of Arizona, and fellow psychologists found that when white golfers are told that their golfing performance will be compared with that of black golfers, they perform worse if they believe this is a test of "natural athletic ability" (because here the comparison poses a threat based on the stereotype that blacks are great athletes), but that they perform better if they believe it to be a test of "sport strategic intelligence" (because this comparison suggests the in-group's superiority).[25]

So if people are exposed to stereotypes about the inferiority of an out-group (those who are not part of the individual's in-group) in a given domain, then their performance is typically elevated—a phenomenon they refer to as stereotype lift. In this way, just as a sense of in-group inferiority can impair performance, an ideology of superiority can give members of high-status groups a performance boost.

But we're very sensitive to what's near us all the time. Although the effect can be slight, anything connected to our identity affects us. People prefer people, places, or things that remind them of themselves. Amazingly, even our given name primes us during our lives. As psychologist Brett Pelham has shown, for example, people named Dennis and Denise are, strangely, more likely to become dentists. People named Lawrence or Laurie are a bit more likely to become lawyers. People are more likely to live in places whose names resemble their own first or last names—people named Louis are, in truth—no kidding—slightly more likely to live in . . . St. Louis![26]

Our society can use this knowledge of multiple selves, and how immediate information can change our mind, to effect important changes in how we think about family connections. We shall see how, in the next chapter, that shifting our identity to a larger group promotes behavior tending to benefit all individuals, and since we all have multiple families, adding one that joins to global concerns on top of all the daily ones can be an easy way to steer people to a wider affiliation. Now with the Internet, Twitter, Facebook, and Second Life, our group's size is expanding even faster than our population is expanding, and that could even move us toward becoming a global human family.

CHAPTER 6

It's All Us Now
Closing the Culture Gap and Building a Global Family

WHY do we empathize with a tightrope walker? Nothing we do, whether it's in our facial contortions or "body English," will actually help the tightrope walker, but we respond continuously to the (mostly faked) slips. We're imitating his or her movements, imagining ourselves up there, and we're trying to balance, to help. So is everyone else. It's empathy.

And watching a tightrope walker is just an extreme example of what goes on in our daily life. We're continuously trying to make out what's going on with other people; trying to determine what a friend is thinking; hoping to interpret the wink of your colleague (correctly); determining what your date will think of you, whether that guy on the corner is dangerous, what the scowl of your boss really means.

It's central to our nature; figuring out our relationships with spouse, family, friends, and associates takes up much, if not most, of our time. It is that ability to connect with others, to imitate and thus learn from others, that has been vital to the success of humanity. That ability, which has its basis in imitation and brain structures such as the mirror neurons and the specialized face-recognition network, served our ancestors well in their early groups, where individuals had to deal with fellow members of a small nomadic band that needed to defend itself from predators and sometimes other bands.

"Locally," that ability to connect serves us well—understanding what's going on with friends and relatives, enabling us to empathize, to share good and ill fortune, to acquire mates. But now, in a world of billions, this default position of having but one relatively small family, needs to expand even further to regard everyone, not just members of "us" with a higher degree of common concern—to expand our caring to "them."

Comparing the behavior of primates that have not evolved the chimp-gorilla-orang "constant contact" child-rearing route* with human groups led Sarah Hrdy to her conclusion that other caregivers† in addition to mother (and/or father) are the secret both to the survival of young *Homo sapiens* and to human beings' relatively high reproductive rate. In short, the road to success for early human beings was to get lots of help supplying and protecting the young, who were too slow growing and expensive for a mother, or often even for a couple, to rear by themselves.

Hrdy's conclusions are reinforced by evidence that early hunter-gatherer groups were not centered invariably on males, with females joining other groups to breed,‡ as was once supposed. A careful analysis of a key early anthropological database shows that in only six of forty-eight hunter-gatherer groups studied, the females moved, while in twenty-six groups the results were mixed—sometimes males, at other times females moved to breed.[1] Thus the potential for breeding females to have the most valuable helpers—female kin, especially their own mother—available often seems to have been present.[2] Indeed, the flexibility of breeding arrangements was so well timed that when the woman was pregnant, she and her mate were living with her family.

Further, recent discoveries indicate that the other great apes are more flexible in such arrangements than previously thought, with breeding females sometimes staying with their mothers rather than transferring groups to reproduce. All this helps remove one difficulty with the cooperative breeding hypothesis: if mothers always found themselves surrounded by unrelated female strangers, recruiting of other caregivers would have tended to be more difficult.

It makes sense then that much of our characteristic human behavior started in infancy as offspring of our ape ancestors learned to evaluate and attract the attention of potential caregivers. Presumably in our ancestral line cooperative breeding preceded the astonishingly rapid evolutionary enlargement of energetically expensive brains. Not only did we become upright before we got smart, but our brain expansion was made possible by the evolution of the new (for great apes) cooperative breeding pattern, the most "human" aspect of our family structure. Hrdy supports her hypothesis

---

* Especially the New World Callitrichidae—marmots and their relatives.
† Also known as alloparents.
‡ Or patrilocality, in the jargon of anthropologists.

with evidence that both our ancestors and people today are amazingly flexible in the seeking and recruiting of caregivers, moving quickly to replace, for example, ones that have died.

Our ancestors thus evolved a fine sensitivity to what other individuals thought and felt. Among the skills learned would have been conflict resolution, something even found in close relatives that are not cooperative breeders.[3] Bonobos, for example, often settle disputes with sex; they form same-sex coalitions for mutual aid, pleasure, and relaxation; and the females use sexual favors to obtain food. All those activities require detailed information about their companions—and especially about members of their group of closest associates, members of their families —and human beings are much more skilled at acquiring and evaluating such information than our great-ape relatives.

Human beings are Earth's dominant animal because of two evolutionary innovations: we produce big-brained offspring and have extraordinary skill at divining and dealing with the intentions of others. Those changes that enhanced cooperation include evolving language with syntax, agriculture, writing, printing, industrialization, and such. Those basic innovations led also to other key human attributes: empathy, and then notions of ethics, and then improved communication, all of which we see as central to solving the us-them hangover from our original family structure.

The current human quandary has its roots in our evolution and history; human beings seem most suited to live as small-group animals. Now this "default position" of our nature is making it difficult for us to adapt rapidly to life in ever more gigantic groups. And, like the coalescence of the dozens of "Germanies" and "Italies" two centuries ago, humanity is adapting, but the pace of technological and environmental change is leaving us behind. We are in a race with ourselves, and we are losing.

It's apparent that humanity has to revolutionize its ways, and quickly. Luckily the basis for change seems to exist in our brain cells that recognize others and mirror them. We act on this recognition almost constantly, and it forms the source of our social life. We know that sounds mysterious, so let us explain. The evolutionary depth of our commitment to empathy can be seen in how common it is, in less developed forms, in other animals. We think of empathy as unique to higher primates, possibly to humans alone, but a recent study shows that a form of empathy is found in mice.[4] This empathy is produced solely by exposure to their cage mates, but not to strangers, in pain. In one study, when mice in a group were given noxious stimuli of different intensities, their pain was influenced by their neighbor's status. They gave a strong response to cage mates in pain and not to strangers' distress.

And this pattern continues up to more complicated organisms, even up to us. New brain research shows that when we see emotion in others, it activates our own internal neural mechanisms of emotions. So we "resonate" with the emotional state of another individual. A few functional magnetic resonance imaging (fMRI) studies show that observing pain in others involves the same brain areas that are active in ourselves when we experience our own emotions and pain.*

It's common lore that females are more empathetic than males, and studies generally confirm that females perform better in tests of empathy, interpersonal sensitivity, and emotional recognition than do males. And it may have something to do with brain differences—young adult females have significantly larger gray matter volume in an area of the brain named the pars opercularis (in the frontal lobes near Broca's area) than do young adult males. We'll explain why this is important in a second. The larger the pars opercularis in all females and males, the more empathy they experience in certain circumstances. So this brain structure seems important to our connections with others.

We are focusing on this because the pars opercularis is also *smaller* than normal in people who suffer from autism. Autism is actually a range of behavioral difficulties that include low emotional sensitivity and a high ability to "systematize"—that is, to calculate events. It's no accident that many autists are math geniuses.

In one brain study, high-functioning children with autism and matched controls underwent fMRI while imitating and observing a set of slides of facial expressions of emotion. The children with autism showed no activity in the pars opercularis. Of "normal" kids, those with more autism-like symptoms have the least activity. That suggests that a dysfunctional frontal lobe may underlie the social deficits observed in autism. And, we'd assume, such a difference between people might underlie an empathy deficit in some.

Cambridge (UK) psychologist Simon Baron-Cohen describes this as a contrast between empathetic ways of viewing the world and systematic— "bloodless" or analytic-logical, cool—ones. The view is that autism is at the extreme of the systematic and reaches the logical extreme in some male brains. It's true that the great majority of autistic people and

---

* Basically, fMRIs measure ongoing brain function. When neurons fire they consume oxygen. The oxyhemoglobin protein that carries the oxygen is of course delivered by blood flow. Brain firing removes the oxygen from the blood, producing de-oxyhemoglobin protein. The amount of oxy and de-oxy is what the fMRI measures, giving a view of ongoing brain work.

high-functioning ones of this spectrum (called Asperger's syndrome) are male, and the standard joke is that all engineers are really Aspergers who have found a suitable job.

But the distinction is important even if empathy is found to be more characteristic of females than males. This might possibly be due more to upbringing than genetics. We can't tell, but if you dress little boys in pink and little girls in blue, observers rate the pink boys as more empathetic. Perhaps the differences in upbringing enhance any existing, genetic predisposition. Important, though, is that *what has been traditionally regarded as a "female" approach to the world now needs be stronger in all of us*, at the expense of a calculating, analytic, systematic view.* Times change, and we all need to adapt and develop the empathetic side.

Adaptation is clearly possible, even among those with strong motives not to change. For example, the ideas of our major religious leaders have changed drastically on a long time scale. In the eleventh century, Europe faced a growing threat from the Muslim world. The Holy Land had long been under Muslim control, and Christian pilgrims were in danger in their travels. Pope Urban II called the Council of Clermont to respond to this threat as well as other pressing issues, and on the last Tuesday of November in 1095, Urban began the council with an electrifying speech. The pope used highly abusive language when referring to the Muslims, calling them an "accursed race," and commanded his followers to go to the Holy Land to fight for its liberation from Muslim control. He promised that God would grant them a full remission of their sins if they died while on crusade and that killing heathens was God's work.

The crusaders were convinced by Urban and his minions that their struggle would earn them the reward of eternal paradise in heaven. (Does this sound like something we hear today from another religious source?) So, when the crusaders reached the holy city of Jerusalem in 1099, they were freed to unleash an unholy wave of brutality, and they slaughtered thousands of Muslims—men, women, and children—in the name of Christianity:

> In the minds of the crusaders, religious fervor, barbaric warfare and a self-serving desire for material gain were not mutually exclusive experiences, but could all exist, entwined, in the same time and place.... In

---

* Of course, the counterexample is women who rise in politics, for instance, like Indira Gandhi, Golda Meir, or Margaret Thatcher—all women who were not exactly known for their bleeding hearts. But they may well be at the extreme of their sex's range or just learned what they had to do to get ahead.

a moment that is perhaps the most vivid distillation of the crusading experience, they came, still covered in their enemies' blood, weighed down with booty, "rejoicing and weeping from excessive gladness to worship at the Sepulchre of our Saviour Jesus."[5]

It's impossible to think that the current church would be so blatant and bellicose.* Christianity has changed. It gradually evolved away from advocating mass murder, doubtless partially due to the bloody internal strife connected with the Reformation and the advent of the Enlightenment. And the prospect of suffering sanctions has accelerated many other forms of social change, from the abolition of slavery (promoted by Christian evangelicals) to the increasing of gender and racial equity encouraged by civil rights legislation. These changes have often coincided with external drivers, such as the increased need for workers to replace the men who became soldiers in the Second World War that led to more women in the work force and thence the "Rosie the Riveter" phenomenon. That brought rapid change to the glacial movement for women's rights, which by then was a century old. Many women then had job opportunities previously denied them, and the process eventually helped increase gender equity. Working together showed once and for all what women were capable of, even though most were thrown out of their wartime jobs when the men returned. Top-down restructuring helped the women's rights movement, and despite a setback in the 1950s, women in the West were at least on their way to equal rights. Similarly, a variety of sanctions has helped millions of people give up that most addicting of habits, smoking.

Today the external drivers requiring a functional global family are much more powerful than a desire to conquer or convert others, a need to win a gigantic war, or even a threat to individual health. Those drivers are too many people; the rich consuming too much; the poor, in misery, having too little; and all using environmentally malign technologies. Combined, these drivers threaten civilization as we know it.

And there are a lot of difficulties ahead, as Paul Krugman, among others, points out: "And as I watched the [climate] deniers make their

---

* Of course, not everything about the papacy is bang up to date. The current pope, when a cardinal only a few years before assuming the crown, said in his "Letter to the Bishops of the Catholic Church on the Collaboration of Men and Women in the Church and in the World" (www.vatican.va/roman_curia/congregations/cfaith/documents/ rc_con_cfaith_doc_20040731_collaboration_en.html) speech that women should concentrate upon "feminine values" like "listening, welcoming, humility, faithfulness, praise and waiting."

arguments, I couldn't help thinking that I was watching a form of treason—
treason against the planet."[6] Acts of treason against a nation-state is something we all can understand; such would qualify as treason against what is
in most minds now the largest extended family. Krugman has the scale of
the imagined family we must develop right, but a better way of expressing it
would be "treason against humanity." That's a form of treason that should
be, in everyone's minds as soon as possible, treason against our most inclusive family.

Individuals change behaviors when they see that doing so is in their
best interest. People didn't stop smoking when cigarettes were often called
"coffin nails"—they changed because of the increasing and well-publicized
research that indicated that smoking really did greatly amplify the chances
of disease and early death. Most people did not start recycling because it
was "good for the environment" but because it was first made mandatory in
some jurisdictions, with sanctions for those who did not.

Many governments and corporations have recognized that humanity
faces serious problems, ranging from the depletion of mineral reserves to
the destruction of tropical forests and the modification of global weather,
and some have taken steps to conserve resources (especially energy) and
protect the environment. Many millions of people realize that nuclear
weapons threaten everyone, including their owners, and some powerful
groups are at least talking about finding ways of eliminating them.[7]

Humanity has managed to stay more or less a small-group animal by
constant subdivision, associating in much smaller, overlapping groups, more
limited bands, than the populations in which we're physically embedded,
and considering other members with various forms of affiliation as familial,
part of us. Dunbar's number, that we have approximately 150 people in our
local world, gives us a basic idea of how many we can directly deal with in
our lives. Of course, modern communications make it possible to have many
fragmentary relationships, an important development that may help spread
the specific kinds of empathy needed to create a sustainable society.

Trying to live in groups of any size inevitably involves politics—in
human beings politics is normally thought of as group decision making
in situations of differential power, and the tactics used by different groups
maneuvering to achieve their ends. There is, as all of us know, much political action within families—when the kids cooperate to play mom against
dad, and mom and dad determine the tactics to keep the kids away from
drugs or driving drunk. We rarely call that politics, but it is.

Primatologist Frans de Waal pointed out the seeds of politics can
be seen in our closest relatives. Remember Jane Goodall's study of the
Kasakela-Kahama chimpanzees—where groups of chimp "us" warred

against "them." The behavior was very humanoid, and it showed the total lack of empathy that is all too frequently seen in *Homo sapiens*, even today. In *Chimpanzee Politics*, de Waal tells a famous story of complex inter-male political action. A long sequence ended when two male erstwhile enemies, Yeroen and Nikkie, eventually ganged up on a pesky rival named Luit, bit off all his toes and his testicles, lacerated his body, and caused his death. Lots of politics, little empathy, and little opportunity for scientists to empathize with any of them and do anything but guess at their "motives."

Malevolent intra-family violence makes the news every day in the United States, with hundreds of people killed annually by their husbands, wives, or lovers, and lesser family violence (especially wife battering and physical abuse of children) being much more common. But unlike chimp groups, human societies have much more empathy for the victims and impose a variety of social sanctions on the perpetrators, even when empathizing with the feelings that led to the crimes.

Americans find it very hard to understand the motives of al Qaeda suicide bombers; the bombers fail to appreciate the "needs" of an empire struggling to maintain its "way of life" by maintaining military forces in the Middle East. Overall, humanity is not doing very well at putting together a cooperative global family to settle their differences peacefully. But, short of a global catastrophe, we're stuck with gigantic groups "forever." So we need to ask ourselves how to maintain the small-group coherence and interests that make us comfortable—the families we invent and join—and to reduce competition between families and enhance their empathy and cooperation. We've got to learn to work more with them, if a world suitable for us is to persist. We think that means creating a new, science-based, compellingly attractive worldview. Elements of that view are that

1. there is a real world out there,
2. we can understand and manipulate that world,
3. reason will aid us in making that world a better place, and
4. emotion will continue to play an important and partly understood role in our reasoning.

Recent research in neuropsychology has made clear the importance of emotions in our cognitive processes in, for example, decision making. Human beings are not, as many once imagined, rational actors. We're swayed by the immediate, "primed" to shift ideas, and often fooled by the way a question is posed or how choices are framed.[8]

And if you share our values, whatever we do to better organize a global family and develop a vision should be done democratically.* All of that means that closing the empathy gap and developing a better set of family values inevitably involves politics. And, as we will see, it will involve a redefinition of patriotism.

This sounds good as a vague generality, as does the famous financial advice to "buy low, sell high." But when we try to settle large governance dilemmas with substantial ethical content, there's always the problem of practicality. On crucial issues like ethnic cleansing, population limitation, ending most uses of fossil fuels, and so on, the global community will be able, ideally, to form consensuses, through the sorts of processes we discuss here. Ideally, all will agree that some behaviors are ethically correct and that other behaviors, for example, homicide by individuals or governments, should not be allowed.

Unhappily, however, "allowed" implies an agency, someone or something that allows and that in turn implies some sort of global regime—a transnational entity with enforcement power. It means dampening love of nation-states and putting patriotism back into the category of "the last refuge of scoundrels." It means supporting the pie-in-the-sky democratic world government movement to help keep the need to solve global problems with global institutions at the forefront. The United Nations hasn't excelled in this department. So we face the unenviable task of trying to spread empathy and substantially weaken national sovereignty while leaving nations, subnational groups, and individuals to make their own choices in areas where their behavior does not carry serious implications for the good of others.

The need is crystal clear. We know that recent developments have placed us all in the same family, in the same boat, like it or not. The worst problems are common to all of us, from climate disruption and poisoning of the environment to pandemics and the threat of nuclear war. Like it or not, we're all balancing on that same global tightrope—and more than one on a tightrope implies substantial coordination if fatal falls are to be avoided.

There is, of course, no magic bullet for avoiding a fall of civilization from its tightrope, but understanding family values and moving them into the realm of open discourse can help. Let's start with some bad news. Many interfamily issues have very deep roots. Evolving culturally in semi-isolation and in different environments, human groups viewed speaking the "right" language, having the "right" skin color, being a fan of the "right" soccer

---

* Or, more accurately, through some form of republican (representative) government.

team or citizen of the "right" nation, as being just the way things should be. A lot of "rules" are programmed early on, from language to proper behavior. Human beings learn from childhood an astounding number of cultural rules, from what's good to eat and to the polite way to serve dinner, to the appropriate ways to dress, make love, and worship the "right" gods.

References to family loyalties and rules are even engraved on belt buckles ("Gott Mit Uns") or in lyrics of patriotic songs ("A real live nephew of my Uncle Sam, born on the fourth of July") and love songs ("Your cheating heart"). Abortion is an outstanding example of variation in what is "right." Some people consider life to begin at conception, others that life is a continuum and define the start of a human individual as somewhere between conception and birth, and still others, such as the Masai and some Latin American slum-dwellers, really only consider a child's life to have begun after he or she lives through dangerous early infancy.

Opinions on what is the right way to treat abortion legally are all over the map. So are views of what's right in many other areas, from tolerance of minority religions, different sexual preferences, treatment of women, and standards of beauty to ownership of guns, public exposure of body areas, hair styles, and the death penalty.

It won't be easy to make the necessary changes with the needed speed in the most critical of these loyalties and rules, especially those that differ dramatically from group to group. After all, few people are even aware of the narratives—the embedded stories we all develop as children in social contexts—that dictate much of their behavior. There is no single, simple solution to the human predicament, no quick fix that will install an empathy-based morality on a global civilization.

Note that most people learn some a version of the golden rule as children, but children's brains are much more impressed by the non-golden-rule behavior they actually observe repeatedly among their kin and pseudokin. Thus parents have much less influence on their children than they and we might have thought.[9] And the lesson much more often is "do unto them before they can do unto us." Embedding a new ethic, growing the right synapses in childhood, should involve the creation of new institutions and other forms of social capital that start to operate at birth.[10]

Obviously, no combination of such steps will suddenly transform a world of people raised in nation-states, religious sects, divergent cultures, and often other competing interests into a peaceful sustainable global society. But a world population better educated in regard to the common threads of its humanity and the common threats to the human family might be better able to manage inevitable change. Society must seek ways to raise the odds of successful management and to fine-tune child rearing and educational programs to minimize the production of future warmongers or terrorists like Osama bin Laden.

Ok, so what do we do now? Only Pollyanna would think we can establish a sustainable society quickly, easily, with no expense and no deadly arguments. But we're discussing what is *required* to reach sustainability, not what will be easy or even possible. Humanity is faced with a complex problem of conscious evolution. It is time now to put aside our species' childish things and develop a plan for social survival. It means at last actually doing something about installing a new narrative, a new ethic of reciprocity, or adopting a "veil of ignorance" approach (finding ways to plan a society by those ignorant of what their station in it will be[11]) as a basis for all family relationships—the ultimate family value.

Humanity needs a many-wedge plan for success in levering people away from a them-us mentality to the degree that formation of a true global family becomes possible.[12] So let's examine what *could* be done to make a cooperative, empathetic, and sustainable world. Remember, we're all looking at the same world, society, and environment, at the very nature and future of humanity. It's a future we must face, for the sake of humanity, teetering on a tightrope right now.

CHAPTER 7

The Beginnings of a New Stage in History

HUMANITY has reached an important point in its history. As we've indicated, we're at the end (perhaps a bit past the end) of the adolescent "all you can eat" era on Earth. While many feel that it's time for big changes, there isn't a clear idea of the *what, how,* and *where* of the changes needed. Many now realize that the main drivers of the deterioration of humanity's life-support systems—overpopulation, overconsumption by the rich, and the use of environmentally malign technologies—all must be dealt with. But despite abundant warnings from the scientific community,[1] increasing population and consumption remains ignored by politicians, economists, and the general public. We've pointed out the adaptability and great capacity of the human mental system, but now it's time to specify social and political recommendations that could lead to an attractive and possible human future.

There is an authentic conservative view of human nature and its consequences for politics and social action, one more traditional than ours. It holds that competition and conflict are innate and predominant in human affairs, and individualism and individual action will always dominate social concerns. (This view is *not* that of the lunatic fringe, "birthers," and "death panelers" who are influencing the modern Republican Party in the United States and the neo-Nazis who are gaining adherents in Europe.) This view sees it as a mistake, often counterproductive and certainly unwise, to try to change something as deeply rooted as what its holders view as "human nature."[2]

It's a point of view, traced as a rule to the eighteenth-century British parliamentarian Edmund Burke, that is respectful of the status quo. It assumes that public and government institutions and the society's norms of behavior have developed over millennia to good effect and shouldn't be overthrown capriciously. It is "conservative" in the true sense as to how society should approach change.[3] So, any dream of an overarching or global (in both senses) management of human action just can't happen, and to think otherwise is just indulging in 1960s "Kumbaya" wishful thinking, and possibly would open the door to such radical catastrophes as the slaughters that followed the French and Russian revolutions.

The influential conservative philosopher Michael Oakeshott ridiculed as "rationalism in politics" the reconstruction of traditional social institutions, customs, and morals on the basis of theory.[4] In his view, attempts to force a society to change due to an intellectual idea are likely to do damage to traditions grounded in centuries of practical experience. Oakeshott expressed scorn mostly for the social schemes of the planners on the Left, but he also criticized right-wing plans.

In modern America, one major justification for the conservative approach was the failure of several attempts to change society. One was the attempt, through the Eighteenth Amendment to the Constitution, to prohibit the sale of alcoholic beverages in the United States. "Prohibition" led to large illegal operations controlled by gangsters who made fortunes selling illicit hooch. The amendment failed so disastrously that it was repealed in 1933. Another failed attempt to change society, this time more influential, was the urban renewal movement of the 1940s, 1950s, and 1960s that also led to gang formation. While social planners' housing developments sprang up throughout the United States, England, and France, the most famous of these was the Chicago (housing) "projects."

The aim was empathetic and compassionate: Get rid of the shacks that the poor (predominantly black) people lived in, dwellings lacking good sanitation, good heating, good services. Put the people in well-constructed, well-heated, and well-cooled apartments in well-designed, large high-rises (to keep cost down), and it would be a great improvement in their lives. Out of the favelas, into safe, secure, solid apartments. It sounded good.

But the devil lay in the details. One of the main building projects was placed between two of Chicago's wealthiest neighborhoods, Lincoln Park and the Gold Coast, close to Michigan Avenue's high-end shopping district. So this made Cabrini-Green, begun in 1942 and completed in 1962, a great place for selling drugs, and with a population largely of young people who didn't have jobs, it produced gang violence and conflict. In one nine-week period in 1981, ten residents were murdered and thirty-five wounded by gunfire.[5] Vandalism flourished as gang members covered walls with graffiti, broke doors and windows, and jammed the elevators to foil their competitors.

The architectural design didn't help: the planners fenced the buildings to prevent residents from throwing garbage over the railings, from falling, or from being thrown off. This made it look like, well, a prison. There were famous photos of the piles of garbage, which once made it up to the fifteenth floor, and the water and power often went out. Did the social planners' compassion for the poor improve their lives? It seemed a great day for people living in squalor when these "projects" were built, and another, greater day when they were dynamited and demolished.*

Conservatives could make a similar case for the poor results from the trillions of dollars of foreign aid that the West has spent, with generally good intentions, for development in poverty-stricken countries. Of course, empathy alone isn't enough; good intentions mixed with good analysis is what's needed. We're beginning to see this in foreign aid, where the different "traps" that countries suffer from are better understood. The remedies are different for countries suffering from bad governance or from civil war, or for those with rich natural resources and the corruption, theft, and arms acquisition that result from exploiting those resources. It's been well said that "diamonds are a guerilla's best friend."⁶

When aid funds are tracked, the situation can seem very bad indeed; one study found that of those funds given to the Ministry of Finance in Chad for rural health clinics, 99 percent didn't reach the clinics. Empathy and compassion are nothing without competence,† so due diligence needs be applied.⁷

But on the thought that it's not desirable or possible to change or tinker with "human nature" and established social mores, the conservative view is simply wrong. Indeed, the conservative idea that past arrangements are best for the present grows more untenable every day as human behavior and technologies transform the world and produce new opportunities and dilemmas. We must learn from history but not be paralyzed by it.

---

* But a good example of rather nonempathetic urban development is Robert Moses's plans to have New York build seemingly every possible highway in the city, plans that were stopped due to protests. The best book on Moses is probably Robert A. Caro, *The Power Broker: Robert Moses and the Fall of New York* (New York: Vintage Books, 1975).

† Alex de Waal, for instance, documented that our initial humanitarian and liberal tendencies have gone wrong in Darfur. It would seem obvious that bringing war crimes charges against Omar Hasaan al-Bashir, the head of the Sudan, was a good idea. De Waal counseled against it, saying that al-Bashir would react violently and the rebel groups would be emboldened. Sure enough, it was a disaster; al-Bashir shut out Oxfam and Save the Children, expelled aid workers, and allowed violence to increase. Alex de Waal, ed., *War in Darfur and the Search for Peace* (Cambridge, MA: Global Equity Initiative, Harvard University, 2007).

The term "human natures" is properly plural; they always change generation to generation as the environment develops people with very different views.[8] We get prepared early on for a certain lifestyle, for our future behaviors. Like George H. W. Bush, most people think our current way of life is inevitable and unchangeable. Indeed it's a common function of the human mental system to simplify the world and to produce a kind of psychological inertia, to assume the future will be like the past and that it has always been the same. This is obviously wrong, and our adaptations to the changing world begin, actually, before birth.

In the first few days of their lives, French infants cry differently than do German babies. The French infants cry with a rising intonation; Germans with a falling one. Kathleen Wermke analyzed more than twenty hours of recorded cries: "Newborns prefer exactly the same melody patterns that are typical of their respective mother tongues. . . . As a result, they reproduce exactly the same intonation patterns that are typical of their respective mother tongues."[9]

A key to changing human nature and expanding empathy for others may be found in research on how people respond to their surroundings. David Hume, the eighteenth-century Scottish philosopher, noted that "[it isn't] possible for any set of men to converse often together, without acquiring a similitude of manners."[10] In Hume's philosophy, people (sometimes called "Humean" beings) are sensitive to changes not only in their immediate personal environment but also in the social and the global environment.

That understanding of the crucial role of environments led to tests of the so-called broken window theory. That theory postulates that the more disorder, even petty disorder like broken windows or graffiti, is evident in an environment, the more that incidents of petty crime and further disorder will spread among people. The same theory predicts that favorable trends will also spread. New York was counting on the spreading of positive trends in the mid-1990s when they started an anti-graffiti and street cleanliness crackdown. This campaign coincided with a decrease in petty crime, but since this was a quasi experiment (at best), we can't really know what the cause of the decline in crime was and it produced much consternation among those graffiti artists and litterers who felt discriminated against.

The crackdown was and is controversial, for it was initiated in the administration of Rudolph Guiliani, which often harassed innocent people who were deemed to be antisocial by the predominantly white police department. And no one has defined the term *disorder*. Psychologist Kees Keizer and colleagues set about trying to test the broken window theory. They conducted their experiments on unsuspecting members of the public in two situations: either a norm was violated or not (example of norm violation: graffiti right next to a "No graffiti" sign). They tested whether seeing disorder isn't just priming people to commit the same crime, but to commit crimes in general.

So what did they find? In six experiments, they found the percentage of people violating the norm was consistently two to three times greater when the norm was violated in the environment to which they were exposed. The violations included littering, trespassing, and even stealing money from a mailbox.[11] The experiments suggest interesting possibilities for creating environments that expand empathy, in which improved environments and sprucing up areas, fostering larger groups and cooperative ventures, can increase empathy.

But there are a lot of determinants for antisocial or criminal actions, of course, even for something as important as suicide: people commit suicide more when it's nice out more than when the weather is poor.[12] So our immediate surroundings affect us greatly: runners go faster when they are paced; women eat one hundred calories less per meal when they are eating with men than if they are dining only with other women (men don't care so much who they eat with, the animals).[13] Now the challenge is to further redesign our surroundings in order to redesign our behavior.

One way of redesigning surroundings to move to a more cooperative human society might be to adopt the Sabido method, based on research by Stanford University social psychologist Albert Bandura.[14] His techniques have been successfully employed to increase the acceptability of family planning. It involves writing and producing serialized dramas on radio and television that can win over audiences while imparting socially beneficial values. The method bears the name of the pioneer of this entertainment-education strategy, Miguel Sabido, who was vice president for research at Televisa in Mexico in the 1970s. Character development and plot lines provide the audience with a range of characters—pseudokin—that they can relate to. Some characters are good, some not so good, and the plots lead them through evolutionary changes. Characters may begin the series desiring to have large families, and then through interaction with other characters, twists and turns in the plot, and sometimes outside intervention, they may end up deciding to stop at two children. Under the guidance of Bandura's findings, the serial dramas are not soap operas in which characters wallow endlessly in the seamy side of life. The serial dramas portray people's everyday lives and realistic solutions to their problems. The dramas are aimed at increasing empathy, altering norms, reducing discrepancies in power relations, linking people to support groups, and so on.

Sabido took the classic literary device of character growth and developed the process in a way that enabled TV series to tackle the most sensitive of subjects—sex, abortion, family planning, AIDS—in a nonthreatening and even enlightening manner. By transmitting values through the development of pseudokin, the Sabido method has proven able both to attract large and faithful audiences and to stimulate thoughtful discussions throughout Africa, Asia, and Latin America.

Sabido's first soap opera to promote family planning was *Acompáñame* (*Accompany Me*). *Acompáñame* was a nine-month dramatic series that showed the personal benefits of planning one's family by focusing on the issue of family harmony. The Mexican government's national population council (CONAPO) reported the results as follows:[15]

- Phone calls to the CONAPO requesting family-planning information increased from zero to an average of five hundred a month. Many people who called mentioned that they were encouraged to do so by the soap opera.
- More than two thousand women registered as voluntary workers in the national program for family planning. This was an idea suggested in the *telenovela*.
- Contraceptive sales increased 23 percent in one year, compared to a 7 percent increase the preceding year.
- More than 560,000 women enrolled in family planning clinics, an increase of 33 percent (compared to a 1 percent decrease the previous year).

During the decade 1977 to 1986, when several Mexican soap operas on this theme were on the air, the country experienced a 34 percent decline in its population growth rate. As a result, in May 1986, the United Nations Population Prize was presented to Mexico as the foremost population success story in the world.

Thomas Donnelly, then with United States Agency for International Development in Mexico, wrote, "Throughout Mexico, wherever one travels, when people are asked where they heard about family planning, or what made them decide to practice family planning, the response is universally attributed to one of the soap operas that Televisa has done. . . . The Televisa family planning soap operas have made the single most powerful contribution to the Mexican population success story."[16]

Similar programs introduced in Tanzania at the end of the last century provided dramatic evidence of the approach's efficacy. Before the program was broadcast in the test area, many people believed gods dictated how many children they had. Following the broadcasts, there was a significant rise in the use of contraceptives in the test area, and the same was observed when the broadcast was later played in the previous control areas.

There and elsewhere the Bandura approach has also had dramatic effects on changing behavior relative to AIDS.[17] So behavior, even in important matters such as family size, can be changed, and quite rapidly at that.

It's easy to imagine that similar programming could prepare people to join in actions that involve coordination with other nations. Carefully orchestrated media could help direct society toward sustainability, just as it unfortunately moved Rwanda toward genocide. Another wedge that could prove very useful in moving people in those directions is called deliberative polling. It was developed by Stanford political scientist Jim Fishkin.

Deliberative polling is a novel approach to public opinion research that itself could be a useful wedge in changing behavior. A sample of people is polled on some critical issue. Then some of the people are invited to a weekend gathering to discuss it. Before the weekend, carefully balanced briefing materials are sent to the invitees. During the weekend, attendees work in small groups with trained moderators to develop questions that they later use in conversations with competing experts and political leaders. Some of this process is made available to the original sample as television, live or taped (and edited), broadcasts. Then the original sample is again asked the original questions. The changes in opinion observed are an estimate of the conclusions an informed public would reach on the issue.

Software (PICOLA—Public Informed Citizen Online Assembly) has been developed that would allow much wider use of deliberative polling and much wider dissemination of the results. Deliberative polling could clearly be one wedge used to help close the culture gap and speed the spread of empathy.

On issues such as climate disruption, there is both a lack of information in the public media mixed with an excess of disinformation. Conventional public polls reflect this with small economic trends rated as of greater concern than critical issues related to the survival of civilization. In one week, Tiger Woods's car crash and infidelity received more media coverage than the connection between overpopulation and climate disruption has gotten in all of history. Indeed, on a chart of percentage coverage of news stories in the media in 2009, neither overpopulation nor climate disruption appeared. Stories on Woods, the "balloon boy," the murder of a Yale graduate student, and the sex life of South Carolina's conservative governor all got significant coverage, and the death of Michael Jackson occupied about as much media space as Pakistan, Russia, and the Mexican drug war combined.[18]

The public is subject to "rational ignorance," the situation where an individual sees little advantage to educating herself on a subject when there is little practical use to which she can put the information. There's often little or no corrective action available to an individual. "What can I do about more droughts and increasing deserts even if I'm convinced that greenhouse gas emissions by my country are contributing toward them?" People don't like to confront the inevitable trade-offs or don't care to invest time and effort in acquiring information or coming to a considered judgment on issues when they feel powerless to influence the course of events.

Important for changing attitudes is the likelihood of new information or a new outlook persisting and being translated into behavioral change. How "sticky" is culture in certain respects? Does being better informed on environmental issues lead to people making different, more sustainability-friendly decisions? How much does people's moral competency (their capability to be, say, empathetic) determine their performance toward others as opposed to the incentives built into the cultures to which they are exposed? These are difficult issues, to which substantial attention has been paid but with little resolution beyond the historical observation that education does not ordinarily produce action that maps one-on-one with newly acquired knowledge.[19] We don't always do what we have learned is right. History can be a two-edged sword when it comes to empathy and sustainability. Knowing history is important, but inferring the proper lessons from it is even more important. From our viewpoint, the one genuinely positive thing about the U.S. invasion of Iraq—the one proper lesson that could be drawn from it—was the role that empathy played. It was empathy for the Iraqi people's suffering under Saddam Hussein that was one factor (albeit a minor one) in the support many Americans originally gave to the war.

History has its dark side. Some of humanity's most destructive ideas are based in purely imaginary "nostory." Sometimes history is simply faked, as when Hitler had the SS simulate a Polish attack on the Polish-German frontier as a pretext for invading Poland in 1939. More often an entire nation or large group of citizens can believe the imagined history, such as Israel being a gift from a god to the Jewish people, or that the United States has always been on the side of civilization and democracy and that its various adventures from "manifest destiny" to invading Iraq were in support of those two ideas.

An attempt should be made to "end history"—but not in the sense of Francis Fukuyama, that the present form of what he views as liberal democracy terminates the human cultural evolution in the political sphere (a deeply silly idea, in our opinion).[20] What should be ended are historical views that justify past atrocities by implying "they deserved it." Nations and peoples take pride in their histories, even though to a large degree they are fictional.[21] The Trojan War myth helped unify ancient Greece, even though many doubt a war happened, or if it did, that it lasted a decade and ended with an enormous hollow horse containing soldiers.

The United States has had many fine moments, from producing the world's best constitution to building a system of higher education that was once the envy of all nations and, after a delay, opposing Hitler's tyranny. But the United States has had many dismal moments as well in which the empathy deficit was all too apparent. It is hard for Americans to remember that our "land of the free and the home of the brave" has also been the land of slaughtering and impoverishing of Native Americans, holding slaves, lynching blacks, attacking weak nations far from our boundaries to establish our empire, "civilizing the Filipinos with a Krag,"* fighting Hitler with troops segregated by skin color, burning Japanese cities and immolating the innocent women and children who lived there, invading Vietnam and killing its citizens (remember the My Lai massacre), and transferring wealth from poor to rich (that is going on busily today).

Similarly, most peoples have grievances tracing to historical events—the Holocaust and the long history of other persecution of the Jews in Christian countries, the Arab memories of the Crusades, the slaughter of Palestinians during the establishment of Israel, the rape of Nanking by the Japanese army, the defeat of the Serbians at the first Battle of Kosovo in 1389, the murder of millions on both sides during the partition of India, the killing of thousands in the World Trade Center in reprisal for the U.S. presence in Saudi Arabia, and on and on.

The time has come for humanity as a whole to lessen its focus on family issues from the past and look forward to how it can unite as a single family at a higher level to avoid incalculably greater horrors in the future. It is, for example, time for Jews to leave the horrors of the Holocaust behind when it comes to formulating policy, and it's time for Palestinians to put aside what the Israelis did historically in the Middle East and stop acting as if responding to the postwar grant of territory to the Jews.†

Now, unable to rewrite history, both peoples need to move forward and focus on how to solve their difficult disputes in the context of today, build their mutual empathy, the roots of which can be seen in various groups trying to build bridges to the other. They need most of all to work together to

---

* The Krag-Jorgensen was America's first bolt-action repeating rifle.

† Indeed, Mahmoud Ahmadinejad, who isn't our absolute favorite person or political leader, points out that it was the Germans and anti-Semites of Italy, France, Poland, and other European nations who slaughtered the Jews in World War II, and yet the Jews were given land in Palestine as compensation. If past history were to be the quide, why weren't the Jews given Sicily or East Prussia—or even Grenada or Cordoba, from where they were forcibly expelled in the fifteenth century? (Or, as an amusement, think why not Miami Beach, which we had already conquered and occupied?) But they were given Palestine, where of course Jews lived two millennia ago.

stay alive in a world of weapons of mass destruction, as climate disruption, misallocation, and population growth threaten the scanty water supplies both peoples depend upon.

History is overflowing with unfairness; it's time to forget that and to initiate a new history that isn't unfair. And there are many ways, some of them symbolic, that can help all of us put the past behind us. A famous example is Nelson Mandela's classic donning of a gold-trimmed, moss-green Springbok rugby team jersey, a symbol of the apartheid regime, for his appearance at the June 1995 Rugby World Cup game between Australia and South Africa. It had an electrifying effect on the unity of the healing nation. One can imagine similar symbolic gestures that could help spread a feeling of common identity and thus empathy. For example, if the Israelis simply stated that the Palestinians got short shrift when the Europeans solved the "Jewish problem" in their territory, and if the Palestinians announced that the "Protocols of the Elders of Zion" were a fabrication and they were being removed from Palestinian school textbooks, that might help change attitudes that must change if the two peoples will be able to move forward together in an increasingly crowded and environmentally vulnerable area.

Putting the past behind can lead to reconciliation in the wake of historical injustices—as in the Truth and Reconciliation Commission in South Africa and the Gacaca reconciliation court system in Rwanda.[22] Gacaca ("justice on the grass" in Kinyarwanda) is a traditional local justice procedure that the Rwandan government tailored to process the huge amount of local and relatively small genocide cases. Gacaca has helped clear Rwanda's overcrowded prisons and overwhelmed domestic courts using a family- and community-based system of justice—local participation, having the perpetrator confront the victim, community healing. In so doing, Gacaca doesn't focus on punishing the individual, but on agreeing to put the past behind, and the results are mixed, sometimes creating hard feelings rather than community feelings.

Indeed, the power of empathy and the potential for reconciliation can be seen in the history of men of opposing armies who refuse to kill their opponents and to make death-sparing arrangements with them. Those histories put the lie to the common notion that men are born killers. On American Civil War battlefields, it was common to find the standard muskets holding many unfired loads; some men could not bring themselves to shoot the "enemy" but just went on ritually reloading their weapons—stuffing load after load down their barrels—without firing them. Following the Battle of Gettysburg, 27,574 muzzle-loading rifles were picked up from the battlefield, and almost 90 percent of them were still loaded; 12,000 with more than one load; and 6,000 of those with between six and ten loads.[23]

In World War I, German machine gunners at the Battle of the Somme refused to shoot British infantrymen who were retreating after the enormous slaughter. Early in that war, much to the distress of their generals, the soldiers from the two opposing sides had made informal live-and-let-live pacts with each other to avoid bloodshed, and even in 1915 they prearranged Christmas truces. During World War II, it is estimated that as many as 85 percent of soldiers failed to fire at the enemy. In the Vietnam War of the 1960s, the American military had to convince their soldiers to shoot to kill. In all these situations, the soldiers' relationship with their "targets" was very recent history. The machine gunners' empathy was directed at men who a few minutes before were trying to kill them in the course of a desperate assault.

In any case, the big issue is how to reorganize global civilization ethically and consciously evolve its norms to promote the spread of empathy and a transition to a sustainable and fair society.[24] A key to all this, we believe, is making the discussion bottom-up, with the participation of as many people as possible—not a top-down attempt of old, rich, white males to find their preferred solution to the human predicament. Finding convergence will be challenging: there are few ethical universals, and it is highly unlikely that many will be agreed upon soon—although most ethical systems do converge on some basic elements, for example, special circumstances are required before killing is justified.

A typical case where detailed convergence has not resulted is the 1948 United Nations Universal Declaration of Human Rights. There was substantial opposition to that declaration among Muslims originally, and they produced a Universal Islamic Declaration of Human Rights in response. The Muslim version assigned certain rights to women, but not equal rights, and it did not give everyone the right to marry, regardless of religion. It says that Muslims are required not to submit to rule by non-Muslims, allows beating and amputation as punishments, and puts religious restraints on freedom of speech. On the other hand, even some small improvement in human rights can provide an important weapon for the weak, and we believe it would be a better world if basic rights to subsistence and security were accepted while more difficult goals such as gender, racial, and religious equity are pursued.

We clearly need an international discussion of such eco-ethical issues, one that involves not just "leaders" but as much of diverse publics as possible. "Rights" should not be granted from above by those claiming to be in communication with supernatural entities or defined by the powerful, but, we believe, they should be voluntary and agreed upon as democratically as possible by societies—they should not be imposed upon people, and there should not be a right to abuse the weak or the "other."[25]

Indeed, even if some believe rights might stem from supernatural entities, in our current world of many differing religions, rights must nevertheless be harmonized across religions and other belief systems in order for our world to achieve peace and necessary cooperation. Humanity's future hangs on finding some broad agreement on major eco-ethical decisions involving difficult topics like population size and the equity of patterns of consumption.[26]

We need to create a venue to serve as a rallying point for those myriad organizations fighting for environmental quality and social justice, and for the efforts to "cancel" history. It would emphasize that the whole human family has outside enemies, from climate disruption and global distribution of toxic chemicals to the threat epidemics and of ecosystem-destroying nuclear war. These enemies are threats that the global family must cooperatively organize to deal with in order to avoid its own destruction. A new attempt to focus humanity's attention on this crucial issue, the Millennium Assessment of Human Behavior (MAHB), is treated in the appendix.

At the extreme of human family structure questions is how more than seven billion people should organize themselves into a single entity to solve massive global problems. That is, how should we unite the nation-states? Many aspects of this global governance question are reminiscent of the issues in the 1787–1788 debates between the progressive Federalists and conservative Anti-Federalists over uniting the states of North America.[27] Those debates were over the ratification of a then-radical proposed constitution to replace the Articles of Confederation of the thirteen states that became the United States of America. The debates focused on how disparate political units could be united to provide for both common defense and economic prosperity, while retaining personal liberty in a representative political system. They debated whether defense could be left to the individual states, depending on independent militias in times of crisis, or whether it was necessary to have a professional standing army and navy under the control of the central government. A main point of the Federalists was that a strong central authority was needed so that treaty obligations could be met (the states weren't, for example, meeting their obligations with Great Britain agreed to in the Treaty of Paris that ended the Revolutionary War). The Federalists also asserted that a permanent national military was a prerequisite to proper national defense.

A major issue in that long-ago national security debate was how much the nation was threatened by external enemies (more explicitly, European powers). That should be thought analogous to whether today's external enemies (global problems such as climate disruption or lethal pandemics) are serious enough to demand some sort of global governmental regime instead of the ad hoc multiple treaty system in place today.

The Federalists took the position that relative security at the end of the eighteenth century could easily become imperiled at a future point; in the same way, environmental scientists today are concerned that before the end of the twenty-first century, today's relatively benign climate could become a major source of death and destruction. The Anti-Federalists felt that militias could be united and organized in time for defense, fearing government control of a permanent military more than outside enemies. Today's conservatives often seem to fear government intervention more than they fear a threat to civilization. Many conservatives still claim that climate worries are overblown and that people are not contributing to climate change.

Much of the Federalist-Anti-Federalist dispute focused on the relative importance of liberty and security, a live issue today as the United States is being converted into a combination theocracy and corporate plutocracy, with an increasing concentration of power in malign hands.[28] And population entered into the eighteenth-century discussion big time, with the Anti-Federalists pushing for power to rest in the states—as close to the people as possible so that their representatives could be from individuals who lived among their constituencies and would thus be truly representative.

At the time of the debate, the U.S. population was four million people, and it was 95 percent rural. The population is now about 310 million, almost eighty times as large, and 20 percent rural. With a country so much more populous than it was in 1788, with diverse groups of people living cheek by jowl in cities and with instant communications, this issue of representation has become even more problematic. And at the global scale, the ways liberty might be promoted and preserved with seven *billion* people poses a challenge to family organization and empathy spreading that is truly unprecedented.

The main lesson, for us, from the legendary constitutional debates is how they illuminate the need for similar informed citizen participation today. The founding fathers had some distinct advantages in their discourse: it was a discourse among an elite group of men, many of whom knew each other and all of whom had similar educations. All were familiar with the premier discourse on politics of the day—Montesquieu's *Spirit of the Laws*.[29] There was no significant culture gap.

There are reasons to hope. Enthusiasm for the MAHB seems to be growing. Enough people are interested in supplanting complete sovereignty of nation-states with a new sort of planetary regime that a global referendum has begun on a democratic world government (www.voteworldgovernment .org/). Its goals are to abolish war and settle disputes between nations by law, as they are usually settled now within nations; lower taxes globally (without the burden of supporting huge, useless, or positively dangerous military establishments, they easily could be); and solve global problems, especially the environmental predicament.

Of course, the idea of a world government goes back thousands of years, was mentioned in the Bible (Isa. 2:2–4), and was an especially hot topic a couple of centuries ago when Immanuel Kant wrote his essay "Perpetual Peace: A Philosophical Sketch" (1795). Kant was perhaps inspired by the founding of the first democratic union of states in 1782. Needless to say, the world of Rush Limbaughs and Mahmoud Ahmadinejads hardly seems ready for a global government of any sort, or more global influence in national affairs, which is much more likely, any more than European nations and their colonies seemed ready for democracy in 1700. Yet, with all its governance flaws, the United States has now been a republic for well over two hundred years. Europe itself, a mere sixty-five years after the defeat of Hitler, has moved, with all *its* governance flaws, toward being a union of states.

But, of course, today there is a much more pressing need for global governance (and thus a global "family") than there was in Kant's time. Then, there was no possibility of a nuclear winter, the chance of sudden climate disruption from human activities was extremely remote, there were no synthetic toxins spread from pole to pole, economic transactions in New York could not influence markets in New Delhi in a tiny fraction of a second, and a fatal disease from the Congo could not be transmitted to an Englishman in London in less than a day. Clearly, there isn't time to wait for the institution of a new, powerful global government to deal with pressing problems such as climate disruption, but it clearly is the time to bring the overall issue of world governance to the forefront.[30]

So, can we further foster developing the global human population as an imagined community of pseudokin?

New tools are becoming available. PRE attends meetings in Second Life (http://secondlife.com/support/downloads.php) in which difficult issues are discussed in beautiful surroundings. Participants can be totally anonymous, with no accent or appearance factors entering into the discourse. A woman who wears a burkha in real life can be represented by a male avatar in biker's dress. And a discussion group often forms a group of pseudokin. The building virtual world represents both a threat and an enormous opportunity for humanity.

Cross your fingers. Such technological devices can help, but, unhappily as we have pointed out, there seem to be no silver bullets. Working on all the many wedges seems the best way to go, while working to create positive interactions among the different approaches to the problem and among families. We can also hope for one of those social transformations such as occurred in racial and gender equity in the United States after the Second World War or in the collapse of the Soviet Union and international communism at the end of the twentieth century. Complex natural and human systems produce those kinds of surprises, but scientists are not sure whether their occurrence can ever be predicted with any accuracy.[31] But by closing key parts of the culture gap, we may encourage the emergence of a social transformation toward sustainability. Watching current events makes the odds of such success seem ever smaller, but salvation may lie dormant in the seeds of growing concern. We certainly hope so.

One important wedge could be a new emphasis in educational, political, and nongovernmental organization campaigns upon the communality of humanity, the important nonrational aspects of our behavior, and how important it is that this be fostered. For the foreseeable future, there'll be families, clans, tribes, religions, team identification, company identification, racial identification, and so on. But for now, a goal needs to be adding courses about human identification and empathy to all school curricula, emphasizing how common are all our problems and interests, and emphasizing how crucial to our decision making are our emotions.[32]

In theory, education from kindergarten on could be revised to make the general public more conscious of the us-them impacts of our family heritage. Ideally, the key elements of what has been learned about human perceptions, cognition, and emotion (and their interactions) should be woven into early school curricula and emphasized to all college students. Other changes could greatly improve the quality of education and at the same time improve the levels of empathy and the sense of community in societies. Children are often schooled in too much isolation, without a mix of adults. Efforts should be made to bring more adults with time on their hands into the schools, especially in the early grades, to increase the ratio of caregivers to students. Today the United States, with its badly decaying educational system, could take advantage, for example, of unemployed and retired executives and the elderly, to the benefit of both young and old.[33]

Cooperative rather than competitive children's games should be encouraged by governments, perhaps (among other things) with subsidies in rich nations to toy makers to engage with and follow the advice of cooperative game theorists and those who design cooperative-play video games. The focus would be not cooperation to vanquish other teams, but cooperation within the team to outwit humanity's worst enemy—us.

Early science fiction stories had the population of a threatened Earth come together against weird extraterrestrial enemies. Now our society has need of unity against the enemy from within. While modern media, especially racist Internet sites, exaggerate the differences between people and peoples, now they need encouragement to work for a human reunion.* Given appropriate incentives, many could also increase awareness of our similarities and the boat we're all in. Much is known about the techniques of changing awareness (the entire marketing profession is dedicated to developing them); what is less clear is how to develop the incentives.

---

* In today's world, should running a racist Internet website be considered the ethical (or legal) equivalent of crying "fire" in a crowded theater?

CHAPTER 8

Getting to "Alike" One Another

A N important component of generating the necessary global family awareness is finding new ways to concentrate on the commonality of being human. Since the more alike we see each other, the more we like each other, society needs to develop additional ways of educating about the essential similarity of all peoples, in texts and films as well as new courses in schools, using the insights of the social sciences, reorganization of outdated university curricula, and, of course, revitalizing the mass media.

Most people do not understand how similar are seemingly "different" peoples. Much more attention in both schooling and the media could be placed on the basic biological and cultural "alikeness" of all *Homo sapiens*, as well as the fascinating variation that develops on extremely similar backgrounds. After all, there are more genetic differences within than between populations, and we all have common needs physiologically and psychologically. There are also many cultural universals (equally advanced languages with syntax, making and using diverse tools, decorative art, rites of passage, sex role differentiation, kinship terminologies, competitive games, use of fire, etc.[1]) about which people should be educated.

And more attention could be focused on a near universal desire to help other people—demonstrated by everything from babies offering to help adults to almost everyone wanting to help the earthquake-devastated people of Haiti. Despite all our conflicts, despite the actions of the bin Ladins and Milosevics, there are many organizations and individuals in most countries struggling to help the poor, damp down conflict, preserve the environment, and generally make the world a better place. It's common human behavior, and everyone should be urged to deliberately get involved in something that will affect more than themselves.

Remember, we're all great at connecting with others, at knowing what's going on inside them, and we're wonderful imitators. The closer one is to identifying oneself with a group making positive changes, the better the result. Take one current example—the results of experiments testing different effects of messages urging hotel guests to use less energy. The standard message asked guests to do it "for the environment." A second asked them to "cooperate with the hotel"—this was 12 percent less effective than the environmental appeal. Third was the statement that "most people in the hotel reused towels"; this was 18 percent more effective than the standard message. The fourth message was that "most people *in this room*" did so (italics added). This was 33 percent more effective* than the first.[2]

Now this method is being used to reduce energy consumption in Sacramento, California, and has had a positive effect. This principle, making people identify with a group more closely, can produce energy saving that would otherwise take years to effect and cost millions in, say, converting to more environmentally benign energy mobilization systems.

Here's what was done: Positive Energy, which is a company headed by the social psychologist Robert Cialdini, has created a software program that evaluates energy usage neighborhood by neighborhood. But instead of the usual "You've used 22 precent less electricity than the same month last year," the reports document a homeowner's energy use in relation to the usage of one's neighbors, making it what people like "us"—in one's neighborhood, in the same-size houses—are using. Here is one communication that was sent to a customer in Palm Springs: "You used 72 percent more than your efficient neighbors," the report said. In a twelve-month comparison with one hundred neighbors of similar-sized homes, "you used 125 percent more natural gas than your efficient neighbors. This costs you about $381 extra per year."

And these messages have had the same effect as in the hotels; those people who found out what "people like us" are doing reduced their energy use by more than 2 percent over the course of a year. For one hundred thousand homes, this is the equivalent of taking two thousand homes off the grid. As Cialdini explained it, "These are the people who are most like me—we share the same circumstances."[3]

---

* Our colleague, neuroscientist Robert Sapolsky, suggests this could reflect a residue of small-group worries about reputation, fear that the cleaning lady will know you're not protecting the environment and will tell people about it. In any case Robert Cialdini, who directed the research, used it as an example of the power of "provincial norms"— which fits well with our view of human beings behaving as small-group animals.

Everybody who's been through a college psychology course knows about the experiments of psychologists Stanley Milgram and Philip Zimbardo.[4] In Milgrams's most famous study, unsuspecting people were induced to give horrific shocks to a person in the other room (of course they didn't, really). In Zimbardo's Stanford Prison Experiment, Stanford students, like the brown-eyed/blue-eyed students in Jane Elliot's classroom, quickly became bullying and sadistic to a group of other students selected to be prisoners (they did, really). The studies are held to be echoes of the Nazi camps and Abu Gharib, and they are. Extreme behavior can be elicited from most people when placed in an environment with similar stimuli.

But what you probably don't know is that Stanley Milgram conducted *many* experiments on more than a thousand people of different sexes, schooling, and backgrounds.[5] While 90 percent in the famous study delivered the maximum 450 volts to the miserable victim, the situation changed when someone (like them) was in the same room. Just the presence of another person dropped the numbers who shocked to 10 percent. But the biggest determining factor is the perceived similarity of the person delivering shocks to the "authority." The more alike, the less we'd punish. As psychologist Jerry Burger wrote about in a recent study repeating the procedure (and the results), "Milgram . . . argued that people follow an authority figure's commands when that person's authority is seen as legitimate. Moreover, our culture socializes individuals to obey certain authority figures, e.g., police officers, teachers, parents. Milgram's experimenter was granted the legitimacy of authority by virtue of his association with the experiment, the university, and perhaps even science."[6]

During the days of his prison study, Dr. Zimbardo himself became affected by the abuse students inflicted on others, and he became inured to the depth of the cruelty going on. He strongly resisted stopping the experiment and himself became enmeshed in it; he continued to carry on until REO's grad student classmate Christina Maslach, then a close friend of Dr. Zimbardo, made Zimbardo see that he was also a victim, and he stopped the study.[7] Christina Maslach was the ultimate "us" in this study, for Zimbardo married her afterward.

Remember what happened when Jane Elliot separated students in her classes into blue-eyed and brown-eyed kids? And the problem of skin color is, of course, the first and strongest kind of grouping in society, just ahead of sex. While the race and sex discrimination problems aren't going to be eliminated any time soon, an innovative study shows that families can change, and quickly. In a study called "Can Race Be Erased?" psychologist Robert Kurzban showed a group photos of different people of varying skin color and had them read a sentence about conflict on the computer screen—"They started it" and the like. The two sides of the fight were racially mixed, but when Kurzban asked the viewers to recall the two groups, they divided the groups by skin color, black with black, white with white.

Then Kurzban changed the conditions of the study. Instead of using a plain photo, he "dressed" the individuals via computer program, in either yellow or green jerseys. When the same question was asked after reading the sentences about conflict, the jersey colors trumped race! And we see this daily in team sports; people who are of similar background, once they are on a different team, see those who were once "us" as "them," and those of different races come together, as the different races and ethnic groups of the 1979 Pittsburgh Pirates baseball team used to say, "We are family." So race can be "erased," but it will take a lot of work to get more of us on the same "team."[8]

A prerequisite of such erasure would be seeing oneself as one piece of the puzzle, as was promoted by the well-known experiments of jigsaw and High Point (North Carolina). Jigsaw is a system, which has been shown for several decades to be effective, that makes sure that individuals learn how to work together and to empathize with each other. It was developed by the social psychologist Elliot Aronson to help in schools where the students were in conflict. He stated that "the jigsaw process encourages listening, engagement, and empathy by giving each member of the group an essential part to play in the academic activity. Group members must work together as a team to accomplish a common goal; each person depends on all the others. . . . This 'cooperation by design' facilitates interaction among all students in the class, leading them to value each other as contributors to their common task."[9]

Seeing oneself as part of a common system, a piece in a common puzzle, reduces racial conflict and increases educational outcomes. As a piece in a jigsaw puzzle, each student plays an important part, and as a result, each student is essential; this in particular is what makes this strategy so effective. The jigsaw classroom was first used in 1971 by Aronson and his colleagues. The schools in Austin, Texas, had just been desegregated at that time, so the students—white, African American, and Hispanic—at that moment found themselves in the same classrooms for the first time. So the initial process of school desegregation began with fear, distrust, and fistfights, and other conflicts broke out all across the previously quiet Texas city. After studying the schools, Aronson concluded that the competitive environment of the classroom contributed in great part to the clashes and to the many incidents of aggression.

The jigsaw program attempted something new: to shift the classroom emphasis from competition to cooperation. Aronson and his colleagues and the teachers divided their students into small groups, who were diverse in terms of race, ethnicity, and gender, and they made each student responsible, in the first exercise they tried, for a part of Eleanor Roosevelt's biography. Needless to say, at least one or two of the students in each group were already viewed as "losers" by their classmates. In these assigned tasks, everyone was responsible for their particular piece of the entire puzzle. And no one could solve the problem alone.

Aronson's jigsaw technique has now been used in lots of different classroom situations. A history class, for example, could be divided into small groups. Suppose their task is to learn about World War II. In one jigsaw group, Linda is responsible for researching Hitler's rise to power in prewar Germany. Another member of the group, Steven, is assigned to cover concentration camps; Pedro is assigned Britain's role in the war; Melody is to research the contribution of the Soviet Union; George will handle Japan's entry into the war; Clara will read about the development of the atom bomb.

Eventually each student will come back to her or his jigsaw group and will try to present a well-organized report to the group. The situation is structured specifically so that the only access that any individual member has to the other five assignments is by listening closely to the report of the person reciting. Thus, if George doesn't like Pedro or if he thinks Linda is a nerd and tunes her out or makes fun of her, he cannot possibly do well on the test that follows.

It's an important paradigm that needs be expanded to different cities and to different areas of work. A recent survey concludes (ignore the jargon),

Use of the jigsaw classroom will facilitate a recategorization process by which members of racial-ethnic groups other than one's own ("them") will begin to be seen as being members of a more inclusive "we."
. . . [So] why do we not make the jigsaw classroom required course work for all students in colleges and universities? This could easily be done by integrating the jigsaw classroom into course work that is offered to undergraduates. Although there are a number of possibilities, here, one potential means of doing this would be to offer a course in cooperative learning, possibly from within the Education Departments of colleges and universities, where those doing scholarly work in the area of cooperative learning could be recruited to instruct such course work. This cooperative learning course work could then become required for all students who are completing undergraduate degrees. Students would be required to complete cooperative learning

requirements (much like they are required to complete English and science requirements) to complete a degree.[10]

Being part of a jigsaw makes it relatively easy to see those who were "them" as being part of the same system as "us." That helps, because all of us have a major problem seeing people who live in different cultures, and even different groups in our own country, as being in any way like us. For most of us, that's dramatically true of those who live in a culture of crime. *We often have no idea, even, how they see themselves.* We never learn about them in school. For instance, the sociologist Sudhir Venkatesh began what was to become a compelling study of the gangs in Chicago. He did this over a ten-year period and uncovered the hidden structure of these gangs, how they function as their own alternative community, how disputes are settled, even why most drug dealers live at home with their mothers because they don't make much money. But Venkatesh began with a different view, one that saw "them" as far away from his life as a sociology student at the University of Chicago.

In one of his first times interviewing a gang member, Venkatesh acted as a good "objective" student and asked, "How does it feel to be black and poor?"

Then Venkatesh gave the multiple choice answers: very bad, somewhat bad, neither bad nor good, somewhat good, very good.

"'Fuck you!' he said. The guy . . . began to laugh which prompted others to start giggling. He told me, 'You got to be fucking kidding me.'"

So Venkatesh tried again with the same question to a man who was to be the major figure in his work, a gang leader named J.T., who returned from college to this life.

"I'm not *black*," he answered looking around at the others knowingly. "Well then how does it feel to be *African American* and poor?" I tried to sound apologetic, worried that I had offended him.

"I'm not African American either, I'm a nigger."

Now I didn't know what to say. I certainly didn't feel comfortable asking him how it felt to be a *nigger*.

"Niggers are the ones who live in this [poor] building," he said, "African Americans live in the suburbs. African Americans wear ties to work. Niggers can't find no work."[11]

So how can those who "wear ties," who don't see "these people" as part of "us," cross the divide if they do not understand what's going on within different parts of society? But sometimes the tie wearers do have an understanding of the other.

Assimilation of gangsters into the community can also have a surprisingly positive effect. In 2003 the West End neighborhood in High Point, North Carolina, was an open-air drug market rife with crime and disorder. The streets were crammed with drug dealers, and gunshots often rang out, the result of fights for territory among the dealers. Sometimes a local church congregation could not park their cars because the street was jammed with addicts looking for drugs. The High Point police acted as police usually did: seeing the dealers as "them," and so the police would stop the men, pat them down, and arrest the ones with drugs in their pockets. Many went to jail and returned to the street when they got out, so the police and the justice system never shut down the drug market and the disorder.

But then the police tried something different, "focused deterrence." At the suggestion of David Kennedy, director of the Center for Crime Prevention and Control at John Jay College of Criminal Justice, police started talking to community leaders in West End. They found out who the street drug dealers were. There were fewer than they had expected: only sixteen, of whom three were habitually violent. The police arrested and prosecuted the violent ones, and invited the rest in for a chat.

The young dealers were shown the evidence against them, and given a choice. If they stopped dealing drugs and carrying guns, they would not be prosecuted. Then prosecutors warned them that if they did not stop that day, they would be sent to jail, possibly for the rest of their lives.

The nonviolent dealers saw that the community wished to include them, and they would be treated as "us." The dealers' neighbors and family told them that what they were doing was wrong and had to stop. They faced a roomful of community figures, parents, relatives, and others with close, important relationships with particular dealers. The drug dealers were told that they were valuable to the community. They were told that local law enforcement had worked up cases against them, and that if they continued to deal the drugs, the cases against them would be prosecuted.

Making this connection between the dealer and the wider community—giving dealers the sense that there was real empathy—worked. In High Point and in other cities, the drug markets have declined or, in some cases, even closed. In most cases there have been great reductions in violent and drug-related crime, 20 percent in High Point, and there has been no sign of the return of the scourge. Many other cities are now using this model, making a more inclusive family and spreading empathy at the same time.[12]

But High Point–type projects alone can't move us far enough toward sustainability. One reason is that a factor that separates the complex world of today from the simpler one of the hunter-gatherers is that rapidly increasing culture gap. The gap traces in part to our crisscrossing family networks. An individual person doesn't need to possess most (or, it seems sometimes, *any*) of the society's information because that knowledge is housed with groups of pseudokin (physicists, mechanics, song writers) who can employ it for the benefit (or detriment) of all.

In plain English this means that you don't need to know dentistry in order to have a root canal, and you can use a computer, watch TV, drive a car, or be defended (or threatened) by an intercontinental ballistic missile without the vaguest notion how those devices work.

Key parts of our culture are increasingly segregated in the hands of various specialist families, because our culture has developed technology rapidly over the last two centuries and not progressed in ethics and governance. But aside from selected members of such groups as environmental scientists, philosophers, anthropologists, or psychologists, very few people have even thought about the deeply inconvenient truths of society's peril, the role the empathy shortfall and pseudokin structures play in creating that peril, and the part changing those things must play in averting utter disaster.

It was said, perhaps not with complete accuracy, that John Stuart Mill was the last person to "know everything," but, of course, there was less to "know" then, and achievements of different civilizations like India and China weren't included in "everything." Now many, if not most, "highly educated" persons can't describe how the basic process of evolution works, give a coherent description of the threat climate change poses to civilization and how climate disruption differs from stratospheric ozone depletion, explain how population size influences vulnerability to novel pandemics, give a discourse on why we don't behave "rationally," or tell why racism is biological nonsense. In short, it is commonplace for people to be clueless about how the world works, how our minds work, and how threatened our society is by its unsustainable patterns of behavior.

However an increased breadth of knowledge alone is unlikely to get humanity on the way to sustainability in the nick of time. But clearly one of that gang of wedges needed to solve the predicament facing the human family is to close the culture gap on key aspects of how our life-support systems work and how human beings are related to one another. Unfortunately, these are among the most difficult parts of the gap for us to feel any real concern about because of our biological inheritance. Human beings evolved to deal with the immediate: the clear and present problems—a rock thrown by an adversary, a dangerous animal approaching, sudden changes in weather, a sharp noise, and being short-changed. The australopithecine who did not become aware of the leopard's approach did not contribute her genes to the next generation.

However, our ancient ancestors did not evolve mechanisms to allow them to perceive changes in the climate that took decades. If the climate were changing, it was not because they were causing it, and there was little they could do about it anyway. It seems likely that natural selection long favored our brain's tendency to habituate—to tune out all but "big news" recent changes in the world or nearby events. This tendency is still with us. We notice the air conditioner start up, but then its steady hum disappears from consciousness. This process, in which we cancel out ongoing unchanging activity, allows us to focus on sharp and immediate changes, like a sudden appearance of a leopard or a Jaguar sedan driven across our path, but it makes the environmental background seem even more constant than it is.[13]

What's more, an australopithecine female who had to be alert for leopards had no reason to be concerned about the fate of individuals beyond her immediate band. Her brain system was tuned to deal with those who are close biological kin and those females from outside the band (if any) who had mated with her kin and might help her raise her own offspring. There was little or no reason to extend her empathy beyond those with whom she had daily lifelong contact. Indeed, our female ancestors very rarely had contact with "others." But that calculus has changed dramatically. Now the modern version of the early woman, as a rule, has more contact with non-kin, even non-pseudokin, than she has with her extended family.

Those factors worsen the problems of the culture gap in a species (us, that is) that is still dealing with the small-group family structure grounded in the Pleistocene and earlier. And the very gradual change of the us-versus-them structure does not make educating people about the need and possibility to extend empathy to all any easier.

In our view, the educational systems all through the world are in dire need of reorganization. Both the dramatic gap between the educated and the basic knowledge of how the world works and the difficulties of getting individuals to focus on long-term trends and to be less inclined to find problems with "them" cry out for remodeling how schools and universities work so that they refocus their efforts on closing those key areas of the culture gap.[14] Remodeling them makes Hercules' task of cleaning the Augean stables trivial by comparison.

While what needs to be produced (e.g., the kinds of knowledge and information and its transmission) has changed dramatically, the intellectual development of school and university structures has been a classic demonstration of cultural inertia. It is as if modern military organizations were not (as usual) planning to fight only the last big war, but were planning to refight the Peloponnesian War, complete with tightly massed and superbly drilled phalanxes of hoplite citizen-soldiers who knew the other members of the phalanx well—families, then.

That the antique departmental structure of universities is no longer adequate for dealing with the major problems of a global community has been apparent for decades. There have been haphazard attempts to modernize, such as was suggested by the 1996 Gulbenkian commission on restructuring the social sciences, with little success.[15] One of the worst problems in the social sciences is a failure to define overall goals and take a sampling approach to meeting them—that is, to focus on a limited set of carefully selected situations that are relevant to major societal problems. A good place to see this is in one of our favorite disciplines, history.

PRE, a war history buff, was recently reading an interesting historical paper on the Russian Brusilov offensive in the First World War.[16] The details of the blunders made by both Tsarist and Habsburg leaders were of "hobby interest"—they had the same sort of relationship to behavioral science that describing new species of mites from Borneo have to ecological science. Both lack a sampling approach to nature.[17] Historians have produced many thousands of accounts of military blundering—and they are accumulating continuously. It clearly will never be possible to detail them all in print.

Historians need to decide what are the critical big questions in our past that remain unanswered, and design programs (and give out rewards) for those who do the best job of tackling them. The kind of analysis that should be encouraged includes that in Jared Diamond's now-classic *Guns, Germs, and Steel* and *Collapse,* and his new *Natural Experiments of History;*[18] Joseph Tainter's *Collapse of Complex Societies;*[19] or more conventional works like those of Eric Hobsbawm, David Kennedy, and, of course, the classics of Karl Marx, Oswald Spengler, Arnold Toynbee, and William McNeill.[20] All of these scholars focused on the big picture and tried, with varying success, to illuminate how *Homo sapiens* weathered (or did not weather) past times of crisis.

Perhaps it would be a good idea to "reboot" sociology, political science, economics, anthropology, and psychology by combining all into a single discipline of behavioral sciences with separate subdisciplines.[21] Universities might follow the suggestion of the Gulbenkian commission—that every professor be required to have an appointment in at least two of the subdisciplines.[22]

In the humanities, rebooting could give universities a much larger role in dealing with family-structure and empathy issues, especially by integrating closing the key parts of the culture gap into the curricula. Perhaps most importantly, universities could be central to developing a vision of what sort of world people could enjoy. We don't know what the best answers are;

the need for dramatic change presses from without, but the changes must come from within.

The structure of the university disciplines is only one small part of the problem; the contemplative scholar model of an ideal faculty member needs revision, as time to contemplate is running out. Because of that model, universities and academic training often produce followers, not leaders. Feelings of urgency tend to be limited to small groups of faculty and students (as, for instance, those who oppose U.S. wars).

In the main, universities operate on "Council of Basle time." That church council met from 1431 to 1449 and, like most university committees, accomplished little or nothing of real importance. Even the Catholic Encyclopedia commented that "the valuable time and energy which should have been given up to useful legislation were spent in useless discussions."[23] In contrast, today universities should be reorganizing to work more on "World War II mobilization" time, where in roughly five years the United States went on to a full wartime footing and then back to a civilian economy. And that change in university policies will need to involve changes in academic reward systems, so that more credit goes to those scholars who actually produce results applicable to solving problems of the human family—as opposed to the all too common pattern of serving the interests of industry or researching trivia. It is often said that university research should be "curiosity driven," but a key thing for scientists is to have a sound judgment of what to be curious about.

We don't know if adapting university structures and curricula to our new and dangerous world is possible given the conservatism, entrenched interests, tenured professors whose minds stopped working when they got job security, departments that reward miniscule published ideas as "contributions," evaluation of departments by members of the same inbred disciplines who have a vested interest in promoting their privileged pseudokin, and the frequent sloppy thought and political competition endemic to universities and all other ancient institutions. The classic response to the question of why politics within universities is so nasty is that "there is so little at stake." We do know that if universities continue to avoid reorganizing to meet the challenges of this century and do not change their system of scholarship, research, interdisciplinary work, and rewards, they will become irrelevant except as factories for producing components of a crashing socio-political-economic machine, and humanity will suffer greatly as a result.

The culture gap is lethal where it keeps most human beings—average Joes and U.S. senators alike—ignorant of the biophysical facts of life. But most of Americans also suffer from an enormous culture gap in understanding how we run our extended families, indeed how we select and organize that very Senate. Most of the citizens who don't know how television sets are made also do not know how laws are made, or the way their extended family is governed. They don't know the history of the governance system either. The latter is much more important, rarely taught except as myth in civics classes before college, and totally distorted in most media. But one does not need to educate and persuade a majority of citizens to change a society.

Much of the spread of empathy in recent centuries has been through laws—such as the British abolition of the slave trade in 1803 and of slavery itself in 1833, or the late twentieth-century civil rights laws passed in the United States. Groups of citizens deeply interested in the issues got laws passed, then the laws led the way, and eventually the culture followed. Interest groups are key to some of the most needed changes, and the culture gap can make it difficult to find the power to change laws in those areas. For example, only some groups of lobbyists, a few reporters, some business executives and academics, and members of certain nongovernmental organizations (NGOs) are reasonably informed in the critical area of governance, one that requires much more attention if empathy is to be spread and relations among pseudokin families made more cooperative.

This part of the culture gap was essentially nonexistent for hunter-gatherer groups and early farmers. They governed themselves and settled disputes either en masse in public or in councils of elders. Even the Greek city-states made their major decisions in assemblages of all its eligible citizens.* If Athens decided to go to war, six thousand people voted on it, and the "deciders" went out and fought. For example, Socrates was renowned for his valor in battle.

Well over two centuries ago, drafters of the U.S. Constitution proposed the idea that the ultimate source of political power was not a monarch or an aristocracy, but the people.[24] It was, in essence, a first in the West, following a long hiatus since the era of direct democracies like those in classical Athens and the mix of democracy and oligarchy in the Roman republic. But as we noted, since the days of the debate between Federalists and Anti-Federalists, the quality of discourse among even the politically active portions of populations, in the United States and other republics, has declined dramatically. There is much that Americans could learn about balancing powers, allotting responsibilities, representative government, and the like from revisiting that debate today.

---

* Of course, these "eligibles" did not include women, or the male slaves, or the conquered who did most of the work—the *polis* were the landowning elite males—about six thousand of them.

The governance part of the culture gap has expanded hugely since the golden age of Greece, alongside of media that don't expose the deep deceit of "swift-boating" and hires ex-military hacks being paid by the arms industry to pretend to be neutral commentators on issues of war and peace.[25] It is sad to think that with the improved technologies of communication today, very few Americans are aware of the building concentration of executive power in their government (contrary to the intent of the Constitution) or the role of lobbyists in actually drafting legislation, and that few congressmen read most legislation.[26] And this makes it all the more important that the basics of governance in the United States be carefully reexamined and that ways be found to improve public knowledge of and restore a more republican form of government.[27]

The culture gap in American understanding of governance, the manipulation of family values in relation to it, and the impact of an empathy shortfall were demonstrated dramatically in the health care "debate" of 2009–2010 in the United States. It is clear that caring for the health of citizens is a classic government function, and that an empathetic government—especially in a rich nation—should extend health care to all its citizens regardless of ability to pay. To turn it over to private industry and allow many people to go without care or have only substandard care is a bad idea. It adds high salaries and corporate profits to the total of health-care costs, and it puts people at the mercy of organizations (particularly the insurance companies) that aren't actually in the health-care business, but the moneymaking business, and for that reason have incentives to deny care and encourage death, rather than treat the sick. And having a substantial part of the population denied proper care lowers the standards of health of the entire population, putting everyone at higher risk of infectious disease.

That health care should be in the domain of industry because business is more efficient than government is "conventional wisdom," which, like much such wisdom, is very often wrong (think General Motors, Kellogg-Brown, Enron). Obama was trying to reform the staggering and inefficient (from the viewpoint of social values, not the profits of the insurance companies) health-care system. But the governance culture gap allowed members of Congress and others to impede the process with a flood of disinformation at little risk that their constituents would detect them.

Outside of changes in school, more movies like Al Gore's *An Inconvenient Truth* and more Sabido-type telenovelas are needed, which emphasize the common dilemmas of humanity. But unlike Gore's technically excellent movie, they need to be accompanied by realistic analyses of what should be done to solve the dilemmas. Then these programs could help spread the feeling of belonging to a single family threatened not by another family of "them," but by its own corporate behavior. The fascinating discoveries made about our minds and our relationships could be interwoven into various forms of entertainment. And it goes without saying that in the United States, news media should be primarily funded by the government—something that is characteristic of other democracies. The BBC has not become a spokesman for government, nor have the public-supported media of Germany, Canada, or other nations. Americans deserve much better than a steady flood of Faux News or MSNBC.[28] We rarely, if ever, see coverage of the "extremely inconvenient truths" we deal with later—such as the impacts of having corporate executives determine what information reaches us. What's "mainstream" is what the corporate media want us to believe is mainstream.

Thus, one can see that the culture gap is just not a function of the educational system; it is also a function of a media that has largely become a disinformation system of the sort that will need to be disabled or bypassed if we ever are to create a global human family.

CHAPTER 9

Revitalizing Empathy and Staying on the Tightrope

ONE of the major problems related to our extended family structure is that of fundamentalist's power over governments. A recent example is the situation in the Aceh Special Autonomous Area (ASAA) of Sumatra, Indonesia. Its establishment was in one sense a blessing. The Aceh area, which had been devastated by the 2004 tsunami, had been the scene of a decades' long insurrection by the Free Aceh (separatist) Movement.

But the condition of women in the ASAA is compromised by the institution of Sharia law, one of the demands of the separatists who objected to the religious tolerance of a secular central Indonesia government. Following the law spawns public floggings and makes stoning the penalty for adultery. The increased intolerance and reduced empathy that can result from fundamentalist religious families makes it difficult to move toward an imagined global family in which all religions are tolerated if they do not try to impose their views on others by coercion or force.

It would be a mistake to believe that religious governance problems are for faraway places like Aceh. The most powerful nation in the world has, over the past few decades, become more and more influenced by fundamentalist Christian ideals, many of which are decidedly short on empathy for nonbelievers.[1] This is especially bad in a democracy where the norm is that it is impolite to criticize someone else's religion—indeed, even to discuss it. Professor of religion Charles Kimball put his view of that norm bluntly: "We must quickly unlearn that lesson. Our collective failure to challenge presuppositions, think anew, and openly debate central religious concerns affecting society is a recipe for disaster."[2] This is especially true since the political power of the fundamentalists promotes proresource war and antiscience political postures. This power threatens our ability to treat either Earth or other human beings in ways that might make a sustainable society possible.[3]

Nonetheless, there is benefit in believing human beings were created by gods or by processes set in motion by gods. Getting prepackaged norms and a fixed (if mythical) understanding of events like thunder is one way that our brains are able to function effectively. We need quick explanations for events, and we need to tune out continuing events else we be overwhelmed by all that's going on outside of us. Our personal version of reality is a very small abstraction from the external world: the eye, for instance, passes on to our brain only one trillionth of the information that reaches the retina. We need to keep our world simple. If someone refuses to kill, for instance, because she believes she will be punished in an afterlife, that is a benefit to society and, especially, to her potential victims.* Such norms are generally passed down through families and acquired from peers with whom one has frequent contacts, and they help make small groups more stable and functional.

Religions help explain the world,[4] but unfortunately the explanations dreamed up in the distant past have understandably been different from each other, at least in mythology and ceremonies.† Today there are many thousands of religions; there is no known exact number, in part because there is no exact definition of a "religion."[5]

There has been a degeneration of organized religions from the development of wisdom and spirituality in the teachings of Zoroaster, Moses, Jesus, and Mohammed to today's "ethical" monotheisms. Pagan religions, like animistic religions, were concerned with worshipping gods properly to get their assistance in daily life. Henotheistic Judaism (worshipping one supreme god, but not denying the existence of others) had ethical considerations—how to live, a set of desirable rules (the Torah)—but didn't prescribe following those rules as a way to gain a more desirable afterlife. The latter view became solidified in Pauline Christianity along with an intolerance of other belief systems that was alien to both animism or paganism.‡

---

* Of course, we see the reverse in the exhortations of the pope during the Crusades and in the beliefs of contemporary Islamic fanatics.

† For example, numbers of gods, presence or absence of demons or angels, possibility of ghostly ancestors or "saints" intervening in current affairs, systems of appeasement and their potential efficacy, afterlives and reincarnations, importance of appropriate behavior versus predestination, required dress/life style of leaders, and so on.

‡ Of course, many early adherents to Christianity believed in more than one god, and today Christian sects have a trinity; a plethora of minor gods, from angels to saints; and so on—so Christianity is in many ways henotheistic, and Hinduism presents an even more complex god-counting picture.

Besides introducing heresy, the organized religions have an awful lot to do with control by and aggrandizement of their leaders, restriction of empathy to members of the cult, and the subordination of women to men, and too little to do with wisdom or spirituality.[6] We can hardly count the killings done in the name of one god or another, or because people belonged to the "wrong" religion, but they include those who perished and are perishing in the Israeli-Palestinian conflict, the battles between Sunni and Shia in Iraq, the Buddhists and the Tamils in Sri Lanka, and the Russian Orthodox Christians and the Chechen Muslims, to name but a few. In the recent past, there is the slaughter of millions of Jews by Nazis and the roughly ten million murdered by both sides in the separation of the Muslim state(s) of Pakistan from dominantly Hindu India.* Sadly, as a recent study put it, "The revival of religion is multiplying the numbers of people who are willing to kill and die for their faith."[7]

And we in the Abrahamic traditions of the highly civilized West are often shocked, by some of the bellicose sayings of "those" Islamist clerics, with reports of their fire and brimstone sermons sometimes quoting (and, sadly, most often out of context) the Koran. We read texts like this:

> [If you find someone saying,] "Let us go and serve other gods" unknown to you or your ancestors before you, gods of the people surrounding you . . . you must not consent, you must not listen to him, you must show him no pity, you must not spare him or conceal his guilt. *No, you must kill him, your hand must strike the first blow in putting him to death and the hands of the rest of the people following. You must stone him to death* [italics added].

This is pretty rugged stuff, but it isn't from one of those "wicked" Shia Imams, or one of those primitive Tamil warlords, or from a wild Borneo shaman screeching this out, or even the writings from the intimate diary of one of the September 11 terrorists. It comes from Deuteronomy 13:6–11, the West's own Bible. Not exactly "all in one happy human family."

We need a new view of religion with an emphasis on enhancing human sympathy and empathy, on caring for the physical and mental well-being of all human beings and the health of the planetary life-support systems we all depend upon. To do this we need to switch from overconsuming to "satisficing." Rather than maximizing consumption, satisficing means being content with satisfactory results—having a nice apartment and good public transport available as opposed to a ten-thousand-square-foot mansion, two summer homes, and ten cars parked at each.

---

* Bangladesh came later on.

Satisficing is the exact opposite of the philosophy embodied in the "he who dies with the most toys wins" view. Once basic needs are satisfied, more and more money and more gadgets do not translate into much greater happiness or satisfaction, and sometimes more is less. Lottery winners who get windfalls are no happier two years after than before.[8] Nonetheless, in the face of gross inequity, societies claiming religious family values still support overconsumption.[9]

But few sermons are preached against such, to us, clearly unethical activity. Rebooting religion will require widespread recognition that the three major religions (and almost all of the minor ones) are products of much earlier times, when today's fact-based explanations for how the mind works and how the world works weren't available. Those religions have fairly well-known histories of gradually, with enormous effort and argument, inventing doctrine. There is a gigantic literature on this, sometimes deriving from long series of meetings (some lasting years) in which equivalents of shamans produced their interpretations of mixes of texts and myths (think Council of Nicaea or orthodox Jewish rabbis still arguing over how to view the Talmud today).

In the early days the major religious organizations served to bind communities into large groups of pseudokin. They served much of the function that local government business and charities now offer, so they can give up providing this ancient umbrella. Today, we're left with a situation in which many religious conceptions—often presented originally as metaphors—tracing from seven thousand, two thousand, and over one thousand years ago are taken literally by some, often to the great disadvantage of humanity.

And more recent doctrines can also sometimes interfere dramatically with what most of us think of as "normal" family behavior. In her 1993 work *Death Without Weeping*, anthropologist Nancy Scheper-Hughes describes the horrors and violence faced by women in a desperately poor Brazilian shanty town. Out of roughly ten pregnancies, an average woman suffered loss of more than half the offspring to infant death and miscarriages. The result was that, like the Masai, women didn't bond to their children until they were one year old or so and had a reasonable chance at survival. This illustrates the ease with which environmental factors can override what genetic determinists assume to be normal human behavior—instant mother-child bonding.*

Scheper-Hughes blames the Catholic Church for contributing to the mothers' indifference toward the deaths of their babies by teaching fatalistic

---

* Such bonding may be variable in our own society, depending on many circumstances, and its lack may explain cases of postpartum depression.

resignation. Deaths of "angel-babies," as they were called, were treated as a cause for festive celebration. Meanwhile, the church maintained, as it does today, its strictures against birth control and abortion, demonstrating a large empathy shortfall recognized even within the church.[10]

Going at least back to the early Mesopotamian civilizations, and likely much further, people have used religion in defining "us" and "them," have converted people to increase the former and killed people to get rid of the latter. Enmity seems almost built into religion. Indeed, when PRE lived with the Inuit in the 1950s, the contempt of Roman Catholic Oblate missionary Father Rio for the Inuit religion was fully reciprocated by Tommy Bruce and other Inuit, who stuck with their complex animistic nature worship and thought Father Rio's idea of a virgin birth hysterically funny. They expressed amazement at the enmity between Rio and the native Anglican missionary (they shot at each other's dogs when they "trespassed" on the wrong church's land), finding it inexplicable in terms of the "love thy neighbor" talk of both cults.[11]

In today's world of crisscrossed family structures, things are little different from the time of Sargon more than four millennia ago. Empathy for the religious "them" is all too rare. Members of Nazi *Einsatzgruppen* walking small Jewish children into the woods and shooting them in the back of the head, Islamic zealots cutting the heads off of "infidels" on TV or murdering thousands of innocents in the World Trade Center, Jewish zealots killing Palestinian civilians or assassinating Prime Minister Yitzak Rabin because he was seeking peace in compromise—all underline how the religious "us" are comfortable, even joyous, at turning the other weapon on the religious "them."

Religion's overall social impact, despite it being one of the few loci of ethical discussion in our society, has been, unfortunately, a minus. Rather than binding humanity into a single family today, the groups of pseudokin based on religion lead to isolation and conflicts that could threaten society if something is not done to counter its most damaging influences.

But we don't think all is lost. People have been inventing and appeasing spirits and gods for one hundred thousand years or more. During almost all that time, religion was doubtless instrumental. Viewing phenomena without understandable causes, people concluded, logically, that the causes were invisible entities. It would be reasonable then to make attempts to manipulate those ancestral spirits, gods, and other supernatural entities to achieve luck in the hunt, rains in the drought, and sexual attractiveness in the ugly. After all, those big-brained ancient primates were already experts at manipulating each other. It all made sense considering how little our distant hunter-gatherer ancestors knew of how the world worked. But our species is 2,500 years past the Greek revolution in rational thinking and analysis,

200 years past the enlightenment, and 150 years since Darwin began to end humanity's intellectual childhood.

It may surprise you that on the whole, those hunter-gatherer societies were more egalitarian than societies that developed after the agricultural revolution. The basic reasons are clear. Without stark divisions of labor and with the necessity of moving frequently, individuals had little opportunity to accumulate power beyond their own share. A successful hunter got a ration of prestige, and differences in status developed. But that prestige might not carry over to power to settle disputes or to deal with the supernatural.

Hunter-gatherer societies were also, in general, not able to support full-time leaders or skilled artisans. Their successes were also transient: abundant supplies of meat that were killed and dragged home by the most adept hunter could not be passed on to future generations. Settling down to farm and specializing changed all that, and humanity moved into today's more familiar pattern of economic inequity and disparity in power between individuals—more than ever as priestly castes and states evolved and gradually produced the opportunity for hereditary classes to arise as a brand-new human invention.

That sequence suggests that it is not some built-in and immutable "human nature" that divides societies into rich and poor today, but that specific environmental circumstances moved humanity in that direction. This view is supported by the development of hierarchical structures in the hunter-gatherer era in societies such as the Haida of northwestern America. The Haida lived in such a food-rich coastal environment that they could afford to settle down. That environment opened the door to economic inequity and social stratification. The Haida-type cultural exception also suggests, on the positive side, that given the appropriate environment, our behavior could be shifted back toward a more equitable, empathetic society. One of the requirements would be to reduce financial inequality and to reduce the opportunities for families to become dynasties.

Some hunter-gatherer individuals, especially those with schizoid tendencies (e.g., hearing voices inside their heads), often were thought better able to communicate with the supernatural world, but these shamans did not adhere to complex doctrines of "right" and "wrong" behavior or belong to hierarchical organizations.[12] Those phenomena only developed after the invention of agriculture permitted large-scale specialization. Farming that paved the way for the invention of many groups of pseudokin and those monotheisms whose shamans now claim the ability to interpret and intervene in a spirit world. They, of course, use the claim to dictate to others how to act and manipulate the behavior of their large numbers of pseudokin, often to their own advantage.[13]

Nonetheless, there is hope. Many religious leaders care for their kin and pseudokin, even for all of humanity, and many have already taken positions helpful in dealing with the environmental predicament. In 1997 the Orthodox patriarch of Constantinople declared forcing another species to extinction was a "crime against the natural world" and a sin.[14] Indeed, protecting biodiversity ("the creation") was endorsed by the Greek Orthodox, Protestant, and Catholic hierarchs of the Standing Conference of Canonical Orthodox Bishops in the Americas (SCOBA) at their meeting in New York City on June 21, 2005, following approval of the statement by the SCOBA Social and Moral Issues Commission and recommendation by the SCOBA Study and Planning Commission.[15] In March 2008, the Vatican added "pollution" to the list of deadly sins, although the pope continued to condemn abortion and did not mention what we could consider an equally deadly sin, over-reproduction. And there is now a draft of a "Muslim 7 Year Action Plan" to deal with global climate change.[16]

There is a great diversity of Christian (and other religious) worldviews in relation to central issues of sustainability, just as there are outside of religious extended families.[17] There has even been substantial convergence between the views of some evangelical Christian religious groups and those of environmental scientists. The Reverend Richard Cizik has become an important crusader on environmental issues in the evangelical Christian community:

The climate change crisis that we believe is occurring is not something we can wait ten years, five years, even a year, to address. Climate change is real and human induced. It calls for action soon. And we are saying *action based upon a biblical view of the world as God's world*. And to deplete our resources, to harm our world by environmental degradation, is an offense against God. That's what the Scriptures say. Therefore, if we are to be obedient to the Scriptures, there is no time to wait, no time to stall, no time to deliberate [italics in the original].[18]

Equally important, some of the most effective international aid is now provided by organizations with fundamentalist roots. World Vision, a Seattle-based Christian organization, now has forty thousand staff members in nearly one hundred countries. As columnist Nicholas Kristof explains, "That's more staff members than CARE, Save the Children and the worldwide operations of the United States Agency for International Development—combined."[19] Kristof also points out the bravery and persistence of members of Catholic charities operating in horrendous conditions, caring for the ill and even passing out condoms to help stem the tide of AIDS or to give poor women relief from continual childbearing. As he says, "A growing number of conservative Christians are explicitly and self-critically acknowledging that to be 'pro-life' must mean more than opposing abortion." No matter what one's position on faith-based charity, we need to be supportive of this kind of thinking, especially when some of the best religious charities do not tie their efforts to attempts at conversion and when governmental aid is lacking.

In the twentieth century, the Soviet Union tried to replace the Eastern Orthodox religion of the country with a new religion of their own design. The effort was a total failure. Some have concluded that such an outcome indicates that belief is coded into our genes—part of "human nature." But countering that is a widespread fear tracing to Friedrich Nietzsche at the end of the nineteenth century, that if common people realized there were no gods, society would collapse into nihilism. This is not such a crazy fear, since science is often a poor source of ethical guidance. But remember, our species has only had a few centuries during which the original basis of religion—the ignorance of causes of things like lightning, volcanic eruptions, and the death of individuals—has been gradually removed by the development of science. In part, a new social reorganization could build further desire for universalism of major churches. Some of the largest religions have tried, through conversion and murder, to create a single global family of pseudokin based on the religion. But others are more tolerant and strive to assemble pseudokin on the basis of ethical considerations that fit perfectly into a movement to develop human family values. Friends of ours belong to a Unitarian congregation (not church)—an extended pseudokin family where discussions are not about angels and sin, but about human relationships and how to improve human lives. The congregation provides frank, no-questions-barred sex education for young teenagers—not sets of rules developed by old men to favor males in ancient patriarchal societies.

There are other signs of positive religious change. More and more women are being made leaders in various sects, Protestant and Jewish, as are gay individuals. Also cheering has been the persistence of challenges to traditional and rigid belief. Indeed, in Europe today it is estimated that between a quarter and half of all people are not involved in organized religion.[20] Given another few centuries, religion based in the views of supposed supernatural "fathers" might well fade away and be replaced by more adult, ethical discourse—but can humanity afford to wait?

One way to speed the process toward a world family would be to find ways to close the religion culture gap since the power of religion rests so much on counterfeit history and myths, instead of on biophysical realities. If religious leaders become more educated about how the world works, they would see, as some have already, that their goals require the creation of a real global family with an emphasis on spirituality, empathy, and sustainability rather than on trying to spread ancient inventions about the universe.

Perhaps most daunting of all is getting broad agreement on ethical issues from diverse families—be they Vatican bureaucrats, Texans, Uighurs, fundamentalist Hindus, Cubans, Salafi Muslims, Inuit, or Democrats. Even in areas where a naïve person might expect little controversy, as in support of the United Nations' Universal Declaration of Human Rights, the assumption of easy agreement could be wrong, as we have seen.

It might be possible to keep the community benefits of religion and rid our species of the toxic us-them division. One surprising ray of hope is in crowd behavior. Far from the popular "madness of crowds" or "unruly mob," there is building evidence that mobs are not mad or unruly but act surprisingly rationally. In an emergency situation, for example, crowd members more often cooperate to solve the problem rather than panic.[21] Although mobs can be led into violent and counterproductive extremes by instigators, even then most of the violence is committed by a few, and a more general pattern is sensible action, recent studies show.

The focus has shifted toward trying to figure out "the psychological processes that can transform hundreds or thousands of individuals into a unit."[22] A wide range of events, from a fire in a theater to simply being brought together in a tour group can forge a new social identity, transforming the group into a psychological family unit. And social scientists are learning more about ways formation of such a unit can be triggered. The phenomenon also seems to work when members of the crowd are different in many ways, including racially and politically. We've already seen how familiarity can produce unifying feelings in a family setting. That the same process can also work in crowds gives further hope that once much of humanity recognizes it is faced with horrendous common problems, a global psychological family unit can be formed—a unification of the scattered individuals who seem already to possess that allegiance.

After all, human nature changes and so societies have changed throughout history to suit the reality of life as it's being lived at the moment, from humanity's early days as the "terminators" of the large land fauna of Europe, Asia, the Americas, and Australia, through an era of wild expansion of Western capitalism and the decimation of indigenous people, to dealing with conditions in the current crowded cities of Chicago, Mumbai, and Beijing. It has been *Homo sapiens* all the time, but *Homo sapiens* with very different human natures.[23]

Adaptation happens all the time, and the rate of change is increasing, so the possibility of more radical, as opposed to conservative, change seems more probable. The signs are everywhere. There is a current generational attitude change toward the number of children one should have, a change that is being seen around the world; in Iran, for example, families have dropped from having 7 children in 1984 to 1.9 in 2006, and the rate in South Korea has dropped from 5 to 2 in 20 years—a change that took Britain 130 years. Poor countries are changing quickly (although not quickly enough) with increased income and the liberation of women. And changes in sexual behavior are hardly restricted to family size—many have altered attitudes to same-sex unions.

Pope Urban's invocation to slaughter unbelievers wouldn't exactly be greeted with open arms by the Vatican today. We don't go for much animal torture now and decry and punish it when we see it. Hangings no longer get great audiences out for the day's fun in England, the Parisians no longer take pleasure in the sport of cat burning, and conflict diamonds are a no-no. The conservative impulse is correct when change seems too sweeping, as in Prohibition, or is done from a top-down approach with no feel for what's happening "on the ground" in the daily lives of those so affected; aid given to dictators by democracies and disasters such as Cabrini-Green attest to that.

But times and needs have changed drastically, and reasonable conservatism is no longer so reasonable. Not tinkering with society may have been all right in the relatively stable world of our remote ancestors, but in our postindustrial age, it isn't all right in a world when deforestation in Brazil contributes to desertification in Kenya. To be a new conservative, or a true conservative, humanity needs to evolve consciously to conserve our planet, and ourselves.

The encouragement of empathy, to see us all connected, doesn't mean that every one of our affiliations, connections, and actions needs be governed globally. It's only those that affect all humanity that matter. We're proposing, in truth, a new level of awareness *additional* to our complex selves and family organizations. The world is too full now to allow the untrammeled individualism that may have worked well in the past as our modal behavior.

It can't work, not now when one person can blow up an entire city, when smokestacks in China can contribute greatly to droughts in Australia and smog in California, when cow farts in Texas help change the climate in Sweden, and when plagues can circle Earth in days. Individualism could work when any group's action was isolated, and then the dangers to the world were unstoppable (such as the ancient volcanic eruption at Santorini that may have destroyed the Minoan civilization), but not now when the acts of us all threaten not only ourselves but the rest of humanity.

A change away from being a political animal should not be our aim; we're not talking about a change in the tribes in which we take such pleasure, be they the Dodger fans or the foodies or the Hell's Angels or the Republican Party or the nations we love, like France, Alabama, or the Sudan. It is not a new ideology but a change in consciousness about the need for much more rapid political progress in a direction we're already going.

Human beings have been organizing themselves into ever-larger family units and extending empathy for a very long time. If some closure of the now-gigantic culture gap can be achieved in key areas, humanity might cross the tipping point where most people can make the mental jump from small-group animal to global animal. After all, we have brains prepared for connections with others, and media developed to connect those brains worldwide. So we have the ability and we have the technology; now can we find the determination and the leadership from below to make that new mind take over?

One thing seems certain—basic change must be accomplished with new or highly altered institutions. Those we have today, even the ones like private foundations with totally beneficial goals, are fixed on incremental change in the existing institutions that have been steadily driving civilization toward collapse.

This inconvenient problem can be seen in the rolling script at the end of Al Gore's important documentary film *An Inconvenient Truth*. The movie was scientifically accurate and socially transformative—it helped to awaken public concern about the potential for climate disruption. But the recommended "solutions" presented in that terminal script were weak in terms of their direct effect on the problem. They were not as strong as Gore's analysis in his more recent book *Our Choice* (which will reach fewer people).[24] The final movie script suggested many individual actions, such as drive less, be sure your tires are properly inflated, recycle more, heat and cool your home less, put in more efficient light bulbs, and unplug your cell phone charger.

These *An Inconvenient Truth* suggestions for reducing climate change were what we like to call "brick-in-the-toilet-tank" solutions. Placing bricks in toilets is sometimes recommended during droughts in California, to save water each flush. The idea has largely been replaced by low-flow toilets (and shower heads). But toilets account for a tiny fraction of the water use in the state, and the total domestic use is in turn a small fraction of the entire state's water use, since as much as *80 percent of California's water goes to agriculture*. Using such limited, personal techniques as controlling toilet flushes to deal with droughts is like trying to bail out Lake Superior with a thimble.[25] Now, we're not pooh-poohing these small steps,* since such actions do get people involved and, as we have noted, this can be very important. But it is also critical that everyone recognize that such actions alone won't come close to doing the job. After all, the energy saved by unplugging your cell phone charger for a *year* could also be saved by driving a few *seconds* less.

Similarly, people can get a feeling of participation by buying "greener" automobiles. Their gas consumption gets great attention, and laws are passed with fanfare mandating that vehicles improve their efficiency in the next decade. But all forms of transportation use only 28 percent of the energy used in the United States, and personal automobile use makes up two-thirds of the transportation use. So cars use on the order of 18 percent of the total, and replacing half the fleet by 2020, given the incremental increases in standards, could decrease that 18 percent of total consumption by 20 to 25 percent. That will make a 4 percent difference in total. Furthermore, it is not at all clear that many of the greener vehicles will be all that more efficient when their entire life cycles, from obtaining the raw materials to build them to disposing of the remains (such as toxic substances in batteries), are calculated. And the calculation may not give enough weight to Jevons paradox—that increasingly efficient use of some resource can also *increase* the rate of its use. People driving more efficient cars may drive a lot more than those behind the wheels of clunkers.

Unfortunately, the situation is a bit more than, well, just "inconvenient": the human impact on Earth simply must be reduced if human life is to persist anywhere near the current luxurious one enjoyed by a billion or so people. To be ethical, such a reduction in scale would have to involve some redistribution to help the people suffering from underconsumption, and doubtless this reorganization would need to continue to until the population and its consumptive impact has declined substantially. And to do all that without plunging off the tightrope requires that final expansion of empathy.

So what can you do personally? Everything you can among your family, friends, local community, and nation to force politicians, decision makers, and society as a whole to face the fact that "siloed" decision making must be go the way of the dinosaurs. Siloed decision making (a cute term now common in business) is that which is done in isolation, apart from other related decision making—as if, for example, the decision to fire the intercontinental ballistic missile in one silo were made without regard for what was done with the missiles in other silos. We talk a good game of saying everything is tied to everything else, but like universities that praise interdisciplinary courses of study and research but preserve the sanctity of

---

* We couldn't resist.

antique departments, we do precious little about it. It's very important that humanity work on all the wedges that can tilt us toward sustainability at once and keep as close an eye as possible on the related impacts of progress on each. If we wish to join a global family, one that has allegiance to and strong empathy for all other human beings, it will take a lot of effort.

So, how can we sum up this mélange of information and suggestions? Human beings have always been a small-group animal, and they still are. But unlike lions, wolves, or even chimps, for the last few thousand years human beings have organized into ever larger groups, from thousands to millions to billions—and have found ways, for better or worse, to retain its small-group character. The "family values" conception, much spouted by conservative politicians, is only a century or so old, and peoples' ideas of nationhood are not much older, but they have distant roots in the behavior of our mammalian and, especially, our primate ancestors.

Human beings evolved as the only cooperatively breeding great ape, with an enhanced capacity for rapid reproduction and a built-in capacity in our brains to be empathetic with the members of our small hunter-gatherer groups.

Our forbears lived out their childhoods (and in many cases their entire lives) in those isolated small groups. But then, starting about sixty millennia ago, our ancestors went on the move, going "out of Africa," and leaving their African homeland to occupy a world empty of their own kind.*

When some ten thousand years ago hunter-gatherers took up farming, settlements enlarged and specialization that created families within families grew apace. Peoples of the Nile Valley, Indo-Iranian region, and elsewhere began to contact one another, and individuals, for a variety of reasons ranging from building projects to defense, acquired allegiance to ever larger family groups from bands to clans to tribes to states to empires.

All those diverse families had and have values, and those family values defined who they were and today define who we are. But, sadly, those values also stored in our history and even in our brains and perceptual systems who they weren't and who we aren't—the "them" who seem to have caused, and still drum up, so much trouble in the world. People can get their social comfort in diverse ways—even though the ways of those others may seem weird, unnatural, or heretical to those of "us" who live in the "proper" moral culture. Thanks to our evolutionary history, we have carried with us that long-standing us-versus-others approach to the world. That

---

* Of course, it wasn't quite empty of our closest relatives; there were the remnants of the earlier migration of *Homo erectus*, who had occupied much of the Eurasian continent and may have even left a miniature version in the Indonesian archipelago—nicknamed "the Hobbit"—although evidence for this is questionable.

approach expanded in Mesopotamia and at Thermopylae, caused misery for millions in the Crusades, the Mongol conquests, and perhaps hit a peak in Nazi Germany during World War II, where the tribal value of German *kultur* brought death to tens of millions, including many millions of German citizens who were caught up in the consequences of Nazi policies.

So humanity is now struggling to organize itself to live successfully in more and more colossal groups. Those giant groups have evolving cultures that are still burdened by the us-them mentality, and by problems with forming the complex and overlapping personal and group identities that our evolutionary backgrounds as small-group social animals necessitate. And despite several centuries of scientific progress, most human beings are still unaware of the biological and physical facts of life. Finding ways for them to acquire that knowledge would help close a lethal part of the culture gap, which in turn would provide an intellectual basis for pursuing increases in empathy and cooperation.

The latter proves very difficult for many societies to accept; some strains of cultural evolution, especially the evolution of religious notions, make the very existence of them threatening. Nonetheless, we need to reorient our common cultural evolution toward removing the threat of them— both actually and psychologically. How we should try to accomplish this seems clear; whether it is possible seems much more cloudy.

We all need to take a deep breath and take giant steps, or really leaps, to produce greater familiarity and empathy with others. Education, both formal and informal, must enhance the sense that we're all genetically, socially, and environmentally related. It must close those key parts of the culture gap. That sense and additional knowledge could be the opening key for people to start to make the behavioral changes needed for societal survival. We must replace the threat of "them" with the threat of the real enemy, us, or, more accurately, our collective behavior.

Know it or not, all of us are now walking the same tightrope, and we need to keep our balance together. At the circus, our mirror neurons keep us squirming in our chairs, and we are almost overwhelmed with empathy. But now we need to generalize that emotion from circus to the globe. We must act as one with those with whom we share the now-swaying civilization tightrope, with millions of fellow citizens of our nations, with seven billion fellow citizens of Earth, and with trillions of *Homo sapiens* who, if we succeed, will have the opportunity to try to walk the tightrope in the very long-term future.

The good news is that we're going with the tide of history. Our human families have been extending and our empathy expanding for thousands of years. For the final step to save civilization, everyone must strive to transform that tide into a tidal wave.

Acknowledgments

WE thank Albert Bandura (Psychology, Stanford), Scott Barrett (School of International and Public Affairs and Earth Institute, Columbia), Robert Brulle (Sociology, Drexel), Douglass Carmichael (Visiting Scholar, Stanford), Lisa Daniel (Hudson Cook LLP), Timothy Daniel (NERA, Inc.), Lawrence Goulder (Economics, Stanford), Dennis Pirages (Political Science, University of Nevada, Las Vegas), Gene Rosa (Sociology, Washington State University), Lee Ross (Psychology, Stanford), and Robert Sapolsky (Biology, Stanford) for extremely helpful comments on the manuscript. PRE is grateful for the support of Pete and Helen Bing and the Mertz Gilmore and Winslow Foundations; REO for the continuing support of the Will J. Reid Foundation. And we are once again indebted to our wives, Anne Ehrlich and Sally Mallam, for hard work on the manuscript, patience, and putting up with us.

Appendix: Going Further
Reading, Informing, Acting

BOTH of us have worked with institutions that try to help produce a new understanding of ourselves, society, and the possibilities for the future.

There is a growing consensus among environmental scientists that the scholarly community has explained the basic issues of the human predicament repeatedly and more than adequately. These issues include climate disruption, toxification of the planet, the deterioration of the epidemiological environment, and the potential impacts of nuclear war, as well as racism, sexism, economic inequity, and other factors that impede finding solutions to those problems. Those scientists believe humanity must take rapid steps to ameliorate these and related threats and have shown the directions society should be moving. But little is being done to develop policies that would avert a collapse of civilization—as exemplified by much talk and slight action on climate disruption. The central need is clearly not for more natural science (although in many areas it would be helpful) but rather for a better understanding of human behaviors and how they can be altered to direct humanity toward formation of a global family and a sustainable, empathetic society before it is to late.

PRE has been active with a group of natural scientists, social scientists, and scholars from the humanities in organizing the Millennium Assessment of Human Behavior (MAHB). This was so named to emphasize that it is human behavior, toward one another and toward the ecosystems that sustain all of us, that requires rapid modification. The MAHB (pronounced "mob") hopes to deal with the big "What are people for?" questions, and focus on how we need to change our treatment of each other and the environment that supports us. It, or any similar effort, should look forward, not only over a couple of decades but over centuries, even over a thousand years. The need is to increase public education on inconvenient truths (including those about "family values" and the scope of empathy) and their significance in today's world and that of the near and long-term future. The MAHB is seeking ways to shrink critical parts of the culture gap, educating people on the full range of population-environment-resource-ethics-power problems. It hopes to help create a better informed and more empathetic world that could move toward sustainability and survive the challenges of the next millennium.

The idea is that the MAHB might become a sponsor of broad global discussion on how to deal with the human predicament, involving the greatest possible diversity of people. It would also bring together people from different disciplines to build research programs that will help show how to convert the discussions into action that would redirect civilization away from collapse. The global discussion of the human predicament would focus on what people desire and what actions are required if the goal is a sustainable society with agreed-upon attributes. The MAHB differs from most international efforts in seeking input from both the scholarly community and the general public on how to organize itself, and it plans to remain open to such input.

Some of the interrelated questions that need to be considered include the following:

1. How much should the MAHB critique current institutional and social practices and suggest directions for the necessary changes? Should it assume that if humanity is to change course toward sustainability, this change must be accomplished with new or highly altered institutions (e.g., for governance, control of corporations, income distribution, and education)? What would success in this area look like?
2. Should the MAHB make the claim that incrementalism by major institutions has failed to deal with almost all the most serious environmental problems we face, and without a change in focus, they will continue to fail?
3. Should the MAHB (more modestly) use conversations and publications to nudge existing organizations to modify their behavior in a more empathetic and sustainable direction, including helping others to become sustainable?
4. Should the MAHB be more revolutionary and concentrate its efforts on grassroots groups in an effort to compel governments and other

organizations to take a more direct and effective course that would avoid a collapse of civilization?

5. How much should the MAHB focus on proposing routes to sustainability through large (often global) organizations and how much on encouraging experimentation at community and regional levels?

6. Should the MAHB give high priority to exploring potential scenarios for going forward? No one appears to have a coherent plan for eliciting political, economic, and social behaviors that will ensure that human life-support systems are properly maintained so that civilization becomes sustainable.

7. How can the critical parts of the culture gap be closed quickly? If there also is to be a global discussion of "What are people for?" and "How should we treat each other and the environment that supports us all?" then what can be done to have those discussions become global on a timescale of months and years rather than decades?

Ideally, the MAHB would be kicked off with a world mega conference like the United Nations Conference on Environment and Development, held in Rio de Janeiro in 1992. The purpose of this conference, perhaps to be held as early as 2011, would be to initiate a continuing process; the MAHB would then be solidified into a new, semipermanent institution. The MAHB is now at a preliminary stage, and the need for input from those accustomed to working in the social sciences and humanities, in the media, in the business community, in nongovernmental organizations (NGOs), and (especially) the general public is obvious.

The diversity of the MAHB is, we think, fundamentally a good thing and should be expanded and not narrowed. The issues, like those discussed in *Tightrope*, are the broadest ever to confront human society, and they need to be investigated in many ways by as complete a cross-section of humanity as possible. Some people will be attracted to conferences that deal with the issues, others will want to participate in discussions on Second Life or Facebook, others will join meetings at their college or high school, and others will be influenced by reports of MAHB activities in the media or NGO newsletters. The hope is that from such foci, MAHB issues will begin to diffuse throughout societies.

If you're interested in knowing more or in participating, visit the MAHB website (http://mahb.stanford.edu/). Whether the MAHB will prove to be a successful wedge for generating the needed eco-ethical discussion and behavioral change remains to be seen. A global consensus on the most crucial issues is unlikely to emerge promptly from any single international forum or NGO. But since an ongoing effort is required, not all the goals would need to be reached immediately, and changing minds in the populations of one or a few major players like the United States and/or China could provide an excellent start. If you can't help get the MAHB to work, try organizing your friends and associates in another way—the MAHB is just one possible form of a "hail Mary" pass. If the scientific diagnosis of humanity's approaching collision with the natural world is accurate (and we and our colleagues believe it is), what alternative is there to trying?

REO is generating The Human Journey (http://humanjourney.us), a new website of the Institute for the Study of Human Knowledge, which he founded in 1969. This website follows humanity from our origins in Eastern Africa and the Middle East to the present day, with an eye to what comes next: between about one hundred thousand and two hundred thousand years ago, modern humans (*Homo sapiens*) appeared in East Africa and then about forty to fifty thousand years ago spread to the Middle East, Europe, Asia, and Australia.*

The website overlays the significant stages of this journey with what we know of how we adapted physically and culturally to conditions along the way.

Knowing these determinants reveals a better understanding of who we are and why we do what we do. The site covers genetics, evolutionary biology, anthropology, and linguistics to follow the major routes taken by modern humans in their expansion from Africa to the present day. Where did our journey take us? How did we change along the way? How did our journey affect us all so differently and in so many ways: skin color, languages, cultures, customs, beliefs? Eventually peoples crossed paths, influenced each other, and began to come back together.

READING

We now live in a world in which a real understanding of other cultures and other ways of looking at the world are imperative. The survival of our planet involves global decisions; very few people will spend their whole lives without meeting and attempting to communicate with people from a different country or with a different cultural background. In order to be more effectively involved in the big changes described in this book and on the MAHB and Human Journey websites, it will be helpful and interesting to sample the literature on the human condition and how it has and can be

---

* For details, see the most comprehensive recent source on this rapidly changing story, Richard Klein, *The Human Career: Human Biological and Cultural Origins*, 3rd ed. (Chicago: University of Chicago Press, 2009).

changed. Here we give you an introduction to some of our own favorite sources—with the warning that it represents a drop-sized sample from an ocean of wisdom.

Edward T. Hall's work is unique in that it pinpoints the nonverbal and therefore hidden aspects of culture, such as our experience of time and space, giving us structure from which to examine what is really happening in our own and in other cultures, rather than what is said to be taking place.

In *Beyond Culture* (New York: Anchor Books, 1976), Hall argues that for too long, people have taken their own ways of life for granted, ignoring the international cultural community that surrounds them. Humankind must now embark on the difficult journey beyond culture, to the discovery of a lost self and a sense of perspective.

In *The Dance of Life* (New York: Anchor Books, 1985), Hall looks at how time is consciously and unconsciously structured in various cultures and how time has been experienced by humans from prehistoric times to the present. Hall looks at time as a language, organizer, and message system revealing people's feelings about each other and reflecting differences between cultures.

Another important writer, Marvin Harris, answers such cultural riddles as Why do Hindus worship cows? Why do Jews and Muslims refuse to eat pork? How is it that a peaceful Messiah flourished at a time in Jewish history when military messianism was traditionally and consistently prophesied? Why did so many people in post-medieval Europe believe in witches?

All these riddles are considered in *Cows, Pigs, Wars, and Witches: The Riddles of Culture* (New York: Harper and Row, 1989). Harris's work, which he called cultural materialism, proposes a new way of thinking about and looking at cultures. No matter how bizarre a people's behavior or attitudes may seem, they can be shown to have roots in identifiable physical needs of the culture: Hindus don't eat cows because their products—milk, dung—are more valuable than their meat.

We suspect, because you selected this book, that you are already quite knowledgeable about the origins of *Homo sapiens* and our environmental predicament. If you want to brush up or have a handy reference volume, Paul and Anne Ehrlich's *The Dominant Animal: Human Evolution and the Environment*, 2nd ed. (Washington, DC: Island Press, 2009), is the only book designed explicitly to close those key parts of the culture gap. Naturally, PRE thinks it should be read by every college freshman.

A fascinating (and sometimes horrible) read that reveals much about the human tendency to empathize is Lieutenant Colonel Dave Grossman's *On Killing: The Psychological Cost of Learning to Kill in War and Society* (Boston: Little, Brown, 1995). It will change your view of infantry warfare.

A classic, technical treatment of cooperating to provide collective goods (and thus a main reason for joining groups) is Mancur Olson's *The Logic of Collective Action: Public Goods and the Theory of Groups* (Cambridge, MA: Harvard University Press, 1971). Related to collective groups is the problem of "free riders" (nations, for example, that do not cooperate by limiting greenhouse gas emissions but still benefit from the restrictions others place on their own emissions) and the "drop-in-the-bucket" excuse (Lee Ross, personal communication)—for example, why should I bike to work when the carbon dioxide from my car exhaust is such a tiny proportion of emissions?

A readable key reference on how cooperation can emerge even in a world of selfish, egoistic individuals is Robert Axelrod's *The Evolution of Cooperation*, rev. ed. (New York: Basic Books, 2006). There is now a large literature on the circumstances in which cooperative behavior will evolve, much of it grounded in game theory, which is summarized in Ernest Fehr and Herbert Gintis's article "Human Motivation and Social Cooperation: Experimental and Analytical Foundations," *Annual Review of Sociology* 33 (2007): 43–64.

A key source on how and why people evolved to be so empathetic and developed a complex system of pseudokin is Sarah Hrdy's *Mothers and Others: The Evolutionary Origins of Mutual Understanding* (Cambridge, MA: Belknap Press, 2009). Important work on child development, discussed as the origins of cooperation and empathy, is found in Michael Tomasello's *Origins of Communication* (Cambridge, MA: MIT Press, 2008), and in Andrew N. Meltzoff's chapter "Imitation and Other Minds: The 'Like Me' Hypothesis," in *Perspectives on Imitation: From Neuroscience to Social Science*, vol. 2, ed. Susan Hurley and Nick Chater, 55–77 (Cambridge, MA: MIT Press, 2005). Perhaps the best book on "theory of mind" is Simon Baron-Cohen's *Mindblindness: An Essay on Autism and Theory of Mind* (Cambridge, MA: MIT Press, 1997). Frans de Waal has written many terrific books about bonobos and biology, his most recent has similarities to our view: *The Age of Empathy: Nature's Lessons for a Kinder Society* (New York: Harmony Books, 2009).

Some informative histories include one by Karen Armstrong, one of the world's foremost commentators on religious culture. Her book traces the history of how men and women have perceived and experienced God, from the time of Abraham to the present. *A History of God* (New York: Ballantine Books, 1994) deals with important questions: Why does God exist? How have the three dominant monotheistic religions shaped and altered the conception of God? How have these religions influenced each other? Armstrong's book is important reading so as not to dismiss all religious ideas.

Gina L. Barnes's *The Rise of Civilization in East Asia* (London: Thames and Hudson, 1999) is a first synthesis of East Asian archaeology and early history. Barnes charts the critical developments that culminated in the emergence of the region in the eighth century as a coherent entity, with a shared religion, state philosophy, and bureaucratic structure. Barnes challenges simplistic notions of Asian homogeneity and gets readers to think beyond national boundaries when viewing archaeological evidence.

Jared Diamond's *Guns, Germs, and Steel* (New York: W. W. Norton, 1997) is already a classic. It discusses why history is so dramatically different for peoples around the world. Why did Eurasia become the cradle of modern societies—eventually giving rise to capitalism and science—and come to dominate other parts of the world that lagged in technological sophistication and political and military power? In this book of remarkable scope, Diamond dismantles racially based theories of human history and argues that environmental and geographical factors are actually responsible for history's broadest patterns. In a different vein, Sheldon Wolin's classic *Politics and Vision: Continuity and Innovation in Western Political Thought*, rev. ed. (Princeton, NJ: Princeton University Press, 2006), tells the story of how Westerners have organized themselves politically since the golden age of Greece.

David Christian's *Maps of Time: An Introduction to Big History* (Berkeley: University of California Press, 2005) is an introduction to a new way of looking at history, from a perspective that stretches from the beginning of time to the present day. *Maps of Time* is world history on an unprecedented scale. Beginning with the big bang, David Christian views the interaction of the natural world with the more recent arrivals in flora and fauna, including human beings.

Fernand Braudel's *Civilization and Capitalism, Fifteenth to Eighteenth Century* multivolume series (New York: Harper and Row, 1981–1983) presents the origins of our daily lives in detail, the beginnings of the cities we live in, the food we eat, the way we dress—all as they actually developed during the beginnings of the changed world. This background is essential for understanding how we've created our surroundings, and Braudel's work is an introduction to the Annales school of history, which diverted the field from its fascination with sequences of kings and wars to the lives of everyday people. See also Fernand Braudel's *A History of Civilizations* (New York: Penguin Books, 1993).

Benedict Anderson's *Imagined Communities: Reflections on the Origin and Spread of Nationalism*, rev. ed. (London: Verso, 1991), is a classic of how national "families" gain coherence and histories.

Richard Nisbett and Lee Ross's book *Human Inference: Strategies and Shortcomings of Social Judgment* (Upper Saddle River, NJ: Prentice-Hall,

1981) gathers together many of the mistakes we make in judging the world. They give great examples of how vivid information is very influential in judgment. They describe a person who testifies for the Environmental Protection Agency (EPA). She reports on EPA mileage estimates based on samples of ten or more cars, only to be contradicted by a congressman who retorts, "What do you mean, the Blatzmobile gets twenty miles per gallon on the road? . . . My neighbor has one, and he only gets fifteen." His fellow legislators then usually respond as if one EPA estimate equals one from a neighbor.

A more recent and similar book is Carol Tavris and Elliot Aronson's *Mistakes Were Made (But Not By Me)* (New York: Mariner Books, 2008). *The Jigsaw Classroom: Building Cooperation in the Classroom,* by Aronson and Shelley Patnoe (New York: Longman, 1999), is the definitive work on the jigsaw system.

A wonderful book by Richard Nisbett is *Geography of Thought: How Asians and Westerners Think Differently . . . and Why* (New York: Free Press, 2004), which examines the great effects of cultural "families" on our thought processes.

Robert Cialdini's *Influence Science and Practice,* 5th ed. (Upper Saddle River, NJ: Prentice-Hall, 2008), really helps the understanding of how we decide and are "influenced." Have you ever found yourself saying yes to a child selling candy and then wondering why you have just agreed to buy something you really don't want? We like to think of ourselves as being in control of our opinions, decisions, and actions, but Cialdini identifies six basic psychological pressures almost guaranteed to influence us: reciprocation, consistency, social proof, liking, authority, and scarcity.

Ben Barber's *Jihad vs. McWorld* (New York: Ballantine Books, 1995) is relatively old, but is still a good read about the tensions between building a global family and focusing on much more restrictive ethnic groupings. More recent is Scott Barrett's *Why Cooperate: The Incentive to Supply Global Public Goods* (Oxford: Oxford University Press, 2007), which gives an excellent treatment of ways to move toward a global family without a formal world government. In *The Citizen Is Willing, but Society Won't Deliver: The Problem of Institutional Roadblocks* (Winnipeg: International Institute of Sustainable Development, 2008), Norman Myers and Jennifer Kent examine the way some of the institutions organized by *Homo sapiens* during the transition away from small groups fail to move our species toward sustainability.

Naomi Klein's book *The Shock Doctrine: The Rise of Disaster Capitalism* (New York: Henry Holt, 2007) is a controversial but compelling description of the way neoliberal economic dogma—the idea that market exchange is an ethic in itself, and should be a guide for all human action—plagues our chances of organizing an empathetic world. Another take on the same issue is David Harvey's *A Brief History of Neoliberalism* (New York: Oxford University Press, 2005). It is a stunning indictment of the economic dogma that has helped place so much power in the hands of a few and thus created a major barrier to reaching sustainability

The state of the decaying American empire is vividly described in Chalmers Johnson's *Nemesis: The Last Days of the American Republic* (New York: Metropolitan Books, 2007). This book is a scary treatment of the perils of nation-state families trending toward empire families and their likely consequences. Perhaps even more disturbing is Kevin Phillips's *American Theocracy: The Peril of Politics of Radical Religion, Oil, and Borrowed Money in the 21st Century* (New York: Viking, 2006). Pay special attention to his description of how fundamentalist religious cults are changing the shape of American politics, and read about the frightening signs of a new "endarkenment."

That endarkenment is also described by Sheldon Wolin in his recent *Democracy Incorporated: Managed Democracy and the Specter of Inverted Totalitarianism* (Princeton, NJ: Princeton University Press, 2008). Wolin is a great and radical political theorist, and this is a key reference (along with the works by Harvey and Klein) for those interested in the current struggle of our small-group animal to deal with its now-gigantic groups. Wolin is famous for his criticism of the idea that an empire can be truly democratic, and exposes "democracy" in the United States today as basically fraudulent, but he's sometimes disappointing in his analyses. It contains much traditional progressive thought (with some of its shortcomings)—and interesting parallels to Phillips's conclusions. If you want to know how recent political trends affect those on the short end of the economic stick, you must read Barbara Ehrenreich's *Nickel and Dimed: On (Not) Getting By in America* (New York: Henry Holt, 2001). Reading this book will transform you from sympathizing with the poor to empathizing with them.

INFORMING: TAPED COURSES AND LECTURES

A wonderful way to help close parts of your personal culture gap—especially if you commute to work by car or take long walks where you cannot read but can listen—is to use the audio courses provided by the Teaching Company (www.teach12.com; 1-800-teach-12). A wide variety of courses are offered in science, history, the social sciences, and the arts, and most require only a few weeks of listening for a half hour or forty-five minutes a day. We recommend, for a start, Robert Sapolsky, Biology and Human Behavior:

The Neurological Origins of Individuality, 2nd ed. Another course especially pertinent to our topics is Edward Fischer's Peoples and Cultures of the World. For a look at the long view of history, try Brian M. Fagan's course Human Prehistory and the First Civilizations, and for a view of how the best of religious thought evolved, try Mark W. Muesse's class Religions of the Axial Age.

Many universities provide excellent lectures on a huge variety of subjects; these can be downloaded to your iPod or viewed online.

ACTING

There are a lot of good books and organizations to help change things. *The Stanford Social Innovations Review* is a good place to start.

So what to do? Although we're not in the business of specific advice, we think there are two kinds of action to take: *personal*, as we discussed, isn't going to save the planet or its peoples but every bit helps, and *political*, in which actions are remote but perhaps more powerful. There are many things you can do, from changing your diet and (for many of us) eating and flying less. If you are sticking to meat, try eating less factory-farmed beef, which is far more destructive to ecosystems than are chicken or pork, although eating lower on the food chain is probably better. Anyway, weight loss is key to one's health. Also ask yourself if you need to fly so much. There's always somebody to whom you can compare yourself who is doing worse or guzzling more.

It goes like this. If we ask, "Do you need to fly so much?" people often respond, "Well, I'm not flying first class," which is a gigantic resource hog. The same question to a first classer gets this response: "Well, I'm not renting private jets," and, as you guessed it, one step up (we have heard this any number of times) it's, "I don't actually own a private jet. It's much less damaging to just rent one on occasion." Get the picture?

And once REO was giving a talk to a number of superrich entrepreneurs, and he dared to suggest that they follow the example of one of their number who has decided to live on . . . just twenty-five million dollars and its proceeds. To show how extreme a sacrifice this was, it is for his whole family! When REO mentioned this, one person in the audience said, "That wouldn't even pay the maintenance on my planes and boats." So, what can you do with this kind of extreme self-centered nonempathy?

For the rest of us, we do need to ask ourselves, What is really enough? Do you need as much as your have? Do you have old clothes in the attic and more food than you need? If you spent less, you could support organizations like Grameen, offering microloans that have moved millions out of poverty. Or you could support other organizations like Kiva.org, which allows one to make microloans all over the world, from your computer! And you get repaid. If you want hands-on experience helping others, www .mentoring.org is one good place to start.

Sometimes we think (unscientifically) that the Democrats are really the empathy party. Think of their ex-presidents: The Clinton Global Initiative has helped hundreds of thousands of indigent people get inexpensive life-saving drugs and sponsors energy efficiency and a host of other measures. The Carter Center has eradicated one of the worst scourges of humanity, the Guinea worm. Often known as the fiery serpent, Guinea worm disease has existed since ancient times, but an international coalition is now close to eradicating it. Another disease too awful to describe is obstetric fistulas, endured by African teenagers, where the pelvis is not fully grown. The Worldwide Fistula Fund helps remove the fistulas, as do organizations removing cleft lips that scar people for life.

The most important act of patriotism, to both your nation and your globe, that you can take is to have a maximum of two children (multiple births on a second pregnancy excepted). In public lectures, PRE has frequently been asked whether the good people ("us"—meaning well-off, well-educated, white) shouldn't have more babies while the bad people ("them"—poor, uneducated, dark) have fewer. The question itself shows a profound ignorance of human biology and environmental science. No one should over-reproduce—especially the rich, whose offspring have such a disproportionate impact on our common environment and resources. And we must redesign our education systems so that the crucial parts of the culture gap are closed for all and so that trivial differences such as skin color no longer impede the spread of empathy.

This is just a small sample of possible personal actions that can help move society toward sustainability. But there is no substitute for political action to change the entire framework within which we live. Diets are heavily determined by the actions of a corporate-controlled food industry; personal transport options have largely been dictated by the automobile, oil, rubber, and aircraft industries. Individual action must be turned into collective action, and that's what politics should be about—not corporations buying politicians as it is now in the United States. So do the right things as far as you are capable personally, but also get politically active and use the new communications tools as a way to be effective—as we are using the Web and e-mail lists to spread the news of *Tightrope*.

Notes

CHAPTER 1

1. See, for instance, Paul Ekman, *Emotions Revealed: Recognizing Faces and Feelings to Improve Communication and Emotional Life* (New York: Henry Holt, 2007).

2. Peter Singer, *The Life You Can Save: Acting Now to End World Poverty* (New York: Random House), 2009.

3. John W. Rowe, Dennis A. Cortese, and J. Michael McGinnis, "The Emerging Context for Advances in Comparative Effectiveness Assessment," *Health Affairs* 25, no. 6 (November/December 2006): 593–95.

4. In 2002, the United States ranked nineteenth in quality-adjusted aid and charitable giving divided by gross domestic product; see Anup Shah, "Foreign Aid for Development Assistance," Global Issues, www.globalissues.org/article/35/us-and-foreign-aidassistance#AdjustingAidNumberstoFactorPrivateContributionsandmore (accessed May 11, 2010).

5. Steven Brill, "What's a Bailed-Out Banker Really Worth?" *New York Times Magazine*, January 4, 2010.

6. See, for example, Paul R. Ehrlich and Anne H. Ehrlich, *The Dominant Animal: Human Evolution and the Environment*, 2nd ed. (Washington, DC: Island Press, 2009).

7. See "62% Say Today's Children Will Not Be Better Off Than Their Parents," Rasmussen Reports, October 3, 2009, www.rasmussenreports.com/public_content/lifestyle/general_lifestyle/october_2009/62_say_today_s_children_will_not_be_better_off_than_their_parents (accessed December 2, 2009).

8. One might imagine that this goes against our self-interest, since maximizing the presence of genes identical to ours in future generations is the name of the game in evolution. But genes have far less influence on everyday behavior than many think. And for most of our history, evolution was necessarily shortsighted—what maximized reproduction in the current generation was what counted and what would be adaptive in subsequent generations.

145

9. Sarah Canice Funke, "Joshua Bell Plays D.C. Metro," Suite101.com, April 14, 2007, http://classicalmusic.suite101.com/article.cfm/joshua_bell_plays_dc_metro (accessed October 30, 2009).

10. See, for example, Marshall Sahlins, *Stone Age Economics* (Chicago: Aldine, 1972).

CHAPTER 2

1. Paul R. Ehrlich and Anne H. Ehrlich, *The Dominant Animal: Human Evolution and the Environment*, 2nd ed. (Washington, DC: Island Press, 2009).

2. About a tenth of the CO2 humanity is now dumping into the atmosphere by burning fossil fuels will still be affecting Earth's climate in a hundred thousand years; see David Archer, *The Long Thaw: How Humans Are Changing the Next 100,000 Years of Earth's Climate* (Princeton, NJ: Princeton University Press, 2008). Archer also points out the humanity is becoming a force for climate change comparable to variations in Earth's orbit around the sun that are responsible for ice ages (p. 6).

3. This component of human evolution is discussed in Richard Wrangham, *Catching Fire: How Cooking Made Us Human* (New York: Basic Books, 2009).

4. Viv Groskop, "Not Your Mother's Milk," *Guardian*, January 5, 2007, www.guardian.co.uk/society/2007/jan/05/health.medicineandhealth (accessed June 2, 2009).

5. Sarah Blaffer Hrdy, *Mothers and Others: The Evolutionary Origins of Mutual Understanding* (Cambridge, MA: Belknap Press, 2009), 28.

6. Andrew N. Meltzoff, "'Like Me': A Foundation for Social Cognition," *Developmental Science* 10, no. 1 (2007): 126–34. DOI: 10.1111/j.1467-7687.2007.00574.x.

7. Michael Tomasello, "Why We Cooperate," *Boston Review*, 2009, 3–47.

8. Felix Warneken and Michael Tomasello, "Helping and Cooperation at 14 Months of Age," *Infancy* 11 (2007): 271–94.

9. Michael Tomasello, *Origins of Communication* (Cambridge, MA: MIT Press, 2008).

10. Andy Soltis, "Chilling Find from Nazi Era," *New York Post*, September 2, 2009.

11. Paul Rusesabagina, *An Ordinary Man* (New York: Penguin Books, 2006), 64.

12. Of course, the whole division of the country into the two races was a European innovation, made for the purposes of ease of administration—creating a privileged class of administrators who were a small set of the population. See Rusesabagina, *An Ordinary Man*, note 13.

13. Rusesabagina, *An Ordinary Man*, 134.

14. For Höss material, see Andre Mineau, *The Making of the Holocaust: Ideology and Ethics in the Systems Perspective* (Amsterdam: Editions Rodpi), 134–35.

15. One of the best sources of insight into this is William S. Allen, *The Nazi Seizure of Power: The Experience of a Single German Town* (Chicago: Quadrangle Books, 1967).

16. See, for example, Robert B. Edgerton, *Sick Societies: Challenging the Myth of Primitive Harmony* (New York: Free Press, 1992).

17. Albert Bandura, "Reflexive Empathy: On Predicting More Than Has Been Ever Observed," *Behavioral and Brain Sciences* 25 (2002): 24–25.

18. Hunter-gatherers were very diverse, so generalizations can be very difficult. See, for example, Bruce Winterhalder, "The Behavioural Ecology of Hunter-Gatherers," in *Hunter-Gatherers: An Interdisciplinary Perspective*, ed. Catherine Panter-Brick, Robert Layton, and Peter Rowley-Conwy (Cambridge: Cambridge University Press, 2001), 12–38.

19. Thorkild Jacobsen, *The Treasures of Darkness: A History of Mesopotamian Religion* (New Haven, CT: Yale University Press, 1976). Also see Mark W. Muesse, "Religions of the Axial Age: An Approach to the World's Religions," The Teaching Company Lectures 5 and 6, www.teach12.com/teach12.aspx?ai=16281 (accessed May 12, 2010).

20. The poster features the comics character Pogo by Walt Kelly.

21. Nations as imagined communities is the subject of a classic work by Benedict Anderson (*Imagined Communities: Reflections on the Origin and Spread of Nationalism*, rev. ed. [London: Verso, 1991]), a concept expanded upon by Patrick Geary (*The Myth of Nations: The Medieval Origins of Europe* [Princeton, NJ: Princeton University Press, 2003]).

22. See, for example, "List of Wars and Disasters by Death Toll," Wikipedia, http://en.wikipedia.org/wiki/List_of_wars_and_disasters_by_death_toll#Wars _and_armed_conflicts (accessed February 12, 2009).

23. Navjot S. Sodhi and Paul R. Ehrlich, eds., *Conservation Biology for All* (Oxford: Oxford University Press, 2010).

24. Here is the rest of Mangok Bol's story:

I am a member of the sub-Dinka tribe of Southern Sudan. [Twenty-two] years ago, I was living in the remote village of Gwalla in Southern Sudan with my mother and my siblings. As a young boy growing up, I had never thought of leaving my village for another village let alone coming to the United States of American. . . . Cattle and goat herding among the Dinka people were the usual activities of the boys of my age at 9 to 10 years. One of my favorite daily tasks was looking after the goats. In my village of Gwalla, I use to know all the boys that I used to go goat herding with. Most of these kids were first and distant cousins. Some were from my extended family. The village of Gwalla is a small village of about 800 residents with close kinship ties and related.

My elder brother used to tell me that he knew everybody in the village and that I was going to do the same when I grew. His assertion was primarily based on the fact that all the members of Gwalla community were related by blood and knowing everyone in the village especially those of one's age and prominent village elders was a top priority among the members. I remember I asked my mother a question one time, as why it was so important to know members of your clan and in this case, members of Gwalla clan. She told me in her reply that one of the most important things that elders want their young generation to know was blood relationship in case of future marriages. Marrying from the same clan with common ancestor up to seven lineages is still prohibited among the Dinka people. When I left the village for Ethiopia in 1987 as a result of civil war in the country at the age of 9, I was fully aware of the importance of the kinship ties. . . . My biggest shock in the United States was coming from a small village in South Sudan where I knew everybody to the place where I almost don't know anybody. . . . [The rest of the e-mail appears in the main text.]

(Contributed by Mangok Bol, Brandeis University, originally from Southern Sudan)

25. There is a downside to this, since languages probably influence how people see the world (see John A. Lucy, *Language Diversity and Thought: A Reformulation of the Linguistic Relativity Hypothesis* [Cambridge: Cambridge University Press, 1992]), and it is not clear that the dominant languages are the best possible tools for communication or that we cannot learn things from the languages we're losing.

26. "Sizing Up the Birthers," *Washington Post*, May 7, 2010, http://voices.washingtonpost.com/behind-the-numbers/2010/05/obama_birthplace.html (accessed May 18, 2010).

27. Ross Gelbspan, *Boiling Point: How Politicians, Big Oil and Coal, Journalists, and Activists Have Fueled a Climate Crisis—and What We Can Do to Avert Disaster* (New York: Basic Books, 2005); Chris Mooney, *The Republican War on Science* (New York: Basic Books, 2006); Paul R. Ehrlich, "Ecoethics: Now Central to All Ethics," *Journal of Bioethical Inquiry* 6 (2009): 417–36.

28. Dunbar concludes that the group size identified by this relationship appears to be the maximum number of individuals with whom an animal can maintain personal social relationships.

29. Robin I. M. Dunbar, "Social Systems as Optimal Strategy Sets: The Costs and Benefits of Sociality," in *Comparative Socioecology*, ed. V. Standen and R. Foley (Oxford: Blackwells Scientific, 1989), 73–88; Robin I. M. Dunbar, "Neocortex Size as a Constraint on Group Size in Primates," *Journal of Human Evolution* 20 (1992): 469–93.

30. Joan Oates, "Mesopotamian Social Organisation: Archaeological and Philological Evidence," in *The Evolution of Social Systems*, ed. Jonathan Friedman and Michael Rowlands (London: Duckworth, 1977).

31. Garrett Hardin, "Common Failing," *New Scientist* 102, no. 1635 (1988): 76.

32. F. J. Haverfield "Roman Army," *Encyclopaedia Britannica*, rev. 14th ed. (London: Encyclopedia Britannica Ltd., 1955), 19:395–399.

33. Russell A. Hill and Robin I. M. Dunbar, "Social Network Size in Humans," *Human Nature* 14, no. 1 (2003): 53–72.

CHAPTER 3

1. The dinosaurs, except for birds, were apparently exterminated when an asteroid hit what is now the Chicxulub crater in Mexico about sixty-five million years ago. The crater is 110 miles in diameter, formed in a 100m-megaton explosion by an

object. A much bigger crater has been discovered in India some three hundred miles across. One or the other of these impacts certainly ended a lot of life. See Sankar Chatterjee, "The Significance of the Contemporaneous Shiva Impact Structure and Deccan Volcanism at the Kt Boundary" (paper presented at the GSA Annual Meeting, Portland, Oregon, October 18–21, 2009).

2. Ann Kitchen, Derek Denton, and Linda Brent, "Self-Recognition and Abstraction Abilities in the Common Chimpanzee Studied with Distorting Mirrors," *Proceedings of the National Academy of Sciences U.S.A* 93, no. 14 (1996): 7405–8. This paper shows that not only do chimps recognize themselves in mirrors, but they have the power to first abstract their image from the distorted one in order to recognize themselves.

3. Matt Walker, "Ant Mega-Colony Takes Over World," *BBC News*, July 1, 2009, http://newsvote.bbc.co.uk/mpapps/pagetools/print/news.bbc.co.uk/earth/hi/earth _news/newsid_8127000/8127519.stm?ad=1 (accessed March 13, 2009).

4. A good review is in Martin J. Doherty, *Theory of Mind: How Children Understand Others' Thoughts and Feelings* (New York: Psychology Press, 2008). The original conception is found in Simon Baron-Cohen, *Mindblindness: An Essay on Autism and Theory of Mind* (Cambridge, MA: MIT Press, 1997).

5. Why? The early focus of evolutionary biologists was on the idea that the pair bonding of a male and a female was required to allow secure and rapid production of offspring. In other words, a parent pair-bond was thought to have evolved in response for the need for fathers to hang around to help supply food to the premature young and decrease the chances of early death. That would protect the male's genetic investment—he wouldn't have donated his effort and sperm to an offspring that would die. No fatherly help, no genes from either parent passed on to the grandchildren. The immediate reward, natural selection's way of creating male helping behavior, was presumed to be the sexual favors of the female. Anthropologists once thought all those factors led to the development of bi-parental unions, the start of families. They imagined females would be bonding with the male hunters who were best at supplying the protein-rich food to their children. Also important were the group benefits of hunting, although with males concentrating on sharing meat with their own offspring and not children of other males.

That scenario now seems very unlikely. Mom and pop were probably not the first family members. For one thing, a careful reevaluation of the early information on hunting returns in extant hunter-gatherers reveals that the early anthropologists had often overestimated the amount of highly nutritious meat that the ancient hunters could provide. Both in total calories and in the constant flow of calories required by infant *Homo sapiens*, the less spectacular produce of tubers, berries, turtles, lizards, insects, and the like from the women's gathering and cooking proved more dependable and thus more important than, say, the occasional big antelope male hunters managed to bring home. Pop apparently did not always play the key provisioning role once thought.

6. Sarah Blaffer Hrdy, *Mothers and Others: The Evolutionary Origins of Mutual Understanding* (Cambridge, MA: Belknap Press, 2009), 286.

7. "Frequently Asked Questions," American Society for the Defense of Tradition, Family and Property, www.tfp.org/tfp-home/frontpage/frequently-asked-questions .html (accessed September 19, 2009).

8. Tamar Lewin, "Family Decay Global, Study Says," *New York Times*, May 30, 1995.

9. Hrdy, *Mothers and Others*, 144–45.

10. As a result of the rise of that *stable, small-nuclear-family* ideal, our dictionaries still define families as two different sex parents and their biological or adopted children. We hear a lot from politicians about "family values" these days. In a sense, of course, these values were humanity's first values, be they mother love (the most basic of "mammalian values"), giving preference to siblings (having more empathy with those we see most), or having a position in a dominance hierarchy (which meant knowing all the other group members). Family values— the values that control relationships with those with whom we are in the closest contact—remain the primary values for most of us and, diverse as they are, serve as models for many of our most critical relationships even in today's giant and complex societies.

11. The role of romantic love in marriage is complex and variable even today. For a summary and references, see Gwen J. Broude, *Marriage, Family, and Relationships* (Santa Barbara, CA: ABC-CLIO, 1994), 265–67. Anthropologist Melvin Konner has a wonderful quote to the effect that we are only a century or two into the notion that marriage requires romantic and passionate love—so it's no surprise that we haven't gotten far with a much more recent notion, namely, that passion should last in a marriage. This seems especially pertinent since people now live much longer than they did in the nineteenth century, and in much better health.

12. 1 Kings 11:3.

13. Deut. 22:13–21, 23–24.

14. Material on Na from Cai Hua, *A Society without Fathers or Husbands: The Na of China*, trans. Asti Hustvedt (New York: Zone Books, 2001). It has been subject to some criticism, but not on the points we make (see, e.g., book review by Charles F. McKhann, *Journal of Asian Studies* 62, no. 1 [2003]: 225–27).

15. Hua, *A Society without Fathers or Husbands*, 119.

16. Hua, *A Society without Fathers or Husbands*, 214.

17. Hrdy, *Mothers and Others*, 290.

18. For several decades anthropologists focused on a hypothesis by Sherwood Washburn and C. S. Lancaster that hunting big game, perhaps as long ago as several million years, is what led to families. It presumably encouraged male-male cooperation, and also male-female division of labor—males out trying to kill antelopes and females gathering nutritious roots. The males would bring the dripping chunks of impala steak and share the meat with the females and young. All the latter would occur at campgrounds ("home bases"). These and some other linked characteristics formed, as Washburn and Lancaster put it, "the basis of the human family." But the archeological evidence for this scenario dissolved—what were thought to be the remains of big animals killed turned out to be remains scavenged. Anthropologist Owen Lovejoy then focused on the evolution of wide-ranging males provisioning

stay-at-home females, while female anthropologists Nancy Tanner and Adrienne Zihlman tried to shift the focus to the key role of women. Tanner and Zihlman got a boost from primatologist Richard Wrangham and his colleagues, who speculated that the invention of cooking was a major step toward family formation. Which views are correct? Lacking time machines, we still don't have a fully satisfactory explanation for the evolution of the family.

19. See Edmund Blair Bolles, "Charybdis," Babel's Dawn, http://ebbolles.typepad .com/babels_dawn/2007/01/charybdis.html (accessed December 10, 2008), but when did this start? See also Robert M. Sapolsky, "A Natural History of Peace," *Foreign Affairs*, January/February 2006, www.foreignaffairs.org/20060101faessay85110 -p50/robert-m-sapolsky/a-natural-history-of-peace.html (accessed November 13, 2006).

20. Gerald M. Edelman, *Neural Darwinism: The Theory of Neuronal Group Selection* (New York: Basic Books, 1987).

CHAPTER 4

1. Anthony Wohl, *The Victorian Family* (New York: St. Martin's Press, 1978).

2. To get an idea of the diversity, see Stevan Harrell, *Human Families* (Boulder, CO: Westview Press, 1997).

3. Interestingly the same question applies to other primates—that is, why is it the male baboon who leaves the natal group at puberty, while it is female chimpanzees who wander between groups in adolescence?

4. Frank Newport, "Church Attendance Lowest in New England, Highest in the South," Gallup, April 27, 2006, www.gallup.com/poll/22579/church-attendance -lowest-new-england-highest-south.aspx (accessed May 12, 2010).

5. See, for example, "State Rankings by Divorce Rate, Out-of-Wedlock Birth Rate and Teen Birth Rate, 1998," Oklahoma, www.state.ok.us/osfdocs/budget/ table25.pdf (accessed May 12, 2010).

6. "The Lives and Loves of French Mistresses and Their Masters," Parler Paris Previews, January 25, 2006, www.adrianleeds.com/parlerparis/issues/pparis25-1-06 .html (accessed May 12, 2010).

7. People not related genetically or by marriage but who have an emotional relationship with another individual are sometimes called "fictive kin." We use the term *pseudokin* for people or groups with relationships with others (real or imaginary) that resemble in certain respects those of true kin. We could further divide pseudokin into three categories:

As-if kin. Others beyond the father, technically the alloparents, who in reality act to help the mother to raise her offspring. They are normally physically present with the rest of the family (e.g., mother's sisters, grandmothers, nannies, "courtesy" aunts and uncles, fellow kibbutzniks). As-if kin include other groups affiliated through close contact like members of a street gang, crime family, or infantry squad. Originally as-if kin were almost entirely close genetic relatives, and their urge to help in the rearing of others' children was evolutionarily explicable because those children were carrying genes identical to their own. That is, it was an example of "kin selection"—natural selection favoring individuals who were altruistic toward others carrying a good dose of the same genes. One imagines that the mechanism that selection created for identifying kin was constant contact/familiarity—and that mechanism now is one cause of altruistic behavior toward pseudokin, like falling on a grenade to save fellow members of an infantry squad that have no genetic relatedness to the sacrificing individual. There is a gigantic literature on how cooperation evolves among kin and non-kin. For a recent overview, see Elizabeth Pennisi, "On the Origins of Cooperation," *Science* 325 (2009): 1196–99. We won't attempt to summarize it here.

True pseudokin. People considered to be in kin-like relationships without the presence of shared genes, marriage ties, or personal contact. Pseudokin can be real although remote or characters in a novel or drama; they, of course, have no direct contact with the nuclear family but are viewed psychologically as kin because of seeking "like" company (fraternity brothers at different campuses, white racist groups) or because media/cinema/novels provide the familiarity (pseudocontact) that elicit kin-like responses (Nelson Mandela, Princess Diana, Harry Potter, characters in the detective series *Law and Order*) without any real personal contact at all.

Special kin. A small-group arrangement that is based not on seeking "like" in a personal or family sense or an emotional one but on the need to form groups in order to function—professional colleagues, union associates, or members of sports teams; senators; Friedman's "Chicago boys"—which often evolve family-like characteristics (e.g., pride in belonging and accomplishments, victory, refusal of professional groups to police their members, etc.).

We've seen that early human beings developed a wide variety of nuclear and near-nuclear family arrangements. Matrifocal families consist of just a woman and her children. Nuclear families consist of mother, father, and their kids. Polygynous families are dad, several wives, and their kids. Stem families throw in a small number of other relatives to a nuclear family—say, crazy grandpa living in the attic. Extended families stretch over more than one couple of the same or different generations. There are infinite variations on this theme, as we have already suggested. But what is clear is that human beings, even in the simplest societies, have a strong focus on setting up specific cultural rules that recognize and structure relationships among individuals. That tendency makes us unique among all living animals (in part, of course, because humanity alone has the language to transmit the rules). The agricultural evolution freed many human beings from the strict production-reproduction activities of the family and allowed *Homo sapiens* to be the only mammal to develop specialized occupations and long distance communication—making pseudokin and special kin possible, "families" within "families," but also putting groups in contact with "others."

8. See, for example, Phillip A. Goff, Jennifer L. Eberhardt, Melissa J. Williams, and Matthew C. Jackson, "Not Yet Human: Implicit Knowledge, Historical

Dehumanization, and Contemporary Consequences," *Journal of Personality and Social Psychology* 94 (2008): 292–306.

9. See Barbara Harff, "No Lessons Learned from the Holocaust? Assessing Risks of Genocide and Political Mass Murder Since 1955," *American Political Science Review* 97 (2003): 57–73. That paper contains an interesting model for predicting future genocides.

10. Nicole McPhee, "Doing Diversity Right: Renowned Iowa Schoolteacher and Discrimination Educator Get to the Heart of the Matter," *Gauntlet News*, August 9, 2001, http://gauntlet.ucalgary.ca/a/story/2741 (accessed May 30, 2008).

11. Stephen Ambrose, *Citizen Soldiers: The U.S. Army from the Normandy Beaches to the Bulge to the Surrender of Germany* (New York: Simon and Schuster, 1997), 276.

12. Thomas Kühne, *Kameradschaft: Die Soldaten des nationalsozialistischen Krieges und das 20. Jahrhundert* (Göttingen, Germany: Vandenhoeck & Ruprecht, 2006).

13. J. Goodall, A. Bandora, E. Bergman, C. Busse, H. Matma, E. Mpongo, A. Pierce, and D. Riss "Intercommunity Interactions in the Chimpanzee Population of the Gombe National Park," in *The Great Apes*, ed. David A. Hamburg and Elizabeth R. McCown (Menlo Park, CA: Benjamin Cummings, 1979), 13–53.

14. Paul R. Ehrlich and Anne H. Ehrlich, *One with Nineveh: Politics, Consumption, and the Human Future* (Washington, DC: Island Press, 2005), 238–39.

15. One of the brightest spots in the struggles to maintain a viable environment for humanity is the efforts of the Natural Capital Project to align economic incentives with conservation (www.naturalcapitalproject.org/home04.html).

16. Brian Knowlton and Michael M. Grynbaum, "Greenspan 'Shocked' That Free Markets Are Flawed," *New York Times*, October 23, 2008.

17. Naomi Klein, *The Shock Doctrine: The Rise of Disaster Capitalism* (New York: Henry Holt, 2007).

18. Lansky showed his ethnic as well as his pseudokin relationships when, near the end of his life, he, like some other Jewish gangsters, fled to Israel under the "law of return." Despite pouring millions of dollars into the country, he was soon thrown out.

19. Participants in the activities of the the Royal Swedish Academy of Sciences Beijer Institute of Ecological Economics (www.beijer.kva.se/).

20. "Will Future Americans Salute Us?" Democratic Underground, www.democraticunderground.com/discuss/duboard.php?az=viewall&address=104x 3040597 (accessed April 14, 2010).

21. Which itself raises a series of issues—for instance, women that some of us might consider "abused" might actually be content with their situation.

22. Shaila Dewan, "U.S. Suspends Haitian Airlift in Cost Dispute," *New York Times*, January 29, 2010, www.nytimes.com/2010/01/30/us/30airlift.html (accessed February 17, 2010).

23. There is a good account of this in Farhad Manjoo, *True Enough: Learning to Live in a Post-Fact Society* (Hoboken, NJ: Wiley, 2008).

CHAPTER 5

1. "Donna Brazile Weighs In on the Presidential Race," *North Texas Liberal*, May 3, 2008, www.northtexasliberal.com/2008/05/donna-brazile-weighs-in-on -presidential.html (accessed May 9, 2008).

2. Suzanne Vega, "How to Write a Song," *New York Times* blogs, December 8, 2008.

3. Jon Lee Anderson, "Gangland: Life in the Favelas of Rio de Janeiro." *New Yorker*, October 5, 2009 www.newyorker.com/magazine/toc/2009/10/05/ toc_20090928#ixzz0oWdK2twX (accessed May 20, 2010).

4. Chen-Bo Zhong and Katie Liljenquist, "Washing Away Your Sins: Threatened Morality and Physical Cleansing," *Science Online*, November 2, 2006, www .sciencemag.org/archive/ (accessed May 10, 2010). The opposite is true; a bad smell, sitting in a disgusting room makes people have stricter moral judgments.

Simone Schnall, Jonathan Haidt, Gerald L. Clore, and Alexander H. Jordan, "Disgust as Embodied Moral Judgment," *Personality and Social Psychology Bulletin* 34, no. 8 (2008): 1096–1109.

5. There are hundreds of studies of priming. One good review is Wido La Heij, Jaap Dirkx, and Peter Kramer, "Categorical Interference and Associative Priming in Picture Naming," *British Journal of Psychology* 81 (1990): 159–77.

6. A good review of this study and many other confirming ones is in Bert S. Moore and Alice M. Isen, eds., *Affect and Social Behavior* (Cambridge: Cambridge University Press, 1990).

7. Emab Salib and Mario Cortina-Borja, "Effect of 7 July 2005 Terrorist Attacks in London on Suicide in England and Wales," *British Journal of Psychiatry* 194 (2009): 80–85.

8. See, for example, Detlef Siebert, "British Bombing Strategy in World War II," BBC, www.bbc.co.uk/history/worldwars/wwtwo/area_bombing_01.shtml (accessed December 12, 2009).

9. Jennifer Rast, "Prophetic Signs That We Are in the End Times," Contender Ministries, http://contenderministries.org/prophecy/endtimes.php (accessed August 12, 2009).

10. Vittorio Gallese and Alvin Goldman, "Mirror Neurons and the Simulation Theory of Mind-Reading," *Trends in Cognitive Science* 2 (1998): 494–501.

11. In her otherwise excellent *The Philosophical Baby: What Children's Minds Tell Us about Truth, Love, and the Meaning of Life* (New York: Farrar, Straus and Giroux, 2009), Alison Gopnik makes this assertion.

12. Richard Wilkinson and Kate Pickett, *The Spirit Level: Why More Equal Societies Almost Always Do Better* (London: Penguin Books, 2009).

13. As reported on BBC News on October 23, 2009. See "Rich Germans Demand Higher Taxes," *BBC News*, October 23, 2009, http://news.bbc.co.uk/2/hi/ europe/8321967.stm (accessed December 12, 2009).

14. Willard Gaylin, *Hatred: The Psychological Descent into Violence* (New York: Public Affairs, 2004), 163.

15. John Hunning Speke, *Journal of the Discovery of the Source of The Nile*, repr. ed. (1863; repr., Ann Arbor: University of Michigan Library, 2009).

16. David Brooks, "Clinton, Obama Enter Final Stretch in Pa. Primary Fight," analysis by Shields and Brooks, *PBS Newshour*, April 18, 2008 www .pbs.org/newshour/bb/politics/jan-june08/sbdebate_04-18.html (accessed May 19, 2010).

17. Jeremy N. Bailenson, Shanto Iyengar, Nick Yee, and Nathan A. Collins, "Facial Similarity between Voters and Candidates Causes Influence," *Public Opinion Quarterly* 72, no. 5 (2008): 935–61.

18. Our colleague Robert Sapolsky has pointed out to us that there is another aspect of today's group relationships that did not occur in hunter-gatherer societies (and was relatively rare until much more recently). Turnover in human groups, for most of our history, was gradual. An individual died, a woman married into another group, and so on. Today, groups may totally dissolve at a given time—the cruise ship docks, the class graduates, the firm goes bankrupt, the military unit is demobilized. There have been no scientific studies of the results of such (in historic terms) unique behavior.

19. Richard L. Moreland and Robert B. Zajonc, "Exposure Effects in Person Perception: Familiarity, Similarity, and Attraction," *Journal of Experimental Social Psychology* 18, no. 5 (1982; repr., 2009): 395–415.

20. CNN, *Crossfire*, November 15, 2002.

21. Andrew N. Meltzoff, "Imitation and Other Minds: The 'Like Me' Hypothesis," in *Perspectives on Imitation: From Neuroscience to Social Science*, vol. 2, ed. Susan Hurley and Nick Chater (Cambridge, MA: MIT Press, 2005), 55–77.

22. Steven J. Spencer, Claude M. Steele, and Diane M. Quinn, *Stereotype Threat and Women's Math Performance*, *Journal of Experimental Social Psychology* 35, no. 1 (January 1999): 4–28.

23. Margaret Shih, Nalini Ambady, Jennifer A. Richeson, Kentaro Fujita, and Heather M. Gray, "Stereotype Performance Boosts: The Impact of Self-Relevance and the Manner of Stereotype Activation," *Journal of Personality and Social Psychology* 83, no. 3 (2002): 638–47.

24. Claude Steele's most important and accessible article is in *Atlantic Monthly*: Claude M. Steele, "Race and the Schooling of Black Americans," *Atlantic Monthly*, April 1992. Claude M. Steele and Joshua Aronson, "A Threat in the Air: How Stereotypes Shape Intellectual Identity and Performance," *American Psychologist* 52, no. 6 (1997): 613–29. Claude M. Steele and Joshua Aronson, "Stereotype Threat and the Intellectual Test Performance of African Americans," *Journal of Personality and Social Psychology* 69, no. 5 (1995): 797–811. Joshua Aronson, Diana Quinn, and Steven Spencer, "Stereotype Threat and the Academic Underperformance of Minorities and Women," in *Prejudice: The Target's Perspective*, ed. Janet Swim and Charles Stangor, (San Diego, CA: Academic Press, 1998), 83–103.

25. Jeff Stone, "Battling Doubt by Avoiding Practice: The Effects of Stereotype Threat on Self-Handicapping in White Athletes," *Personality and Social Psychology Bulletin* 28 (December 2002): 1667–78.

26. Brett W. Pelham, Matthew C. Mirenberg, and John T. Jones, "Why Susie Sells Seashells by the Seashore: Implicit Egotism and Major Life Decisions," *Journal of Personality and Social Psychology* 82, no. 4 (2002): 469–87.

CHAPTER 6

1. George P. Murdock, *Ethnographic Atlas* (New York: Macmillan, 1967).

2. But it is not always the female siblings that are the best alloparents: Edward H. Hagen and H. Clark Barret, "Cooperative Breeding and Adolescent Siblings," *Current Anthropology* 50 (2009): 727–37. It would be interesting to investigate if grandmother effects are absent in the six groups in which the females move.

3. Frans B. M. de Waal, *Peacemaking among Primates* (Cambridge, MA: Harvard University Press, 1989).

4. Dale J. Langford, Sara E. Crager, Zarrar Shehzad, Shad B. Smith, Susana G. Sotocinal, Jeremy S. Levenstadt, Mona Lisa Chanda, Daniel J. Levitin, and Jeffrey S. Mogil, "Social Modulation of Pain as Evidence for Empathy in Mice," *Science* 312, no. 5782 (June 30, 2006): 1967–70.

5. Thomas Asbridge, *The First Crusade: A New History* (New York: Oxford University Press, 2004), 30–31; Christopher Tyerman, *God's War: A New History of the Crusades* (Boston: Belknap Press, 2006).

6. Paul Krugman, "Betraying the Planet," *New York Times*, June 28, 2009, www .nytimes.com/2009/06/29/opinion/29krugman.html?_r=2(accessed July 1, 2009).

7. These groups include the unlikely combination of George P. Shultz, William J. Perry, Henry A. Kissinger, and Sam Nunn; see their article "Toward a Nuclear-Free World," *Wall Street Journal*, January 15, 2008, http://online.wsj.com/public/article_print/SB120036422673589947.html (accessed January 17, 2008).

8. See, for example, Amos Tversky and Daniel Kahneman, "The Framing of Decisions and the Psychology of Choice," *Science* 211 (1981): 453–58.

9. Many of the studies are reviewed in Judith Rich Harris, *The Nurture Assumption: Why Children Turn Out the Way They Do* (New York: Free Press, 1998).

10. If societies made increasing empathy a major project, it might be possible to expose all children to a variety of caregivers, or at least to a variety of human images from birth onward. TV programming for young children could shift emphasis from selling oversugared cereals to exposing tots to people with unfamiliar skin colors, hair styles, and modes of dress. Our marvelous technological abilities might find ways to make lightweight, "breathable" face masks of a variety of colors and styles that could be used by parents and alloparents to expose very young infants to a variety of human appearances. Far out? Maybe. But it might help humanity to achieve the levels of empathy, cooperation, and conflict reduction that could permit a sustainable society.

11. See John Rawls, *A Theory of Justice* (Cambridge, MA: Belknap Press, 1971). Finding ways to do that would be a difficult but possibly important exercise.

12. We borrowed the wedge analogy from Steve Pacala and Rob Socolow, "Stabilization Wedges: Solving the Climate Problem for the Next 50 Years with Current Technologies," *Science* 305 (2004): 968–72.

CHAPTER 7

1. See, for example, National Academy of Sciences USA, "A Joint Statement by Fifty-eight of the World's Scientific Academies" (Statement produced at the Population Summit of the World's Scientific Academies, October 24–25, 1993 [New Delhi, India: National Academy Press, 1993]); Union of Concerned Scientists, *World Scientists' Warning to Humanity* (Cambridge, MA: Union of Concerned Scientists, 1993).

2. A near fatal flaw in the conservative view is that they retain the outdated idea that there is an immutable "human nature," whereas in fact there are many human natures, dependent in large part on the environments to which individuals are exposed; see Paul R. Ehrlich, *Human Natures: Genes, Cultures, and the Human Prospect* (Washington, DC: Island Press, 2000). We say "near" fatal since in today's world the unhappy characteristics referred to tend to be very common—whatever the role of genetics as opposed to environment in their generation.

3. Geoffrey Brennan and Alan Hamlin, "Analytic Conservatism," *British Journal of Political Science* 34, no. 4 (2004): 675–91. John Considine, "Constitutional Interpretation: Burke and Buchanan and Their 18th Century Intellectual Roots," *Constitutional Political Economy* 17 (2006): 71.

4. See, for example, Michael Oakeshott, *"Rationalism in Politics" and Other Essays*, rev. ed. (Indianapolis: Liberty Fund, 1991).

5. Donna L. Franklin, *Ensuring Inequality: The Structural Transformation of the African-American Family* (New York: Oxford University Press, 1997), 199.

6. Paul Collier, *The Bottom Billion* (New York: Oxford University Press, 2007), 66.

7. Collier, *The Bottom Billion*, 66.

8. Ehrlich, *Human Natures*.

9. Birgit Mampe, Angela D. Friederici, Anne Christophe, and Kathleen Wermke, "Newborns' Cry Melody Is Shaped by Their Native Language," *Current Biology*, November 5, 2009. DOI: 10.1016/j.cub.2009.09.064 (accessed May 19, 2010).

10. David Hume, *Essays: Moral, Political and Literary* (Indianapolis: Liberty Classics, 1986), www.econlib.org/library/LFBooks/Hume/hmMPL21.html, I.XXI.9 (accessed May 13, 2010).

11. Kees Keizer, Siegwart Lindenberg, and Linda Steg, "The Spreading of Disorder," *Science* 322, no. 5908 (2008): 1681–85.

12. Emad Salib, "Gray Weather Conditions and Fatal Self-Harm in North Cheshire, 1989–1993," *British Journal of Psychiatry* 171 (1997): 473–77.

13. *Consumer Reports on Health*, November 2009, 2.

14. See, for example, Albert Bandura, "Social Cognitive Theory for Personal Change by Enabling Media," in *Entertainment-Education and Social Change: History, Research, and Practice*, ed. Arvind Singhal, Michael Cody, Everett Rogers, Miguel Sabido (Mahwah, NJ: Lawrence Erlbaum, 2004), 75–96.

15. "Sabido Method—Background," Population Media Center, www.population media.org/what/sabido-method/ (accessed April 18, 2009).

16. "Sabido Method—Background."

17. "Sabido Method: Cognitive Social Learning," Shadow blog, www.garyfeng.com/wordpress/2003/04/22/sabido-method-cognitive-social-learning/ (accessed April 18, 2009).

18. "All the News," Good/Transparency, http://awesome.good.is/transparency/web/0912/all-the-news/flash.html (accessed Augst 12, 2009).

19. See, for instance, Daniel Blumstein and Charlie Saylan, "The Failure of Environmental Education (and How We Can Fix It)," *PLoS Biology* 5 (2007): e120; Albert Bandura, Impeding Ecological Sustainability through Selective Moral Disengagement," *International Journal of Innovation and Sustainable Development* 2, no. 1 (2007): 8–35, and references to Bandura's work therein. For a wide-reaching review that deals with Ernest Becker's controversial ideas see Janis Dickinson, *The People Paradox: Self-Esteem Striving, Immortality Ideologies, and Human Response to Climate Change, Ecology and Society* (forthcoming).

20. Francis Fukuyama, *The End of History and the Last Man* (Glencoe, IL: Free Press, 1992).

21. Benedict R. Anderson, *Imagined Communities: Reflections on the Origin and Spread of Nationalism*, rev. ed. (London: Verso, 1991). See also, Patrick Geary, *The Myth of Nations: The Medieval Origins of Europe* (Princeton, NJ: Princeton University Press, 2003).

22. Sarel Kandell Kromer, "The Rwandan Reconciliation," *Washington Post*, October 16, 2005, www.washingtonpost.com/wp-dyn/content/article/2005/10/15/AR2005101500108.html (accessed June 3, 2007).

23. The source of this information, and a fine coverage on empathy and killing is Dave Grossman, *On Killing: The Psychological Cost of Learning to Kill in War and Society* (Boston: Little, Brown, 1995).

24. Robert Ornstein and Paul Ehrlich, *New World/New Mind: Moving Toward Conscious Evolution* (New York: Doubleday, 1989).

25. Paul Treanor, "Liberalism, Markets, Ethics," http://web.inter.nl.net/users/Paul.Treanor/human-righ.ts.html (accessed January 3, 2010).

26. Paul R. Ehrlich, "Ecoethics: Now Central to All Ethics," *Journal of Bioethical Inquiry* 6 (2009): 417–36.

27. For the Federalists' views in detail, see Online Library of Liberty, http://oll.libertyfund.org/index.php?option=com_staticxt&staticfile=show.php%3Ftitle=788&Itemid=27 (accessed November 3, 2009). For the Anti-Federalist views, see "Anti-Federalist Writings," InfoPlease, www.infoplease.com/t/hist/antifederalist/ (accessed November 3, 2009).

28. Kevin Phillips, *American Theocracy: The Peril of Politics of Radical Religion, Oil, and Borrowed Money in the 21st Century* (New York: Viking, 2006); Sheldon Wolin, *Democracy Incorporated: Managed Democracy and the Specter of Inverted Totalitarianism* (Princeton, NJ: Princeton University Press, 2008). No politician wants to discuss these and other extremely inconvenient truths. They do not feel free to call for humanely reducing the size of the world population, or even slowing its growth. They don't want to tell people that the economy cannot continue growing and that some redistribution from rich to poor is essential. They don't

want to recommend requiring big corporations (including the major agricultural producers and big pharma) to modify their production-is-everything programs and develop concern for their employees, the surrounding human communities, and the environment. Politicians, already deeply in their debt, can hardly say that corporations, disliked by Adam Smith and despised by the founding fathers of the United States, are now out of control and largely running the world for the benefit of the already rich. Corporations' most recent antidemocratic triumph was the finalizing of the notion, fought for over years in the late nineteenth century by railroad company lawyers, to give corporations the full rights of empathetic, real human beings.

That ultimate triumph came when, in January 2010, a conservative Supreme Court gave corporations the right, as fictitious persons, to spend as much money as they wished buying the election of politicians under a doctrine of "free speech." In short, corporations in the United States now have the rights of real people without any of the responsibilities (and, of course, without the ability to empathize). Corporations, and those who control them, are not like real persons subject to prison or the death penalty when they poison us or cheat us.

29. Charles de Secondat, Baron de Montesquieu, *The Spirit of the Laws* (1748; Cambridge: Cambridge University Press, 1989).

30. See discussion in Elinor Ostrom, "A Polycentric Approach for Coping with Climate Change," World Bank Policy Research Working Paper 5095, on how to proceed in the absence of global governance.

31. One can think of civilization as the conjoining of two complex adaptive systems: the global ecosystem and the human social-economic-political system embedded within it. And one can view today's situation as unprecedented, for the human system is now so large that it is interacting dangerously with the global ecosystem. A complex adaptive system (CAS) is one where multiple actors or elements, interacting as they pursue their perceived goals at an individual scale, produce collective large-scale consequences, including "self organization," that "emerges" from their behavior. The market is sometimes mentioned as a prime example of a CAS in which an emergent property is efficiency and the collective good of society, a macroscopic phenomenon traceable to individual agents following simple rules.

One of the major problems with a CAS is that the nature and timing of emergences is impossible to predict. That freeways will have traffic jams even if there are no accidents and all obey the traffic rules is a simpler example—in this case, we know they will occur, but we can't predict their timing or scale. The market itself continuously demonstrates such unpredictability. The recent economic downturn triggered by the housing bubble in the United States is a stunning instance. History is replete with such examples; the origin and continuation of the twentieth century world wars is a sad recent example. A similar situation can be seen in the unpredictability of weather relative to climate, and of climate changes in response to alteration in the gaseous composition of the atmosphere. What all this means in relation to spreading empathy and achieving a sustainable society is simple: there is no way of predicting a correct course that guarantees success.

That, however, is not a council of despair. As we have discussed, we do know a series of steps that could reduce the chance of undesirable properties emerging and could be used to deal with them when they do emerge. One obvious conclusion is that sensibly and humanely reducing the scale of the human enterprise is essential. Saying it is easy, but getting started on it is daunting, although not impossible. After all, some populations' sizes have already begun to shrink and the economy is at least temporarily in decline, reducing per capita consumption, but, sadly, more so among the poor than the rich. But the rich with the right encouragement might actually find less consumption a decent trade-off for long-term survival, and supporting green technologies is becoming a norm (as testified by the popularity of hybrid vehicles).

Another step would be to increase the resilience of societies and their modularity so that the spread of everything from epidemic disease or starvation following crop failure to financial disasters and wars can be restricted. These are issues that demand the attention of humanity as a whole, and would require much eco-ethical discussion—an important activity for the MAHB. For example, would people prefer lower-cost electricity from a central grid or electricity less subject to interruption from a disseminated source? Should a nation opt to be food self-sufficient when in most circumstances staple foods can be had at lower prices through international trade? Of course, low price and dependability may be simultaneously attainable, but these are the sorts of resilience choices that are likely to face us, mixed in with a variety of issues in the categories of "freedom" and "justice."

Living in two complex adaptive systems means that we can count on big surprises, but we can't predict when and how they will occur. So when we're trying to steer cultural evolution toward the creation of a global family that is both empathetic and sustainable, we should always be thinking of ways to build redundancy and resilience into the interwoven human and natural economies. We must carefully consider the power that we have as the dominant animal and, needless to say, also how power is wielded both within and between groups—an issue too frequently ignored in our search for sustainability (adapted from Ehrlich, "Ecoethics," 417–36).

32. Ehrlich, *Human Natures*, 121–22.

33. Other nations are making huge investments in education while the United States drops behind; see, for example, Mara Hvistendahl, "Asia Rising: Countries Funnel Billions Into Universities," *Chronicle of Higher Education*, October 5, 2009.

CHAPTER 8

1. Donald Brown, *Human Universals* New York: McGraw-Hill, 1991.

2. Noah Goldstein, Robert Cialdini, and Vladas Griskevicius, "A Room with a Viewpoint: Using Normative Appeals to Motivate Environmental Conservation in a Hotel Setting," *Journal of Consumer Research*, 2008. DOI: 10.1086/586910.

3. Bonnie Tsui, "Greening with Envy," *Atlantic*, July/August 2009.

4. An excellent review is Philip G. Zimbardo, "A Situationist Perspective on the Psychology of Evil: Understanding How Good People Are Transformed into

Perpetrators," in *The Social Psychology of Good and Evil: Understanding Our Capacity for Kindness and Cruelty*, ed. Arthur Miller (New York: Guilford, 2004), 11–30.

5. Stanley Milgram, *Obedience to Authority* (New York: Harper and Row, 1974).

6. Jerry M. Burger, "Replicating Milgram: Would People Still Obey Today?" *American Psychologist*, January 2009.

7. Philip G. Zimbardo, Christina Maslach, and Craig Haney, "Reflections on the Stanford Prison Experiment: Genesis, Transformation, Consequences," in *Obedience to Authority: Current Perspectives on the Milgram Paradigm*, ed. Thomas Blass (Mahwah, NJ: Lawrence Erlbaum, 1999), 193–237.

8. Robert Kurzban, Leda Cosmides, and John Tooby, "Can Race Be Erased? Coalitional Computation and Social Categorization," *PNAS* 98 (2001): 1537–92.

9. Eliot Aronson and Shelly Patnoe, *The Jigsaw Classroom: Building Cooperation in the Classroom*, 2nd ed. (New York: Addison Wesley Longman), 22.

10. Devon Williams, "The Jigsaw Classroom as a Missing Piece to the Puzzle," *Urban Education* 39, no. 3 (2004): 316–44.

11. Sudhir Venkatesh, *Gang Leader for a Day: A Rogue Sociologist Takes to the Streets* (New York: Penguin, 2008), 11–12.

12. David Kennedy, "Drugs, Race and Common Ground: Reflections on the High Point Intervention," *NIJ Journal*, no. 262 (2009), www.ojp.usdoj.gov/nij/journals/262/high-point-intervention.htm (accessed January 11, 2010).

13. Paul R. Ehrlich, *Human Natures: Genes, Cultures, and the Human Prospect* (Washington, DC: Island Press, 2000), 135–36.

14. Universities share many attributes of nations as what the historian Benedict Anderson called an "imagined community." They are, in reality, just as if they were genuine tribes or nations and are divided into primitive and comfortable family groups—but these are called departments, grouped into schools and supplemented by much weaker "programs." Departments often function as pseudokin families. Individuals in these departments see a lot of one another, and they often bond, but sometimes they get annoyed with other family members and form rivalries—just as genuine kin do.

The traditional academic departments are, to a substantial degree, economic production units, and members often can benefit from the activities and reputations of others, especially leaders (given the pretentious title of chairpersons) who may have clout with the leaders of the other families. But they also owe some allegiance to the clan of the discipline—academics who they know personally but belong to different families (academic departments, NGOs, government agencies).

Although the large culture gap and the first threat of a collapse of a global civilization make today's university state of affairs entirely unprecedented, the intellectual organization of higher education institutions still has its family-like foundations in the ancient Aristotelian disciplines. Aristotle organized the study of the sciences into those that were productive, or practical, and those that were theoretical. Productive sciences are those, obviously, that have a product, such as engineering and architecture, and also disciplines, such as strategy and rhetoric, in which the product is conceptual, such as victory in the law courts. In the practical sciences, such ethics and politics direct behavior. The theoretical sciences, however, seek information and understanding for their own sake.

Aristotle classified several approved fields of intellectual inquiry; they were physics, metaphysics (which was his name for the discipline that came "after physics in his books," its meaning in Greek, but, of course, this term has taken on a very different focus nowadays), psychology, zoology, ethics, and politics. These and others' later additions were crystallized into the official sciences by the Royal Society of London in 1664 and in the social sciences and humanities over the succeeding two centuries.

15. Immanuel Wallerstein, *Open the Social Sciences: Report of the Gulbenkian Commission on the Restructuring of the Social Sciences* (Stanford, CA: Stanford University Press, 1996).

16. Graydon A. Tunstall, "Austria-Hungary and the Brusilov Offensive of 1916," *Historian* 70 (2008): 30–53.

17. We should note that our own disciplines are hardly free from this problem. For example, many taxonomists (those concerned with classifying organisms), still think the goal of their discipline is the impossible task of completely describing all of biodiversity. There are ten million or more very distinct kinds of organisms (species), billions of populations, all continually evolving and some going extinct— completing the job of "describing" them is as impossible as recording all military screwups. Ecologists are doing better, but still have not matched genetics in using sample systems to uncover generalities about nature.

18. Jared Diamond, *Guns, Germs, and Steel: The Fates of Human Societies* (New York: W. W. Norton, 1997); Jared Diamond, *Collapse: How Societies Choose to Fail or Succeed* (New York: Viking, 2005); Jared Diamond and James Robinson, eds., *Natural Experiments of History* (Cambridge, MA: Harvard University Press, 2010).

19. Joseph A. Tainter, *The Collapse of Complex Societies* (Cambridge: Cambridge University Press, 1988).

20. See, for example, Eric Hobsbawm, *The Age of Capital* (London: Weidenfeld and Nicholson, 1975); Eric Hobsbawm, *Nations and Nationalism Since 1780: Programme, Myth, Reality*, 2nd ed. (Cambridge: Cambridge University Press, 1992); David M. Kennedy, *Freedom from Fear: The American People in Depression and War, 1929–1945* (New York: Oxford University Press, 1999); Karl Marx, *Capital: A Critique of Political Economy*, vols. 1–3 (1867; New York: International Publishers, 1967); Oswald Spengler, *The Decline of the West* (1923; New York: Random House, 1996); Arnold Toynbee, *A Study of History*, 12 vols. (London: Oxford University Press, 1934–1961); William H. McNeill, *The Rise of the West: A History of the Human Community* (Chicago: University of Chicago Press, 1963).

21. Note that there are already people in those and related disciplines working hard on the human predicament. To mention a few we know personally (with representative publications) in environmental sociology, Bob Brulle (Bob Brulle and Lindsay Young, "Advertising, Individual Consumption Levels, and the Natural Environment, 1900–2000," *Sociological Inquiry* 77 [2007]: 522–42); Tom Burns and Tom Dietz (Tom R. Burns and Tom Dietz, "Cultural Evolution: Social Rule Systems, Selection and Human Agency," *International Sociology* 7 [1992]: 259–83); William Catton

(William R. Catton, *Overshoot: The Ecological Basis of Revolutionary Change* [Urbana: University of Illinois Press, 1980]); Gene Rosa and Robert York (Gene Rosa, Robert York, and Tom Dietz, "Tracking the Anthropogenic Drivers of Ecological Impacts," *Ambio* 333 [2004]: 509–12). In environmental political science, Lin Ostrom (Lin E. Ostrom and Edella Schlager, "The Formation of Property Rights," in *Rights to Nature: Ecological, Economic, Cultural, and Political Principles of Institutions for the Environment*, ed. Susan Hanna, Carl Folke, and Karl-Goren Mäler [Washington, DC: Island Press, 1996], 127–56) and Dennis Pirages (Dennis C. Pirages and Theresa Manley DeGeest, *Ecological Security: An Evolutionary Perspective on Globalization* [Lanham, MD: Rowman and Littlefield, 2003]). Among many others, in ecological economics, Ken Arrow (Ken Arrow, Partha Dasgupta, Lawrence Goulder, Gretchen Daily, Paul Ehrlich, Geoffrey Heal, Simon Levin, et al., "Are We Consuming Too Much?" *Journal of Economic Perspectives* 18 [2004]: 147–72), Partha Dasgupta (Partha Dasgupta, *Human Well-Being and the Natural Environment* [Oxford: Oxford University Press, 2001]), and Larry Goulder (Larry H. Goulder and Brian Nadreau, "International Approaches to Reducing Greenhouse Gases," in *Climate Change Policy*, ed. Steven Schneider, Armand Rosencranz, and John Niles [Washington, DC: Island Press, 2002], 115–49). In international relations, Scott Barrett (Scott Barrett, *Environment and Statecraft: The Strategy of Environmental Treaty-Making* [New York: Oxford University Press, 2003]). In anthropology, Doug Carmichael (Doug Carmichael, *Garden World Politics*, book—in draft).

22. Wallerstein, *Open the Social Sciences*.

23. "Council of Basle," The Catholic Encyclopedia, www.newadvent.org/cathen/02334b.htm (accessed September 30, 2009).

24. While the Constitution begins, "We the people of the United States," the Articles of Confederation start with "Each state retains its sovereignty, freedom, and independence, and every power, jurisdiction, and right, which is not by this Confederation expressly delegated to the United States, in Congress assembled."

25. Sebastian Jones, "The Media-Lobbying Complex," *Nation* 290 (2010): 11–16.

26. This is a pervasive problem. Even fewer Americans are conscious that the declaration of a "war on terror" was a propaganda trick, as it redefined a problem of controlling criminal behavior and it resulted in the recruitment of more terrorists and the goal (desired by the perpetrators) of accumulating more executive power. America, early in the twenty-first century, seems to be undergoing the same sort of transition as did Rome after Caesar crossed the Rubicon. The Roman Republic disappeared then, but as in today's America, its superficial form was retained. You would think that the existence of well over seven hundred American military bases overseas, manned by roughly two and a half million military personnel, would be well known to the general public, but it isn't. Not many Americans know about Centcom (the U.S. military's Central Command), which is tasked to control key parts of Asia and northeast Africa to assure oil and gas flows to the United States and its allies, or realize that Centcom is being armed to contest fossil fuel–rich areas with the Chinese and Russians.

Even fewer Americans are aware of the recently established Africom, the U.S. military's African Command. Officially, "United States Africa Command, in concert with other U.S. government agencies and international partners, conducts sustained security engagement through military-to-military programs, military-sponsored activities, and other military operations as directed to promote a stable and secure African environment in support of U.S. foreign policy." Translation: control the rest of Africa, to keep that continent's oil flowing. You would think these overseas military operations would make an alarmed citizenship aware of the U.S. empire. But these extraordinarily expensive operations, a major factor in creating huge budget deficits, remain on the far side of the governance culture gap.

27. Around 1970, PRE was peripherally involved in a "model U.S. constitution" project at the Center for the Study of Democratic Institutions run by FDR "brains trust" member Rexford Tugwell. The idea was to produce a modified constitution that would be a more effective instrument in view of the dramatic changes that had occurred in the almost two centuries since the original U.S. Constitution was written; changes like the accumulation of executive power, term limits, and the Electoral College system. We discussed the establishment of foresight capability, the representativeness of the Senate, and so on. Tugwell believed that as the bicentennial drew near, the United States would be better governed if the fifty states were replaced with at most twenty regional republics, the president was elected for one nine-year term, and separate planning and regulatory branches of government were established. He was at the time about eighty years of age—an old man with new ideas.

Sadly, the entire project was abandoned. Large-scale changes to the Constitution could probably only be successfully made by state legislatures calling a constitutional convention as dictated in Article V of the current Constitution (for some recent suggestions, see Miguel Sabado, *A More Perfect Constitution: 23 Proposals to Revitalize Our Constitution and Make America a Fairer Country* [New York: Walker, 2007]). It was clear when the project was ended, as it is now, that if a convention were called it would not focus primarily on creating a more effective instrument for governance, one that might even make it easier to spread empathy, deal more effectively with pseudokin relationships, and head us toward sustainability, but would instead be sidetracked into battles over abortion, gun control, taxes, and other "hot button" issues of the day—given that many people's ties to pseudokin families being then, as today, stronger than their ties to the imagined community of the United States, let alone the special (and genetic!) overarching kin of all of humanity.

28. See, for example, William F. Baker, "How to Save the News," *Nation* 12 (October 2009): 21–23.

CHAPTER 9

1. The best summary works on this are Kevin Phillips, *American Theocracy: The Peril of Politics of Radical Religion, Oil, and Borrowed Money in the 21st Century* (New York: Viking, 2006), and John Micklethwait and Adrian Wooldridge, *God Is Back: How the Global Revival of Faith Is Changing the World* (New York: Penguin

Press, 2009). The latter is especially frightening because it does not discuss the threat inherent in a return to a world based on ancient myths.

2. Charles Kimball, *When Religion Becomes Evil: Five Warning Signs* (San Francisco: HarperSanFrancisco, 2008), 7.

3. Phillips, *American Theocracy*, deals with this in detail.

4. Paul R. Ehrlich, *Human Natures: Genes, Cultures, and the Human Prospect* (Washington, DC: Island Press, 2000).

5. "Major Religions of the World Ranked by Number of Adherents," Adherents .com, www.adherents.com/Religions_By_Adherents.html (accessed May 29, 2009).

6. Few Christians seem to realize that none of today's orthodoxies were the orthodoxy of the early church, and that early people calling themselves Christians had an extremely diverse set of Jesus myths. Today's orthodoxies, including the ones embodied in the New Testament, are the myths of the winners of long battles in the second and third centuries. The primary victor was the Roman church, which, because of its wealth and political skills, overcame many views on the nature of Jesus's body and numbers of deities to emerge triumphant. The victors wrote the history, established the basic orthodoxy and the doctrine of apostolic succession, and declared all other Christian myths as "heresy." The basic scholarly source on this is Walter Bauer, *Orthodoxy and Heresy in Earliest Christianity* (Philadelphia: Fortress, 1971). If you are interested in the details of how one set of myths can win over others, or if you'd like to know about such things as the Ebionites, the Marcionites, and the Gospel of Thomas, we can recommend Bart Ehrman, *Lost Christianities: The Battles for Scripture and the Faiths We Never Knew* (New York: Oxford University Press, 2004). None of this political organization around myths, of course, did much to spread empathy, although it did lead to lots of heretics being put to the sword or burned alive.

7. Micklethwait and Wooldridge, *God Is Back*, 308.

8. Julien C. Sprott, "Dynamical Models of Happiness," *Nonlinear Dynamics, Psychology, and Life Sciences* 9, no. 1 (January 2005): 23–26.

9. Robert Brulle and Lindsay E. Young, "Advertising, Individual Consumption Levels, and the Natural Environment, 1900–2000," *Sociological Inquiry* 77, no. 4 (November 2007): 522–42.

10. See, for example, James Kavanaugh, *A Modern Priest Looks at His Outdated Church* (New York: Trident Press, 1967).

11. Ehrlich, *Human Natures*, 219–20.

12. Robert Sapolsky, *The Trouble with Testosterone: And Other Essays on the Biology of the Human Predicament* (New York: Scribner, 1997).

13. For discussion of the evolution of religions, see Ehrlich, *Human Natures*, and Sapolsky, *The Trouble with Testosterone*.

14. "The Green Patriarch," The Byzantine Anglo-Catholic blog, April 22, 2008, http://thebyzantineanglocatholic.blogspot.com/2008/04/green-patriarch.html (accessed December 25, 2008).

15. To see their entire statement, go to "SCOBA Hierarchs Endorse Statement on the Environment," Greek Orthodox Archdiocese of America, July 8, 2005, www .goarch.org/news/goa.news1393 (accessed July 5, 2007).

16. "The Muslim Seven Year Action Plan on Climate Change 2010–2017: Summary," www.bcca.org/ief/activities/ARC/Muslim_summary091020.pdf (accessed May 14, 2010).

17. See, for example, Kyle Van Houtan and Stuart Pimm, "The Christian Ethics of Species Conservation," in *Religion and the New Ecology: Environmental Prudence in a World in Flux*, ed. David Lodge and Christopher Hamlin (South Bend, IN: University of Notre Dame Press, 2006), 116–47.

18. "Interview with Rev. Richard Cizik," The Great Warming, www.thegreat warming.com/revrichardcizik.html (accessed October 30, 2010).

19. Nicolas D. Kristof, "Learning from the Sin of Sodom," *New York Times*, February 27, 2010, www.nytimes.com/2010/02/28/opinion/28kristof.html?emc=eta1 (accessed February 28, 2010).

20. According to the European Humanist Association, in "The Status of Non-believers in Europe" (www.humanism.be/fr/doc/pdfs/Warsaw-Vera-3.pdf), there is continuing pressure to destroy democracy in the name of control by those who think supernatural beings whisper in their ears. As the document summarizes (p. 4),

1. Secularist and humanist citizens have no official status in Europe and do not seek to have one. Were they to have such a status their state would not be more secular, as hundreds of thousands or more citizens who belong to religions different from the established one would go on being discriminated against. The only guarantee of effective nondiscrimination is a totally secular state that abides by the rule of law.

2. The recognition of a role in public life extended to nonrepresentative institutions like churches weakens the authority of Parliament and undermines democracy.

3. A clear-cut distinction must be made between freedom of religion for each and every one and the freedom for religious institutions to penetrate and influence public life. We are witnessing an unprecedented attack by ill-concealed attempts to increase religious influence and these must be repelled.

21. Michael Bond, "Critical Mass," *New Scientist*, July 18, 2009, 38–41.

22. Bond, "Critical Mass," 39.

23. Remember that little of our interesting day-to-day behavior is in some sense "programmed" into our genes—our development is evolutionarily designed to be responsive to our environments; Paul Ehrlich and Marcus Feldman, "Genes, Environments, and Behaviors," *Daedalus*, Spring 2007, 5–12.

24. Al Gore, *Our Choice: A Plan to Solve the Climate Crisis* (Emmaus, PA: Rodale, 2009). In this book, Gore discusses the problem of overconsumption and population growth.

25. Much more effective would be stopping the growing of water-thirsty crops and improving the efficiency of irrigation.

Selected Bibliography

O N such a broad topic, anything like a complete bibliography would be a library in itself. Here we list an eclectic selection of the books that have been helpful to us in thinking about the problems of reorganizing human society and aiming it toward sustainability.

Allen, William Sheridan. *The Nazi Seizure of Power: The Experience of a Single German Town*. Chicago: Quadrangle Books, 1967.

Alterman, Eric. *What Liberal Media? The Truth about Bias and the News*. New York: Basic Books, 2003.

Anderson, Benedict R. *Imagined Communities: Reflections on the Origin and Spread of Nationalism*. Rev. ed. London: Verso, 1991.

Appiah, Kwame Anthony. *The Ethics of Identity*. Princeton, NJ: Princeton University Press, 2005.

Armstrong, Karen. *A History of God*. New York: Ballantine Books, 1994.

Aronson, Elliot, and Shelley Patnoe. *Cooperation in the Classroom: The Jigsaw Method*. 3rd ed. London: Pinter & Martin, 2010.

Axelrod, Robert. *The Evolution of Cooperation*. New York: Basic Books, 1984.

Bacevich, Andrew J. *American Empire: The Realities and Consequences of U.S. Diplomacy*. Cambridge, MA: Harvard University Press, 2002.

Bandura, Albert. *Social Foundations of Thought and Action*. Englewood Cliffs, NJ: Prentice Hall, 1986.

Barber, Benjamin R. *Jihad vs. McWorld*. New York: Ballantine Books, 1995.

Barnes, Gina L. *The Rise of Civilization in East Asia*. London: Thames and Hudson, 1999.

Barrett, Scott. *Why Cooperate: The Incentive to Supply Global Public Goods*. Oxford: Oxford University Press, 2007.

Braudel, Fernand. *A History of Civilizations*. New York: Penguin Books, 1993.

Broude, Gwen J. *Marriage, Family, and Relationships: A Cross-Cultural Encyclopedia*. Santa Barbara, CA: ABC-CLIO, 1994.

Brown, Donald E. *Human Universals*. New York: McGraw-Hill, 1991.

Brulle, Robert J. *Agency, Democracy, and Nature: The U.S. Environmental Movement from a Critical Theory Perspective*. Cambridge, MA: MIT Press, 2000.

Christian, David. *Maps of Time*. Berkeley: University of California Press, 2005.

Cialdini, Robert B. *Influence: Science and Practice*. Boston: Allyn & Bacon, 2008.

Colborn, Theo, Dianne Dumanoski, and John Peterson Myers. *Our Stolen Future*. New York: Dutton, 1996.

Collingwood, R. G. *The Idea of History*. Oxford: Oxford University Press, 1946.

Collins, Randall. *Violence: A Micro-Sociological Theory*. Princeton, NJ: Princeton University Press, 2008.

Daily, Gretchen C., and Katherine Ellison. *The New Economy of Nature: The Quest to Make Conservation Profitable*. Washington, DC: Island Press, 2002.

Daly, Herman. *Beyond Growth: The Economics of Sustainable Development*. Boston: Beacon Press, 1996.

Diamond, Jared. *Collapse: How Societies Choose to Fail or Succeed*. New York: Viking, 2005.

————. *Guns, Germs, and Steel: The Fates of Human Societies*. New York: W. W. Norton, 1997.

Diamond, Jared, and James A. Robinson, eds. *Natural Experiments of History*. Cambridge, MA: Harvard University Press, 2010.

Durning, A. *How Much Is Enough? The Consumer Society and the Future of the Earth*. New York: W. W. Norton, 1992.

Edelman, Gerald M. *Neural Darwinism: The Theory of Neuronal Group Selection*. New York: Basic Books, 1987.

Edgerton, R. B. *Sick Societies: Challenging the Myth of Primitive Harmony*. New York: Free Press, 1992.

Ehrenreich, Barbara. *Nickel and Dimed: On (Not) Getting By in America*. New York: Henry Holt, 2001.

Ehrlich, Paul R., and Anne H. Ehrlich. *The Dominant Animal: Human Evolution and the Environment*. 2nd ed. Washington, DC: Island Press, 2009.

————. *One with Nineveh: Politics, Consumption, and the Human Future*. Washington, DC: Island Press, 2005.

Ehrlich, Paul R., and S. Shirley Feldman. *The Race Bomb: Skin Color, Prejudice, and Intelligence*. New York: New York Times Book Co., 1977.

Ehrman, Bart D. *Lost Christianities: The Battles for Scripture and the Faiths We Never Knew*. New York: Oxford University Press, 2004.

Frank, Thomas. *What's the Matter with Kansas: How Conservatives Won the Heart of America*. New York: Henry Holt, 2004.

Friedman, Milton. *Capitalism and Freedom*. Chicago: University of Chicago Press, 1962.

Gazzaniga, Michael S. *The Ethical Brain*. New York: Dana Press, 2005.

————. *Human: The Science Behind What Makes Us Unique*. New York: HarperCollins, 2008.

Geary, Patrick J. *The Myth of Nations: The Medieval Origins of Europe* Princeton, NJ: Princeton University Press, 2003.

Gelbspan, R. *Boiling Point: How Politicians, Big Oil and Coal, Journalists, and Activists Have Fueled a Climate Crisis—and What We Can Do to Avert Disaster*. New York: Basic Books, 2005.

Gladwell, Malcolm. *The Tipping Point: How Little Things Can Make a Big Difference*. Boston: Little, Brown, 2000.

Godfrey-Smith, Peter. *An Introduction to the Philosophy of Science*. Chicago: University of Chicago Press, 2003.

Goldstone, Jack A. *Revolution and Rebellion in the Early Modern World*. Berkeley: University of California Press, 1991.

Goodall, Jane. *The Chimpanzees of Gombe: Patterns of Behavior*. Cambridge, MA: Harvard University Press, 1986.

Gopnik, Alison. *The Philosophical Baby: What Children's Minds Tell Us about Truth, Love, and the Meaning of Life*. New York: Farrar, Straus and Giroux, 2009.

Gore, Al. *The Assault on Reason*. New York: Penguin Press, 2007.

Gourevitch, Philip. *We Wish to Inform You That Tomorrow We Will Be Killed with Our Families: Stories from Rwanda*. New York: Farrar, Straus and Giroux, 1998.

Grossman, Dave. *On Killing: The Psychological Cost of Learning to Kill in War and Society*. Boston: Little, Brown, 1995.

Harrell, Stevan. *Human Families*. Boulder, CO: Westview Press, 1997.

Harris, Marvin. *Cows, Pigs, and Witches: The Riddles of Culture*. New York: Vintage, 1989.

———. *The Rise of Anthropological Theory*. New York: Thomas Y. Crowell, 1968.

Harris, Sam. *The End of Faith: Religion, Terror, and the Future of Reason*. New York: W. W. Norton, 2004.

Harvey, David. *A Brief History of Neoliberalism*. New York: Oxford University Press, 2005.

Hitchens, Christopher. *God Is Not Great: How Religion Poisons Everything*. New York: Warner Books, 2007.

Hobsbawm, E. J. *Nations and Nationalism Since 1780: Programme, Myth, Reality*. 2nd ed. Cambridge: Cambridge University Press, 1992.

Homer-Dixon, Thomas. *The Upside of Down: Catastrophe, Creativity, and the Renewal of Civilization*. Washington, DC: Island Press, 2006.

Hrdy, Sarah Blaffer. *Mothers and Others: The Evolutionary Origins of Mutual Understanding*. Cambridge, MA: Belknap Press, 2009.

Hua, Cai. *A Society without Fathers or Husbands: The Na of China*. New York: Zone Books, 2001.

Johnson, Chalmers. *Nemesis: The Last Days of the American Republic*. New York: Metropolitan Books, 2007.

Jonaitis, Aldona. *Chiefly Feasts: The Enduring Kwakiutl Potlatch*. Seattle: University of Washington Press, 1991.

Keeley, Lawrence H. *War Before Civilization: The Myth of the Peaceful Savage*. New York: Oxford University Press, 1996.

Kelly, Marjorie. *The Divine Right of Capital: Dethroning the Corporate Aristocracy*. San Francisco, CA: Berrett-Koehler, 2001.

Kelly, Raymond C. *Warless Societies and the Origin of War*. Ann Arbor: University of Michigan Press, 2000.

Kennedy, David M. *Freedom from Fear: The American People in Depression and War, 1929–1945*. New York: Oxford University Press, 1999.

Klare, Michael T. *Blood and Oil: The Dangers and Consequences of America's Growing Dependency on Imported Petroleum*. New York: Henry Holt, 2004.

———. *Resource Wars: The New Landscape of Global Conflict*. New York: Henry Holt, 2001.

Klein, Naomi. *The Shock Doctrine: The Rise of Disaster Capitalism*. New York: Henry Holt, 2007.

Klein, Richard G. *The Human Career: Human Biological and Cultural Origins*. 3rd ed. Chicago: University of Chicago Press, 2009.

Korten, David C. *When Corporations Rule the World*. 2nd ed. Bloomfield, CT: Kumarian Press, 2001.

Krech, Shepard, III. *The Ecological Indian: Myth and History*. New York: W. W. Norton, 1999.

La Barre, Weston. *The Human Animal*. Chicago: University of Chicago Press, 1954.

Levin, Simon. *Fragile Dominion*. Reading, MA: Perseus Books, 1999.

Maalouf, Amin. *The Crusade through Arab Eyes*. New York: Schocken Books, 1984.

Micklethwait, John, and Adrian Wooldridge. *God Is Back: How the Global Revival of Faith Is Changing the World*. New York: Penguin Press, 2009.

Milgram, Stanley. *Obedience to Authority: An Experimental View*. New York: Harper and Row, 1974.

Montesquieu, Charles de Secondat, Baron de. *The Spirit of the Laws*. 1748. Cambridge: Cambridge University Press, 1989.

Mooney, Chris. *The Republican War on Science*. New York: Basic Books, 2006.

Nisbett, Richard. *The Geography of Thought: How Asians and Westerners Think Differently . . . and Why*. New York: Simon and Schuster, 2003.

Nisbett, Richard, and Lee Ross. *Human Inference: Strategies and Shortcomings of Social Judgement*. New York: Prentice Hall, 1985.

Oakeshott, Michael. *Rationalism in Politics and Other Essays*. Rev. ed. Indianapolis: Liberty Fund, 1991.

Olson, Mancur. *The Logic of Collective Action: Public Goods and the Theory of Groups*. 1965. Cambridge, MA: Harvard University Press, 1971.

Ornstein, Robert. *Psychology: The Study of Human Experience*. 2nd ed. San Diego: Harcourt Brace Jovanovich, 1988.

———. *The Psychology of Consciousness*. New York: Penguin Books, 1986.

Ornstein, Robert, and Paul Ehrlich. *New World/New Mind: Moving toward Conscious Evolution*. New York: Doubleday, 1989.

Palast, Greg. *The Best Democracy Money Can Buy*. London: Pluto Press, 2002.

Perrow, Charles. *Normal Accidents: Living with High-Risk Technologies*. Rev. ed. Princeton, NJ: Princeton University Press, 1999.

Phillips, Kevin. *Wealth and Democracy: A Political History of the American Rich*. New York: Random House, 2002.

Prestowitz, Clyde. *Rogue Nation: American Unilateralism and the Failure of Good Intentions*. New York: Basic Books, 2003.

Putnam, Robert D. *Bowling Alone: The Collapse and Revival of American Community.* New York: Simon and Schuster, 2000.

Reeves, Byron, and Clifford Nass. *The Media Equation: How People Treat Computers, Television, and New Media Like Real People and Places.* Cambridge: Cambridge University Press, 1996.

Russell, Bertrand. *"Why I Am Not a Christian" and Other Essays on Religion and Related Subjects.* New York: Simon and Schuster, 1957.

Sapolsky, Robert M. *Monkeyluv.* New York: Scribner, 2005.

————. *The Trouble with Testosterone: And Other Essays on the Biology of the Human Predicament.* New York: Scribner, 1997.

Scheper-Hughes, Nancy. *Death Without Weeping: The Violence of Everyday Life in Brazil.* Berkeley: University of California Press, 1993.

Sherif, Muzafer, O. J. Harvey, B. Jack White, William R. Hood, and Carolyn W. Sherif. *The Robbers Cave Experiment.* Middletown, CT: Wesleyan University Press, 1988.

Singer, Peter. *How Are We to Live? Ethics in an Age of Self-Interest.* Melbourne, Australia: Text, 1993.

Spengler, Oswald. *The Decline of the West.* 1923. New York: Random House, 1996.

Stiglitz, Joseph. *Globalization and Its Discontents.* New York: W. W. Norton, 2002.

————. *Making Globalization Work.* New York: W. W. Norton, 2006.

Tainter, Joseph A. *The Collapse of Complex Societies.* Cambridge: Cambridge University Press, 1988.

Tomasello, Michael. *Origins of Human Communication.* Cambridge, MA: MIT Press, 2008.

Toynbee, Arnold. *A Study of History.* 12 vols. London: Oxford University Press, 1934–1961.

Tyerman, Christopher. *Fighting for Christendom: Holy War and the Crusades.* Oxford: Oxford University Press, 2004.

Union of Concerned Scientists. *World Scientists' Warning to Humanity.* Cambridge, MA: Union of Concerned Scientists, 1993.

Wallerstein, Immanuel. *Open the Social Sciences: Report of the Gulbenkian Commission on the Restructuring of the Social Sciences.* Stanford, CA: Stanford University Press, 1996.

————. *World Systems Analysis: An Introduction.* Durham, NC: Duke University Press, 2004.

Westermarck, E. *The History of Human Marriage.* London: Macmillan, 1891.

Wolin, Sheldon S. *Democracy Incorporated: Managed Democracy and the Spectre of Inverted Totalitarianism.* Princeton, NJ: Princeton University Press, 2008.

————. *Politics and Vision: Continuity and Innovation in Western Political Thought.* Rev. ed. Princeton, NJ: Princeton University Press, 2006.

Index

About the Authors

Paul R. Ehrlich is Bing Professor of Population Studies and professor of biology at Stanford University. An expert in the fields of evolution, ecology, human behavior, taxonomy, and population biology, Ehrlich has conducted fieldwork from the Arctic and the Antarctic to the tropics, and from high mountains to the ocean floor. Professor Ehrlich has written more than one thousand scientific papers and popular articles as well as many books, including *The Population Bomb, The Process of Evolution, The Machinery of Nature, The Science of Ecology, Human Natures, Betrayal of Science and Reason, One with Nineveh,* and *The Dominant Animal.* Among his many scientific honors, Ehrlich is a fellow of the American Association for the Advancement of Science (AAAS) and the American Academy of Arts and Sciences, an honorary member of the British Ecological Society, and a member of the United States National Academy of Sciences. He was awarded the first AAAS/Scientific American Prize for Science in the Service of Humanity, and he received the Crafoord Prize in Population Biology and the Conservation of Biological Diversity, an explicit substitute for the Nobel Prize in fields of science for which the latter is not given. Ehrlich has also received a MacArthur Fellowship, the Volvo Environmental Prize for Environmental Sciences, and the Blue Planet Prize.

Psychologist **Robert Ornstein**'s wide-ranging and multidisciplinary work has won him awards from more than a dozen organizations, including the American Psychological Association and UNESCO. His pioneering research on the bilateral specialization of the brain has done much to advance our understanding of how we think. He received his bachelor's degree in psychology from City University of New York in 1964 and his Ph.D. in psychology from Stanford University in 1968. His doctoral thesis won the American Institutes for Research Creative Talent Award and was published immediately as a book, *On the Experience of Time.*

Since then he has written or cowritten more than twenty other books on the nature of the human mind and brain and their relationship to thought, health, and individual and social consciousness. His books have sold over six million copies and been translated into a dozen other languages. His textbooks have been used in more than twenty thousand university classes.

Dr. Ornstein has taught at the University of California Medical Center and Stanford University, and he has lectured at more than two hundred colleges and universities in the United States and overseas. He is the president and founder of the Institute for the Study of Human Knowledge (ISHK), an educational nonprofit dedicated to bringing important discoveries concerning human nature to the general public.

Among his many honors and awards are the UNESCO Award for Best Contribution to Psychology and the American Psychological Foundation Media Award "for increasing the public understanding of psychology."

Acknowledgements

Thank you to everyone I will now proceed to omit from
the following thanks: there are far too many people to list
here to whom I am forever indebted.
    Instead, here is a sighting of wonderful individuals
without whom these texts and this book would not exist.

Joe Luna, Harry Atkins, Rosemary Atkins, Philip Atkins,
Rupert Friend, Martin McGeown, Andrew Wheatley,
Caroline Friend, James Richards, Mike Sperlinger,
Ian White, Ghislaine Leung, David Raymond Conroy,
Beatrix Ruf, Patrick Ward, Siôn Parkinson,
Rebecca Lewin, Martin Herbert, Steven Bode,
Rebecca Kressley, John DeWitt, Lucia Pietroiusti,
Isabella Bortolozzi, Julia Moritz, Jamie Kenyon,
Tim Griffin, Polly Staple, Jamie Stevens, Beth Collar,
Francesco Pedraglio, Andy Holden, Jacques Testard,
Ray O'Meara, Lizzie Carey-Thomas, Heather Phillipson,
Hans Ulrich Obrist, Simon Thompson, Linda Stupart,
Nicolas Garait, Rebecca Lamarche-Vadel, Paul Buck,
Lumi Tan, Alex Poots, Sarah McCrory, Michael Dean,
Helen Marten, Isobel Harbison, Simon Martin, Zak Kyes,
Nicolas Deshayes, Shonagh Manson, Ben Eastham,
Matt Williams, Mark Leckey, Gavin Brown,
Marta Fontolan, Donna Lynas, Freddie Checketts,
Sally-Ginger Brockbank.

Notes on Suicide by Simon Critchley (Essay)
'An elegant, erudite, and provocative book that asks us to reflect on suicide without moral judgment and panicked response.'
— Judith Butler

Pond by Claire-Louise Bennett (Fiction)
'Elegant and funny and seems to find a whole new space in the form.'
— Eimear McBride, author of *A Girl of Half-Formed Thing*

Nicotine by Gregor Hens (Essay)
Introduced by Will Self
Translated from German by Jen Calleja
'A luminous and nuanced exploration of how we're constituted by our obsessions, how our memories arrange themselves inside of us, and how – or if – we control our own lives.'
— Leslie Jamison, author of *The Empathy Exams*

Nocilla Dream by Agustín Fernández Mallo (Fiction)
Translated from Spanish by Thomas Bunstead
'There is something deeply strange and finally unknowable to this book, in the very best way – a testament to the brilliance of Agustín Fernández Mallo.'
— Ben Marcus, author of *The Flame Alphabet*

Pretentiousness: Why It Matters by Dan Fox (Essay)
'Dan Fox makes a very good case for a re-evaluation of the word "pretentious". The desire to be more than we are shouldn't be belittled. Meticulously researched, persuasively argued – there would we be as a culture if no-one was prepared to risk coming across as pretentious? *Absolument* nowhere, darling – that's where.'
— Jarvis Cocker

This Little Art by Kate Briggs (Essay)
'Kate Briggs's *This Little Art* shares some wonderful qualities with Barthes's own work – the wit, thoughtfulness, invitation to converse, and especially the attention to the ordinary and everyday in the context of meticulously examined theoretical and scholarly questions. This is a highly enjoyable read: informative and stimulating for anyone interested in translation, writing, language, and expression.'
—— Lydia Davis, author of *Can't and Won't*

Insane by Rainald Goetz (Fiction)
Translated from German by Adrian Nathan West
'Rainald Goetz is the most important trendsetter in German literature.'
—— *Süddeutsche Zeitung*

The Second Body by Daisy Hildyard (Essay)
'Part amateur detective, part visionary, Hildyard's voice is so intelligent, beguiling and important. Like Sir Thomas Browne or even Annie Dillard, her sly variety of scientific inquiry is incandescent.'
—— Rivka Galchen, author of *Little Labors*

Essayism by Brian Dillon (Essay)
'[A] wonderful, subtle and deceptively fragmentary little
book ... To borrow from one of Barthes's titles, this is a lover's
discourse, the love object being writing, not only in the essay
but in all its forms. It is also a testament to the consolatory, even
the healing, powers of art. And at the last, in its consciously
diffident fashion – Dillon is a literary flaneur in the tradition
of Baudelaire and Walter Benjamin – it is its own kind of self-
made masterpiece.'
— John Banville, *Irish Times*

Moving Kings by Joshua Cohen (Fiction)
'A Jewish *Sopranos*... burly with particularities and vibrant with
voice... utterly engrossing, full of passionate sympathy... This
is a book of brilliant sentences, brilliant paragraphs, brilliant
chapters... There's not a page without some vital charge — a flash
of metaphor, an idiomatic originality, a bastard neologism born
of nothing... Cohen is an extraordinary prose stylist, surely one
of the most prodigious in American fiction today... his sentences
are all-season journeyers, able to do everything everywhere at
once... A crystalline novelist with a journalistic openness to the
world.'
— James Wood, *New Yorker*

Companions by Christina Hesselholdt (Fiction)
Translated from Danish by Paul Russell Garrett
'An affecting homage to, and a high-spirited literary dissection
of, Woolf's *The Waves* ... *Companions*, translated with care and
élan by Paul Russell Garrett, is not at all a gloomy work.
Hesselholdt's touch is light, even mocking, as much as her
subject matter is grave. There is a dancing intelligence roaming
free here, darting back and forth among ideas and sensations.
Her novel is a deceptively nonchalant defence of modernism
and a work of pure animation.'
— Catherine Taylor, *Financial Times*

Compass by Mathias Enard (Fiction)
Shortlisted for the 2017 Man Booker International Prize
Translated from French by Charlotte Mandell
'One of the finest European novels in recent memory.'
—— Adrian Nathan West, *Literary Review*

Notes from No Man's Land by Eula Biss (Essay)
'Two of the qualities that make Eula Biss's essays in *Notes
from No Man's Land* compelling and beautiful are precision
and independence – independence from orthodoxies of the
right and left and the conventions of literary essays and
their displays of sensibility and sensitivity. And whatever
topic she takes up she dissects and analyzes with startling
insight that comes from deep reading and original thinking.
She's important to this moment, important to the opening
up of what essays can be, important for setting a standard of
integrity and insight, and she's also a joy to read.'
—— Rebecca Solnit, author of *Hope in the Dark*

Flights by Olga Tokarczuk (Fiction)
Translated from Polish by Jennifer Croft
'Olga Tokarczuk is a household name in Poland and one
of Europe's major humanist writers, working here in the
continental tradition of the "thinking" or essayistic novel.
Flights has echoes of W. G. Sebald, Milan Kundera, Danilo
Kiš and Dubravka Ugrešić, but Tokarzcuk inhabits a
rebellious, playful register very much her own. ... Hotels on
the continent would do well to have a copy of *Flights* on the
bedside table. I can think of no better travel companion in
these turbulent, fanatical times.'
—— Kapka Kassabova, *Guardian*

Bricks and Mortar by Clemens Meyer (Fiction)
Longlisted for the 2017 Man Booker International Prize
Translated from German by Katy Derbyshire
'This is a wonderfully insightful, frank, exciting and
heart-breaking read. *Bricks and Mortar* is like diving
into a Force 10 gale of reality, full of strange voices,
terrible events and a vision of neoliberal capitalism that is
chillingly accurate.'
— A. L. Kennedy, author of *Serious Sweet*

Nocilla Experience by Agustín Fernández Mallo (Fiction)
Translated from Spanish by Thomas Bunstead
'The best novel I read in 2016. Thrillingly, incandescently
brilliant.'
— Stuart Evers, author of *If This is Home*

The Doll's Alphabet by Camilla Grudova (Fiction)
'If fairytales could dream, this nightmarish collection
is what you might end up with ... The atmosphere of
her fantastical, semi-dystopian settings is so unique
and persuasive that the day after finishing the book, I
awoke from a dream to realize that it had taken place in
Grudova's universe ... The author's surreal humour, often
delivered via deadpan dream logic, recalls the startling
short stories of Leonora Carrington. Both Carrington
and Grudova excel at a certain well-placed, pedestrian
literalism that works deliciously against the magical
elements in their fiction.'
— Claire Lowdon, *Times Literary Supplement*

This Young Monster by Charlie Fox (Essay)
'Good God, where did this wise-beyond-his-years
25-year-old critic's voice come from? His breath of
proudly putrefied air is really something to behold.
Finally, a new Parker Tyler is on the scene. Yep. Mr Fox is
the real thing.'
— John Waters, *New York Times*

Counternarratives by John Keene (Fiction)
Winner of the 2017 Republic of Consciousness Prize
'We have become accustomed in recent years to the
revisionary spirit of much postcolonial fiction, but the
ambition, erudition and epic sweep of John Keene's
remarkable new collection of stories, travelling from the
beginnings of modernity to modernism, place it in a class
of its own.'
— Kate Webb, *TLS*

Football by Jean-Philippe Toussaint (Essay)
Translated from French by Shaun Whiteside
'Toussaint has established himself as one of contemporary
French literature's most distinctive voices, turning the
existential tradition into something lighter, warmer and
ultimately more open.'
— Juliet Jacques, *New Statesman*

Second-hand Time by Svetlana Alexievich (Essay)
Winner of the Nobel Prize in Literature 2015
Translated from Russian by Bela Shayevich
'In this spellbinding book, Svetlana Alexievich
orchestrates a rich symphony of Russian voices telling
their stories of love and death, joy and sorrow, as they try
to make sense of the twentieth century, so tragic for their
country.'
— J. M. Coetzee, winner of the 2003 Nobel Prize in
Literature

The Hatred of Poetry by Ben Lerner (Essay)
'Lerner argues with the tenacity and the wildness of the
vital writer and critic that he is. Each sentence of *The Hatred
of Poetry* vibrates with uncommon and graceful lucidity;
each page brings the deep pleasures of crisp thought,
especially the kind that remains devoted to complexity
rather than to its diminishment.'
— Maggie Nelson, author of *The Argonauts*

Fitzcarraldo Editions
243 Knightsbridge
London, SW7 1DN
United Kingdom

Copyright © Ed Atkins, 2016
This second edition published by Fitzcarraldo Editions in 2017

The right of Ed Atkins to be identified as the author
of this work has been asserted in accordance with
Section 77 of the Copyright, Designs and Patent Act 1988.

ISBN 978-1-910695-21-0

Design by Ray O'Meara
Typeset in Fitzcarraldo
Printed and bound by TJ International

fitzcarraldoeditions.com

Fitzcarraldo Editions